ECONOMIC POLICY AND INFLATION IN THE SIXTIES

ECONOMIC POLICY AND INFLATION IN THE SIXTIES

Phillip Cagan • Marten Estey • William Fellner
Charles E. McLure Jr. • Thomas Gale Moore

With an introduction by William Fellner

American Enterprise Institute for Public Policy Research
Washington, D.C.

This volume is presented within the framework of the American Enterprise Institute's research project on economic policy and inflation, William J. Fellner, project director. Participants in that project who contributed the studies in this volume are:

CHARLES E. McLURE, JR., associate professor of economics at Rice University.

PHILLIP CAGAN, professor of economics at Columbia University.

MARTEN ESTEY, associate professor of industry at the Wharton School, University of Pennsylvania.

THOMAS GALE MOORE, professor of economics at Michigan State University.

WILLIAM J. FELLNER, Sterling professor of economics at Yale University.

All of the contributors are adjunct scholars of the American Enterprise Institute for Public Policy Research.

Domestic Affairs Study 4, April 1972

Library of Congress Catalog Card No. L.C. 72-81312

Printed in United States of America

CONTENTS

66643 /6

122 0

INTRODUCTION

Origin and Character of the Volume. Discussions held at the American Enterprise Institute in the summer of 1970 led to the conviction that undertaking the studies here presented would serve a useful purpose. Paul W. McCracken, at that time chairman of President Nixon's Council of Economic Advisers, shared this view and he was very helpful in making suggestions concerning the composition of the group that would work on the project. The initiators and the participants of the studies were motivated by the belief that scholars located at a distance from the political decision-making centers can learn a great deal by keeping up with a specific sequence of events in a systematic fashion and that it would be worthwhile to communicate the resulting analysis and conclusions to interested readers.

Since it was our purpose to focus on different aspects of the same broadly defined problem, we met several times to discuss our ideas and to exchange comments on our successive drafts. But it was not our intention to fit our studies together in the way in which five chapters of a book would have been organized. Therefore the reader may well find here and there a statement that in a sense "duplicates" a statement made in one of the other studies in a different context. On the other hand, the reader will also find proofs of the fact that five authors cannot be expected to think alike about all matters requiring analysis in a context as broad as that of the present volume.

The Unfolding of a Story While the Studies Were Undertaken. By the time we first met in 1970 it had become clear that the large inflationary carry-over from the preceding years of overfull utilization with which the new administration had to cope was showing strong resistance to anti-inflationary efforts. An extended past record of significant inflation had created the expectation of further major price increases. Hence in our environment in which the unionization of workers and other institutional factors exert a substantial influence on wage trends, money wage rates continued to rise sharply during the recession that had been brought about by policies of restraint. After the downturn in the late part of 1969, producers had to weigh the relative advantages and disadvantages of trying either to maintain adequate capacity utilization rates by price moderation despite rapidly rising wages or to keep prices more in line with wages at declining utilization rates. In actual fact, price moderation did not follow promptly after the downturn. The administration's policies were designed to keep the cyclical setback mild and short, with the result that output started recovering near the end of 1970, after a 12-month interval of recession. In terms of output the recession of 1969-70 (essentially of 1970) was very mild, though as a result of the continuous increase in the size of the "capacity output" even a mild recession leads to underutilization of capacity and to unemployment of labor. When output started rising again no clear signs of a deceleration of the inflation were as yet observable.

Thus policy makers got into the atypical situation of having greatly to reduce a strong inflationary movement during a period of *recovery*, an objective that could be accomplished only by keeping the recovery slow as judged by past standards. I am now taking it for granted that greatly reducing the inflation which developed in the second half of the sixties was a legitimate high-priority objective of the policy makers, and here I will merely add a reference to my paper in the volume where arguments are presented in support of this view. However, it would be wrong to imply that the correctness of the official view of the matter—a view which I share—goes without saying, because some authors have concluded from econometric studies that it is possible to stabilize a high rate of inflation at high employment levels and to gear the economy to an inflationary equilibrium in which all important economic variables adjust smoothly to the correctly anticipated rate of price increase. In my contribution to the volume I give reasons for considerable skepticism concerning this position. Here I will merely say that several economists suggesting the possibility of significantly inflationary equilibria have added enough qualifications to their reasoning to make me wonder whether they would really be willing to take a chance on that line of policy.

The new administration did not take this chance, nor did it take a chance on using a sledgehammer for curbing inflation (McCracken's phrase). It soon found out, though it was slow to admit it, that if after an extended period of rapidly rising prices a soft touch is being used, then that touch needs to be employed for a long time. Meanwhile political pressures accumulate for experimenting with direct wage and price controls. Indeed they accumulate to a point where even those of us who are highly skeptical about mixing such controls with the basic elements of Western economic-political systems have to admit that the pressures may become politically "irresistible," as seems to have been the case by August 1971. This is especially true if not all government spokesmen can resist the temptation to promise to the public rapid progress at little cost, and if not all government experts genuinely share a negative attitude concerning the usefulness of direct wage and price controls. Yet *if* in spite of the clumsiness of our control mechanism and the inevitable arbitrariness of the decisions of the control agencies we will, by the end of 1972, have made significant progress toward satisfactory levels of resource utilization at appreciably reduced rates of price increase, then the policy makers will deserve a good deal of credit for having done as well as may have been possible. It will then have taken the government four years to achieve that result, but the administration started out with a legacy that can hardly be called enviable.

We should keep in mind that when the first phase of the wage-price control program was announced on August 15, 1971, monetary and fiscal policy had already begun to take effect on the price level. In the decision-making process of firms the objective to raise capacity utilization rates by means of price moderation had by then been winning out over the objective of keeping price trends in line with wage trends. Later in this volume I shall show why, judging by past experience, it was reasonable to expect that in such circumstances the money-wage trend would soon have flattened appreciably without direct interference on the part of the government. Downward escalation of price and wage increases would in any event have required a monetary-fiscal management aiming for a slow recovery, with a gradual reduction of excess capacities and a gradual diminution of the unemployment rate to the vicinity of 5 percent by late summer 1972. But unless we have such a monetary-fiscal management, the naked eye will recognize the control program as a patent failure. If on the other hand we have the required monetary-fiscal policies *and* if the control agencies soon start greatly reducing the scope of their activities, then a long and fruitless debate will take place on whether the contribution of these agencies to gradual progress was somewhat on the positive or the negative side or was negligible. I doubt very much that the present Phase II activities of the agencies, with their extensive interferences in the wage and price structure, could remain in effect for long without major adverse consequences, and I think this view is now being increasingly shared by policy makers and the public alike.

The Five Contributions. When we started our studies it was not hard to guess that the characteristics of the story would include some of those discussed in the preceding pages. So we set out to explore the antecedents of the sequence of events I have briefly sketched; we attempted to trace the development of the difficulties with which the present administration became faced and we tried to evaluate policy measures of various types, those that seemed successful and those that did not.

I will end this introduction with a few hints of the content of the five contributions. During the past months they all appeared as Special Analyses in the American Enterprise Institute series, but for publication in the present form we felt free to make a few changes, in some cases for clarification and in others to take account of recent events.

Charles McLure, while recognizing the effectiveness of monetary as well as of fiscal policies, argues that the inflation and unemployment we are now experiencing had their roots in the failure to raise taxes in 1966 and 1967 for financing the Vietnam war and the rising Great Society expenditures. In spite of some errors made by economists in assessing the strength of aggregate demand between mid-1965 and the time when taxes were raised three years later, the major blame for the fiscal failure of the late 1960s must, he argues, fall squarely upon politicians causing unconscionable delays in the adoption of the needed fiscal policies. Economists must shoulder the blame for failure to predict accurately the economy's response once the desired anti-inflationary policies were enacted in 1968. We do not know well enough how to eliminate inflation of long duration without imposing severe costs in terms of unemployment and this makes it crucial to prevent excess aggregate demand from developing. The author favors adopting a presumptive rule that the full employment budget should be in approximate balance except for extraordinary circumstances, such as the present ones.

Before turning from McLure's to Cagan's paper, I will make a brief comment on differences between the distribution of emphasis in the two contributions. The inclination to attribute inflationary effects primarily to budgetary deficits results in most cases from the use of an analytical apparatus different from that which leads to placing the emphasis on monetary policy, particularly on the money supply. Yet the data usually make it difficult to decide this issue for any specific period because deficit policies tend to become associated with permissive policies of the monetary authority and all types of policy must be expected to take effect with lags.

Phillip Cagan regards the 1965-69 period as one in which a made-to-order experiment was performed in the use of monetary restraints. The sharp reduction in the rate of growth of the money supply in the second half of 1966, and then again in 1969, resulted from deliberate acts of Federal Reserve policy, and a slowdown of economic activity did follow in the wake of these restraints. Yet as a result of poor forecasting and of the Federal Reserve Board's over-reliance on "credit market indicators" many mistakes were made: monetary policy was too expansive in 1964 and 1965 allowing inflation to gain a foothold; in 1967 the restraint of 1966 was reversed too sharply; restraint was carried too far in 1969. What kinds of anti-inflationary policy will be considered acceptable in the future is a question the answer to which depends, in Cagan's appraisal, on the results of the present experiment with direct controls.

Marten Estey traces American wage policy from the 1962 guide-posts to the announcement of the Pay Board's 5.5 percent general pay standard in November 1971. He reviews the record of changes in compensation per man-hour, in wage rates under collective bargaining, in productivity and in unit labor costs from 1961 through mid-1971. Wage policy is analyzed from the standpoint of impact, enforcement and substantive standards. It is concluded that although wages rose less rapidly when the guideposts were used than when they were not, the extent to which that was a result of the guideposts is uncertain. In addition, Estey suggests that in Phase II of the present control program rising productivity will be as essential to the achievement of price stability as wage restraint.

Thomas Moore deals with U.S. attempts to alleviate inflation through incomes policies from the time of the Kennedy administration until the wage-price freeze of August 1971. After describing the early beginnings of such efforts which can be traced back to the Eisenhower administration, the paper considers the origin, development, and abandonment of the guideposts. Governmental efforts during this period to induce appropriate price and wage behavior in particular industries, especially the steel industry, are examined. Finally, the effectiveness of incomes policies in the United States is analyzed. The principal findings are that (1) there is inadequate evidence to conclude that the guideposts had an effect on prices or wages, and (2) the inflations of 1956-58 and 1970-71 are more likely to be explained in terms of lags in the economy than of either administered prices or of cost-push.

The conclusions of the paper I wrote are summarized in its last two pages which are also the last pages of this volume. These conclusions relate in part to the present control program and in part to the need for working out during the recovery process a long-run solution that avoids the recurrence of inflationary instability. Feasible long-run solutions can only be in the nature of a "second best" because while the significant rigidities of our wage structure could be diminished they could in practice hardly be reduced to insignificance. I suggest that the "second best" outlined on pp. 247-50 of this volume is less unattractive than the other available options: less unattractive than alternations of highly inflationary levels of effective demand with periods of under-utilization, or than suppressed inflation with reliance on permanent controls, or than rapidly rising payments to persons not at work (welfare-type payments of various sorts).

I think I may say on behalf of all of us that we have developed a high degree of interest in our joint undertaking, and I can only hope that the volume will succeed in conveying a sense of this to the reader.

William Fellner
Project director

1
FISCAL FAILURE:
LESSONS OF THE SIXTIES

Charles E. McLure, Jr.

Introduction

In the second quarter of 1961, just after the trough of the 1960 recession, prices were essentially stable, but the unemployment rate stood at 6.9 percent.[1] In the corresponding quarter of 1971, somewhat longer after the trough of the 1969-70 recession, 6.0 percent of the labor force was unemployed and prices were rising rapidly.[2] During the intervening ten years, the United States had embarked upon an unprecedented course of massive fiscal stimulation while recovering from recession, had seen the final stages of this "experiment for prosperity" overlap with an unexpectedly large buildup for the Vietnam war, had watched as the fiscal measures necessary to avoid wartime inflation were paralyzed by presidential and congressional inaction on recommended tax increases, had twice been shown that restrictive monetary policy can slow the rate of expansion of economic activity, especially by choking off residential construction, and had witnessed a bold attempt to arrest inflation by intentionally slowing down the economy. Shortly thereafter, the nation saw President

---

[1] From March to June 1961, the consumer price index (CPI) fell from 101.0 to 99.5 and the wholesale price index rose from 104.5 to 105.1. The GNP deflator stood at 115.4 in the first quarter and rose to 115.6 and 116.0 for the second and third quarters.

[2] From March to June 1971, the CPI rose from 119.8 to 121.5, an annual rate of increase of 5.6 percent and the WPI rose from 113.0 to 114.3, or by 4.6 percent at an annual rate. The GNP deflator in the first three quarters of 1971 was at 139.9, 141.3, and 142.4, which indicated an annual rise of 4.1 percent between the first and second quarters and 3.2 percent between the second and third. These figures for the CPI and WPI are based on 1967 prices, while those in footnote 1 use a basis of 1957-59.

Richard Nixon, an avowed opponent of wage and price controls, announce a wage and price freeze.

This essay reexamines the record of the 1960s and early 1970s in order to appraise the performance of fiscal policy during the period. The purpose is not simply to determine who was to blame for the failure of stabilization policy—though blame is in fact assessed in several cases. Rather, the intention is to improve our understanding of what went wrong in order that we may learn from the mistakes that were made.

Section one provides a short survey and appraisal of fiscal action and inaction over the past ten years in order to place what follows in perspective. Section two describes briefly the economic analysis— the so-called "new economics"— underlying the 1964 tax cut and the apparent success of fiscal policy through mid-1965. The next three sections review the years of excess aggregate demand that began in 1966 and the period of softness that followed, with a lag, the eventual adoption in mid-1968 of significant fiscal measures to restrain inflation. The final section discusses what went wrong beginning in 1966, why, and what can be done to prevent recurrences of the experiences that began in the late 1960s.

Fiscal Failure: A Brief Overview.[3] President Kennedy's economic advisers brought with them into office what became known as the "new economics." One of its key elements was the idea that fiscal policy should be used actively to keep the economy operating at or near full employment, rather than just to offset cyclical tendencies. The initial manifestations of an active policy were requests for accelerated depreciation and the investment tax credit, which were initiated in 1962. But its most dramatic product was the $13 billion tax cut requested by President Kennedy in 1963 and finally enacted under President Johnson in early 1964. The tax cut was designed to reduce substantially the restrictive impact of budget policy and thereby permit recovery to full employment.

The new economists judged the tax cut of 1964 to be an unqualified success in the active use of fiscal policy for stabilization purposes. With the support of an "accommodative" monetary policy, the economy expanded vigorously following the tax cut and, by the end of 1965, the promised land of full employment was in sight. Economists began to dream of the repeated "fiscal dividends" (tax cuts, expenditure increases, or revenue sharing) that would need to be declared

---

[3] In large part footnotes are omitted from this section, since the fiscal history of this period and its appraisal are covered in substantially greater detail later in this chapter.

8

if the fiscal drag produced by progressive income tax rates was to be offset and a return to restrictively high full employment surpluses avoided. Of course, the specter of Vietnam was becoming worrisome, but there seemed to be little doubt that rational use of fiscal policy would allow the nation to shift to limited warfare without severe inflationary pressure.

As it turned out, the history of economic policy after 1964 is largely dominated by fiscal failure.[4] Expansion was allowed to continue at too rapid a pace in late 1965, and inflationary skirmishes broke out. But more important, defense production rose rapidly, and was not offset by restraint on the tax side, in part because President Johnson believed that a tax increase would not pass the Congress. Nor was the growth of nondefense spending by the federal government curtailed to offset increased spending for Vietnam.

Although most concerned professional economists called for restraint in 1966, even they tended to understate the magnitude of the inflationary problem, for two reasons. First, an increase in defense production appears in the national income accounts initially as a buildup of private inventory investment, rather than as federal purchases, since it is not recorded as part of government purchases until delivery is made. It was thus easy to fail to appreciate the size and economic impact of the Vietnam buildup. Second, the budget for fiscal 1967 underestimated defense expenditures by about $10 billion. Thus, there would probably have been inflationary pressures even if a tax increase of the size that appeared to be needed had been enacted. As it was, the budget went into deficit in the second half of 1966, at a time when the unemployment rate was below 4 percent of the labor force; in 1967 the deficit exceeded 12½ billion dollars.[5]

During this period monetary policy provided the only brake on the economy. In an open rift with the President, the Board of Governors of the Federal Reserve Bank raised the rediscount rate in December 1965. Concrete evidence of the move to monetary restraint was the fact that in January 1967 the money supply (excluding time deposits) was slightly lower than it had been in April of the previous year. The results were dramatic. Interest rates rose rapidly as the

---

[4] There was an abundance of failure in the use of monetary policy in the late 1960s, as has been documented by Phillip Cagan, chapter 2, this volume. But several of the episodes of monetary failure had their genesis in fiscal failures, which by most measures were quantitatively more important, in any case.

[5] Unless indicated otherwise, all statistics reported in this paper are on a national income accounts basis, seasonally adjusted, at an annual rate. For most purposes, these figures are more useful for economic analysis than conventional budget figures.

"credit crunch" developed, and housing starts fell sharply. The power, but also the unevenness, of contractionary monetary policy, firmly applied, was demonstrated conclusively. Money did matter.

The investment boom ended in late 1966, providing temporary respite from the inflationary pressures of excess aggregate demand. Inflation slowed and unemployment rose temporarily in 1967, though it averaged only 3.8 percent for the year. But demand pressures were expected to resume in the second half of the year. In an effort to head off these pressures, the President requested the Congress to enact a temporary income tax surcharge. Congress refused to act for a year and a half and inflationary pressures built to new levels, confirming the accuracy of the forecasts. Only in the summer of 1968 with the passage of the Revenue and Expenditure Control Act did the nation return to fiscal sanity. A 10 percent surcharge was imposed on personal and corporate income taxes and a tight lid was clamped on federal expenditures, shifting the balance of the federal budget by roughly $20 billion between the first half of 1968 and the first half of 1969.

But even then the results were not what might have been expected. Saving seemed to fall as much as consumption in response to the surcharge, and businessmen continued investing in plant and equipment. The usefulness of temporary changes in income taxes as countercyclical tools, especially in a climate of inflationary expectations, was increasingly questioned. Fiscal policy seemed to fail even when it was applied, though premature monetary stimulus in 1968 had contributed to the buoyancy of private demand. As in 1966, monetary policy was tight in 1969, with its primary impact again falling on home building.

The new administration announced a policy of gradualism, an attempt to reduce the rate of growth of output in order to create back pressures on prices and thereby induce disinflation. Relief was slow in coming, and only at the beginning of 1970 did the unemployment rate begin to rise. But when the rise came, unemployment rose more than expected and persisted longer. In fact, the economy went into recession in late 1969. Not until the first half of 1971 did strong growth toward potential output resume.[6] Equally exasperating, however, was the fact that inflation showed hardly any signs of slackening. Finally, on August 15, 1971, President Nixon reversed his field and imposed administrative controls on wages and prices.

---

[6] These developments are, of course, clouded by the General Motors strike in the fourth quarter of 1970.

Fiscal Failure: Appraisal. The economists advising President Johnson during the period when inflationary pressures were being created made some mistakes, by their own admission: they underestimated the strength of demand in 1965; they may have failed to take full account of the economic impact of the known buildup in Vietnam; and in 1968 they overestimated the restraint that would result from the income tax surcharge. Yet the shortcomings of the economic advice given the President pale in comparison to the shortcomings in political action based on that advice. Johnson did not request the important tax increase clearly required in 1966 to prevent inflation, because he thought it would not pass the Congress. And when the tax increase was finally requested in 1967, Congress delayed action until mid-1968, as much as three years after fiscal restraint had first begun to be needed. Moreover, throughout the period, economic decision making was hampered by inadequate information on the rise in expenditure for Vietnam. Thus, it seems that the bulk of the blame for the inflation must fall squarely on the politicians, rather than the economists.

When attention shifts to the more recent period of trying to wind down the inflation, perhaps the blame must also shift. Nixon's economic game plan of gradually disinflating the economy, unlike the Johnson policy that created the inflation, was proposed by administration economists. Thus, the underestimate of both the persistence of inflation and the extent of the slowdown induced by gradualism, it seems, must be attributed in large part to the economists. In all fairness it must be noted, however, that the Nixon economists had a far more difficult task—that of winding down the inflation—than did the Johnson economists and the politicians—that of preventing it. We simply know very little about how to restore price stability without creating temporary unemployment in the process, if indeed it can be done at all.

The difficulty of restoring price stability without inflicting severe costs in terms of unemployment underscores the desirability of never letting an inflation begin. Of particular importance is the avoidance of excess demand. Two approaches to the objective of moving the economy along the path of full employment with price stability are discretionary fiscal policy and reliance upon built-in stabilizers. Either followed consistently would have avoided the large budget deficits in the two years after mid-1966 and, therefore, would probably have prevented most of the inflation of the last six years. But both require a performance from our political system that was not forthcoming between the end of 1965 and the middle of 1968. Whether the nation has gained the economic sophistication and political maturity to improve markedly upon that performance remains to be seen.

One way to improve the performance of fiscal policy is to adopt a presumptive rule of approximate balance in the full employment budget. Thus, changes in expenditures would be matched by changes in taxes, with the basic balance in the full employment budget being determined by the saving/investment needs of the nation. It may be unwise, as well as impossible politically, to require by statute that a given budget balance always prevail at full employment. But a presumptive rule would spotlight massively inflationary deficit spending of the kind that began in 1966 (as well as deflationary policy of the kind that prevailed during the late 1950s) and, hopefully, prevent it. It would not, on the other hand, preclude either the active use of discretionary fiscal policy or more passive reliance on built-in stabilizers.

If active fiscal policy is to be pursued, it may be worthwhile to consider stronger and more predictable measures than temporary surcharges on the income taxes. Such a measure is the variable-rate tax/subsidy on consumer durables and business fixed investment discussed in the final section of this paper. The incentive such a tax or subsidy would give to postpone or accelerate private spending would provide stabilization potency far beyond what would be indicated by the revenue yield or cost of the measure, and these effects should be predictable.

The Economics of the New Economics

In 1963 President Kennedy requested a general cut in income taxes. He did this on the basis of what has come to be called the "new economics." In fact, the economics brought to Washington by Kennedy's advisers—especially Walter Heller, James Tobin, and Kermit Gordon at the Council of Economic Advisers (CEA) and David Bell at the Bureau of the Budget (BOB)—was the conventional wisdom of the professional economist, and by no means new. No less an authority than Walter Heller, usually identified as the chief architect of the new economics, has stated: "Thus the rationale of the 1964 tax-cut proposal came straight out of the country's postwar economics text books."[7] The novelty consisted primarily in the willingness—even eagerness—to apply the tools of the economist's trade actively to the problem of achieving full employment and strengthening and extending recovery in a noninflationary setting. Taking as their marching orders the mandate of the Employment Act of 1946 that the federal government has the responsibility "to promote maximum employment, production, and purchasing power," Kennedy's advisers sought to bring the economy to full employment by cutting taxes, and then to keep it there by offsetting fluctuations in private demand through appropriately applied monetary and fiscal ease and restraint. Though they were later to disown the term, they referred to their objective as "fine tuning" the economy. They explicitly rejected the idea that budget policy should simply react passively to developments in the private sector.

Before the Kennedy economists could apply their tools to the problem of stimulating recovery, it was necessary to convince a reluctant President, a recalcitrant Congress, and a skeptical public both that the tax cut would work and that it would have no significant undesired side effects.[8] For this reason it was necessary to carry on a massive educational campaign to acquaint the skeptics with the economic analysis underlying the tax cut.[9] The economic concepts

---

[7] Walter W. Heller, *New Dimensions of Political Economy* (New York: W. W. Norton & Company, Inc., 1967), p. 72. The historical development of the "new economics" is traced in Herbert Stein, *The Fiscal Revolution in America* (Chicago: University of Chicago Press, 1969). Quoting with approval the above statement by Heller, Stein writes about the tax cut (p. 380): "As far as ideas on fiscal policy are concerned, Kennedy did not choose from an array of competing doctors; he chose from an array of doctors whose ideas were basically the same. If he had chosen six American economists at random the odds were high that he would have obtained five with the ideas on fiscal policy which his advisers actually had, because those ideas were shared by almost all economists in 1960."

[8] It is worth noting that Kennedy had run in 1960 on a platform of budgetary balance, and very nearly was not persuaded that he should not raise taxes in the summer of 1961 to pay for the military buildup touched off by the Berlin crisis; see Heller, *op. cit.*, pp. 29-36.

[9] Again it is instructive to quote Heller: "In 1961 . . . the problem of the economic adviser was not what to say, but how to get people to listen. . . . The power of Keynesian ideas could not be harnessed to the nation's lagging economy without putting them in forms and terms that could be understood in the sense of fitting the vocabulary and the values of the public. At the same time, men's minds had to be conditioned to accept new thinking, new symbols, and new and broader concepts of the public interest." *Ibid.*, p. 27. Arthur M. Okun has made a similar observation in *The Political Economy of Prosperity* (New York: W. W. Norton & Company, Inc., 1970), pp. 98-99: "A great deal of the effort of the political economist must continue to be concentrated on the

discussed here were prominent both in that educational effort and in the basic decisions on policy, and have come to be considered "the new economics." Readers conversant with these concepts can turn directly to the discussion of historical experience in section three with little loss of continuity.

Defining Full Employment: The Phillips Curve. If it was obvious in 1963 that fiscal stimulus was needed, it was far less clear just how much to stimulate the economy. Overstimulation would result in excess demand and inflation. This could be avoided, at least in principle, by moving gradually to increase the stimulus, but only at the risk of delaying the achievement of high employment.[10] Thus the Council of Economic Advisers chose an amount of fiscal stimulus that would reduce unemployment to a considerable degree without running a very great risk of setting off inflation. It set as its interim goal the reduction of the unemployment rate to 4 percent. In the words of its *Annual Report* for 1962:

> Expansion of aggregate demand is clearly the specific remedy for unemployment caused by a deficiency of aggregate demand. Excessive aggregate demand, however, is a source of inflationary pressure. Consequently, the target for stabilization policy is to eliminate the unemployment which results from inadequate aggregate demand without creating a demand-induced inflation. A situation in which this is achieved can appropriately be described as one of "full em-

elementary pedagogy of stabilization policy. During the surcharge battle, I found it as important to produce homilies about small boys taking medicine and fat ladies munching candy as to work on forecasts and technical analysis."

Stein draws a quite different conclusion from his examination of history, as indicated by the following quotation: "On John F. Kennedy's Inauguration Day in January 1961, the stage was set for the act which, more than any other, came to symbolize the fiscal revolution. The play had been written, a receptive or at least permissive audience was in its seats, and the actors in the wings." *Op. cit.*, p. 372. But on the role of Kennedy and his advisers, Stein adds, "it must be made clear that while the setting, the script, and the audience were prepared, the performance was not easy or inevitable . . . the fact that the times were ripe does not detract from the performance. Decisions still had to be made, and they required courage." *Ibid.*, pp. 373-74.

[10] Moreover, incrementalism in fiscal stimulation may be possible as a practical matter only if income tax reduction is abandoned as the vehicle of stimulation. Given the legislative process, repeated small reductions in income taxes are likely to occur only if all of them are legislated at once, subject to subsequent approval or disapproval by congressional resolution. But this would be difficult to do. Moreover, if it should be determined subsequently that too much stimulus was being produced, the political pressures against repealing previously legislated tax reductions might be too strong to resist.

ployment," in the sense that further expansion of expenditures for goods and services, and for labor to produce them, would be met by only minor increases in employment and output, and by major increases in prices and wages. . . . In the existing economic circumstances, an unemployment rate of about 4 percent is a reasonable and prudent full employment target for stabilization policy.[11]

The 4 percent interim goal was based upon historical evidence on the shape of the so-called "Phillips curve."[12] This evidence suggested that as unemployment fell, prices did not begin to rise appreciably until less than 4 percent of the labor force was unemployed. It specifically denied the view held in some quarters that the unemployment of the early 1960s could not be reduced much by increasing aggregate demand because it was largely structural—in other words, the unemployed were not trained for modern jobs, they were too old or too young to be employed, workers and the available jobs were geographically separated, and so forth. It asserted strongly that those who had been "unemployable" in a loose labor market could and would be employed in a tighter, but not overly tight, labor market.[13] But the evidence also suggested that in order to pave the way for non-inflationary reductions in the unemployment rate to much below 4 percent, it would be necessary to begin at once to improve labor skills, and the functioning of labor markets, in an attempt to shift the Phillips curve to the left.[14]

---

[11] *Annual Report of the Council of Economic Advisers*, 1962 (Washington: U.S. Government Printing Office, 1962), p. 46, hereafter cited as the *Annual Report* for the various years. In this paper administration policy is most often taken from these *Annual Reports*, rather than from the *Economic Reports of the President*, since in most cases the economic analysis and supporting data are reported more fully in the former than in the latter.

[12] The name is derived from the pioneering effort by A. W. Phillips, "The Relation between Unemployment and the Rate of Change of Money Wage Rates in the United Kingdom, 1862-1957," *Economica* (November 1962), pp. 283-99.

[13] See *Annual Report*, 1962, pp. 48-49, and 1963, pp. 41-42.

[14] "The recent history of the U.S. economy contains no evidence that labor and commodity markets are in general excessively 'tight' at 4 percent unemployment. Neither does it suggest that stabilization policy alone could press unemployment significantly below 4 percent without creating substantial upward pressure on prices. . . . If we move firmly to reduce the impact of structural unemployment, we will be able to move the unemployment target steadily from 4 percent to successively lower rates." *Annual Report*, 1962, p. 46. Particularly important in suggesting this shape of the price-unemployment tradeoff or (modified) Phillips curve was an article by Paul A. Samuelson and Robert M. Solow, "Analytical Aspects of Anti-Inflationary Policy," *American Economic Review* (May 1960), pp. 177-94.

Potential GNP and the Gap.[15] The proper interim goal of stabilization policy in the early 1960s may have been to reduce the unemployment rate to 4 percent, as was argued by the Council of Economic Advisers. But even this interim goal did not by itself provide an adequate guide for fiscal policy, unless the economy was to be forced to "feel" its way to full employment. Fiscal policy is, after all, defined directly in terms of tax reductions and expenditure changes, and not in terms of reductions in unemployment. The problem for policy makers was to design fiscal policy so as to provide just the amount of stimulus required to bring the level of economic activity up to its potential—that consistent with a 4 percent unemployment rate.[16] Stated alternatively, the task was to stimulate the economy enough to close the gap between actual and potential GNP. Determining the amount of stimulus required thus involved two steps, (a) estimating potential GNP or the GNP gap and (b) estimating the fiscal stimulus required to close the gap. The first of these steps is outlined here, and the second in the section that follows.

Potential GNP at a given time can be estimated in a number of ways. Most ambitiously, if one knows the total capital stock, the labor force, and the natural resources of the nation, and the technical conditions under which these can be combined most efficiently, he can calculate the nation's potential output of goods and services. More realistically, potential GNP can be estimated by extrapolation from some earlier period in which the economy was considered to be operating at capacity. Knowledge of the growth rate in the labor force, of changes in the average work week, and of the growth rate of

---

[15] This section draws heavily upon Arthur M. Okun, "Potential GNP: Its Measurement and Significance," *Proceedings of the Business and Economic Statistics Section*, American Statistical Association, 1962, reprinted with minor changes in Okun, *The Political Economy of Prosperity*, pp. 132-45. Page references are to the latter source. The official sanction for the analysis outlined here was presented by the Council of Economic Advisers in "The American Economy in 1961: Problems and Policies," *Hearings on the 1961 Economic Report of the President*, Joint Economic Committee (Washington: U.S. Government Printing Office, 1961), pp. 327-29, 373-77. For further discussion, see James W. Knowles, *The Potential Economic Growth in the United States*, Study Paper No. 20 on Employment, Growth, and Price Levels, Congress of the United States, Joint Economic Committee (Washington: U.S. Government Printing Office, 1960), and Michael E. Levy, *Fiscal Policy, Cycles and Growth* (New York: National Industrial Conference Board, 1963), pp. 59-81. For a dissenting view, see Arthur F. Burns, "The New Stagnation Theory and Our Current Economic Policies," *The Morgan Guaranty Survey* (May 1961).

[16] If potential GNP had been defined in terms of a lower unemployment rate, not much of the analysis would be changed. This point is made by Okun, *op. cit.*, p. 133.

productivity per man-hour is sufficient for such extrapolations. The GNP gap is simply the difference between potential and actual output.

A third method of estimating potential GNP and the gap is to ask by how much output would increase if unemployment were brought down to a level defined as "full employment." This approach yields what has been called Okun's Law: "In the postwar period, on the average, each extra percentage point in the unemployment rate above 4 percent has been associated with about a 3 percent decrement in real GNP." [17] Given the actual unemployment rate, it is a simple matter to calculate from this rule of thumb the GNP gap directly and the potential GNP indirectly.

In its 1964 *Annual Report*, the Council of Economic Advisers repeated its earlier statement that "the level of constant-dollar GNP needed to maintain the unemployment rate at 4 percent has been growing at an average rate of about $3^1/_2$ percent a year since mid-1955, when the unemployment rate was close to 4 percent." Because output had grown less rapidly than $3^1/_2$ percent from mid-1955 to the first quarter of 1961, a gap of $50 billion (1963 prices) had developed. Expansion had reduced the gap to $30 billion within a year, but at the end of 1963 the gap still stood at about that level.[18]

The Gap and Fiscal Stimulus. That the GNP gap in 1963 was $30 billion did not mean that fiscal stimulus of $30 billion would be needed to return economic activity to its potential level and restore full employment. Considerably less stimulus would be sufficient, because of induced effects on consumption and investment. These expected effects are described here briefly.

Multiplier analysis.[19] Public and private spending on goods and

---

[17] *Ibid.*, p. 135.

[18] *Annual Report*, 1964, p. 37. Under the third method of calculating the gap mentioned above, we would expect GNP to rise by 4.8 percent, or by about $29 billion, from its level of $600 billion in the fourth quarter of 1963 if the unemployment rate were reduced from the reported 5.6 percent to 4 percent.

[19] The multiplier is perhaps the most purely Keynesian of all the concepts of the new economics. For early exhaustive treatments, see Paul A. Samuelson, "The Simple Mathematics of Income Determination" and Robert L. Bishop, "Alternative Expansionist Fiscal Policies: A Diagrammatic Analysis," both in *Income, Employment, and Public Policy: Essays in Honor of Alvin H. Hansen* (New York: W. W. Norton & Company, Inc., 1948), pp. 133-55 and 317-40, respectively. The multiplier process and the induced response of investment are described by the Council of Economic Advisers in *Annual Report*, 1963, pp. 45-51.

services counts directly as part of GNP.[20] But the contribution to GNP of one dollar of, say, increased public purchases or private investment expenditures is not limited to just one dollar. Part of the dollar becomes the disposable income of households, and over 90 percent of this added household income is spent on personal consumption, making a further addition to GNP; part of the receipts from consumption purchases in turn becomes personal income. This process is repeated until the initial dollar of public expenditure or private investment has induced an additional dollar and a half or so of private expenditures for consumption.[21] Thus the fiscal stimulus provided by about $12 billion of added government spending would be enough to close a GNP gap of $30 billion.[22]

If fiscal stimulus were to be provided through reductions in the personal income tax, rather than through expenditure increases, the multiplier process would begin somewhat differently. The tax cut would not itself enter into GNP, since it represents no demands for goods and services. But it would increase disposable income directly, and would largely be spent on personal consumption. From that point on, the multiplier process would be as described for expenditure increases, and the tax multiplier would be about 2. Thus, fiscal stimulus of about $15 billion would be needed to close a GNP gap of $30 billion if the entire stimulus were to be provided by reducing personal income taxes and if induced effects on investment were ignored.

Investment effects. In fact, however, it was never contemplated that tax reduction be limited to the personal income tax. Corporate tax reduction would increase both the net rate of return on invested funds and the flow of internal funds, thus providing a strong stimulus

---

[20] Only government *purchases* count directly as GNP, transfers and grants-in-aid affecting it only as they are spent by the recipient households or state and local governments. Thus increases in these nonexhaustive expenditures are more like tax reductions than increases in purchases in their effects on GNP.

[21] The Council of Economic Advisers estimated the multiplier for tax reduction to be about 2 (*Annual Report*, 1963, p. 48). Because stimulative increases in expenditures were not being requested, no estimate was given for the expenditure multiplier. Presumably, it would have been about $2^{1/2}$, because the first-round effects of the expenditure increase would be somewhat greater than the expected effect of increasing disposable income by an equal amount through tax reduction.

[22] This ignores both the induced investment discussed immediately below and the question of the monetary policy assumed to accompany the expansive fiscal policy, which is discussed on pages 24 and 25, this chapter.

for investment.[23] This would be accentuated by the "accelerator effects" of investment responding to increased output and higher rates of capacity utilization. This last effect would stimulate investment even if tax reduction were confined to the personal income tax or if fiscal stimulus were provided solely by increasing federal purchases. Increased investment arising from any of these sources would, of course, feed directly into the multiplier process and induce increased consumption spending. Thus it seemed likely that the overall increase in GNP resulting from, say, a $10 billion tax reduction would be considerably larger than the $20 billion suggested by multiplier analysis alone, though it would be difficult to quantify.[24]

Tax Cuts and Deficits. At the time President Kennedy requested Congress to cut taxes in 1963, the U.S. economy was beginning its third year of recovery from the brief recession of 1960. In the absence of the tax cut, the federal budget for fiscal 1964 would be in deficit, and with it, the deficit would be even bigger. Many wondered at the wisdom of cutting taxes in this situation. That taxes might be cut in order to arrest a downturn and stimulate recovery was, in 1963, no longer a revolutionary idea. That they should be cut after recovery

---

[23] In 1962 a change in the tax law had enacted the 7 percent investment credit and the Treasury had liberalized depreciation guidelines. Rate reduction could be expected to augment the attractiveness of the investment credit, if not that of more liberal depreciation.

Almost entirely overlooked in the discussion of tax reduction was the theoretical presumption that business taxation actually increases productive investment from a given pool of funds. See Richard A. Musgrave, *The Theory of Public Finance* (New York: McGraw-Hill Book Co., Inc., 1959), Chapter 14, and James E. Tobin, "Liquidity Preference as Behavior Towards Risk," *Review of Economic Studies* (February 1958), pp. 65-86. For a later restatement of this issue, see Joseph E. Stiglitz, "The Effects of Income, Wealth, and Capital Gains Taxation on Risk Taking," *Quarterly Journal of Economics* (May 1969), pp. 263-83. Of course, by increasing internal funds, rate reduction would increase the pool of funds available for investment.

[24] See *Annual Report*, 1963, p. 51. The CEA's lack of quantification of the impact on investment reflects the state of empirical knowledge at the time. Okun states in *The Political Economy of Prosperity*, p. 19, that "The best example I can offer (of a purely scientific, nonideological controversy among economists) is the disagreement among students of business investment regarding the relative importance of internal cash flow, the cost of external capital, and the growth of final demand as determining factors." With regard to the incentive effect on investment, Stein has written, "The acknowledgement of the incentive effect introduced a camel of considerable size into the Keynesian tent." *Op. cit.*, p. 444. The author's interpretation would be that this particular camel had been present in the Keynesian tent for some time, and—to mix the analogies—had long since become a respectable member of the tribe. Support for this proposition is provided, for example, in Musgrave, *op. cit.*, chapter 19.

was well on its way and with the budget already in deficit was another question, and there were many skeptics.[25]

President Kennedy's proposal was met with especial trepidation in some quarters, coming as it did close on the heels of Eisenhower's identification of the national debt as "our children's inherited mortgage." [26] The Council of Economic Advisers marshaled a number of sophisticated arguments to the effect that the growth in the debt posed no serious problem.[27] This paper focuses upon two aspects of the debate: the contention that the preexisting tendencies toward deficit resulted not from fiscally irresponsible deficit spending, but from the failure to maintain high levels of economic activity; and the increase in the deficit resulting from cutting taxes would be temporary, should be considered as a downpayment on prosperity, and would be eliminated by the achievement of full employment. The next two subsections discuss these points.

The full employment surplus.[28] The budget deficit or surplus recorded in the national income accounts is the result of two inter-

---

[25] As Stein has described it, "The tax cut would be made in 'cold blood'." *Op. cit.*, p. 410.

[26] The reference is from President Eisenhower's State of the Union Message, January 7, 1960.

[27] *Annual Report*, 1963, pp. 78-83. Eisenhower's concern with the size of the national debt and characterization of the debt as a burden on future generations revived a classic controversy, most of the important contributions to which are contained in James M. Ferguson, ed., *Public Debt and Future Generations* (Chapel Hill: University of North Carolina Press, 1964). After the smoke had cleared, the conclusion was more or less what Ricardo and Pigou had said, that financing government activities through issuance of debt, instead of through taxation, burdens future generations to the extent that it reduces the amount of capital stock left for them to use. Stein contends that this is the burden Eisenhower had in mind and that by 1963 references to budget balancing were purely ritualistic (*op. cit.*, pp. 350-51, p. 454). There is, however, room for considerable doubt on both scores.

[28] The *locus classicus* of the CEA discussion of the full employment surplus is the *Annual Report*, 1962, pp. 78-81. For a more complete discussion, see Levy, *op. cit.*, pp. 82-97. Stein, *op. cit.*, traces the development of the concept to its origins, especially to Beardsley Ruml and the Committee for Economic Development's famous *Taxes and the Budget: A Program for Prosperity in a Free Economy*, New York, 1947, and to Milton Friedman, "A Monetary and Fiscal Framework for Economic Stability," *American Economic Review* (June 1948), pp. 245-64. He also points out (pp. 364-65) that in 1960 David Lusher, Charles Schultze, and Edward Denison and he himself were among the first to make public estimates of the contemporary high employment surplus. For details of methods of estimating the full employment surplus, see Nancy H. Teeters, "Estimates of the Full-Employment Surplus, 1955-64," *Review of Economics and Statistics* (August 1965), pp. 309-21.

acting forces: (a) the impact of government policy upon the level of economic activity and (b) the relation of receipts to expenditures at various levels of economic activity. Thus it is a poor indicator of the stance of fiscal policy, which involves (a) alone. For this reason it is useful to measure the surplus or deficit at some standard level of employment, thereby isolating the expansionary or restrictive impact of fiscal policy. The full employment surplus is such a standardized measure of fiscal impact.[29]

In Figure 1 the line marked FF' shows, for a given tax-expenditure structure, the state of budgetary balance (as a percent of potential GNP) associated with various levels of economic activity (also expressed as a percent of potential GNP). The upward slope of this line results from the built-in response of tax receipts to fluctuations in GNP and the relatively inelastic response of government expenditures to changes in GNP. This curve shows the budgetary balance at any level of GNP but it cannot by itself indicate either the actual level of GNP or the budget deficit or surplus that will result and be recorded in the national income accounts. To discover that we need a second curve, GG'. It shows what the level of economic activity would be for different tax-expenditure structures, as measured by the level of budgetary balance at full employment associated with them.[30]

---

[29] The inadequacies of the full employment surplus as a measure of fiscal stimulus or restraint have been well documented—for example in Edward M. Gramlich, "Measures of the Aggregate Demand Impact of the Federal Budget," in Wilfred Lewis, Jr., ed., *Budget Concepts for Economic Analysis* (Washington: Brookings Institution, 1968), pp. 110-27—and need not be repeated here. The point is that in its efforts to sell the tax cut the Council of Economic Advisers focused upon the full employment surplus as the best single measure of fiscal restraint.

[30] To the author's knowledge, this analysis has not appeared elsewhere. It is, of course, a gross oversimplification. Programs of equal full employment deficit or surplus could result in quite different levels of economic activity, depending upon the size of the budget, the combination of taxes used to raise a given amount of revenue, the mix of federal expenditures, and the stance of monetary policy. For expositional purposes these qualifications are largely ignored, as they are in most discussions of the full employment budget as a measure of fiscal restraint.

The slope of FF' (.31) is the fraction of increase of GNP taken by increased taxes, plus the fraction of increase in GNP reflected in reductions in transfer payments. The reciprocal of the slope of GG' (−1.82) is the pure consumption multiplier for tax reduction, assuming constant marginal tax rates. Both estimates are taken from Arthur M. Okun, "Measuring the Impact of the 1964 Tax Reduction," in Walter W. Heller, ed., *Perspective on Economic Growth* (New York: Random House, Inc., 1968), pp. 27-49. Inability to incorporate induced investment is one of the shortcomings of this pedagogic device.

Figure 1

NATIONAL INCOME AND BUDGET BALANCE, USING FULL EMPLOYMENT CONCEPTS

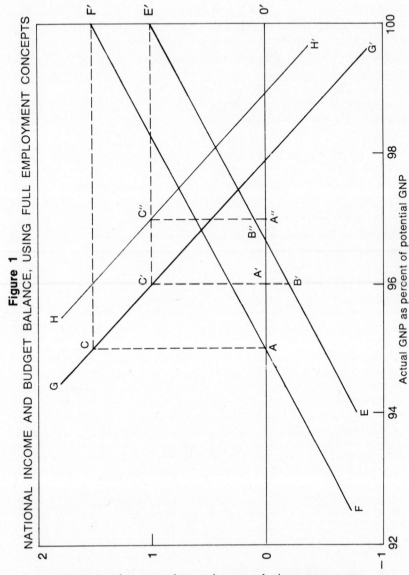

This curve slopes downward because, in general, the greater the level of public expenditures or the lower the level of tax rates, i.e., the lower the full employment surplus, the greater will be the level of economic activity. The actual level of GNP that will result from the tax-expenditure policy indicated by schedule FF' is determined to be OA, the level consistent with the full employment surplus implicit in schedule FF'. (Note that AC equals O'F'.) At that level of output the actual budget is roughly in balance.[31]

When the budget-GNP nexus is cast in these terms, we can see that the actual deficit or surplus is a poor indicator of the stance of fiscal policy. Interpreting the actual budget position as indicating budgetary stimulus or restraint is to confuse it with the first of its determinants, forgetting the second. Line FF' shows that although the actual budget was in balance, a surplus of O'F' would have occurred if the economy had operated at potential. But the economy operated below potential, and the budget was only in balance *precisely* because fiscal policy was too restrictive. A less restrictive fiscal policy—represented, for example, by EE'—would result in a somewhat larger deficit, A'B', but it would also allow the achievement of a substantially greater output, OA'. Thus, far from representing fiscal irresponsibility, the CEA argued, the fiscal policies proposed were essential to meeting the obligations of the Employment Act of 1946.

Revenue recoupment. If fiscal stimulus were applied only through expenditure increases or reductions in personal income taxes, and if induced increases in investment were ignored, the increase in tax collections resulting from the higher level of economic activity would be extremely unlikely to wipe out the increase in the deficit (or reduction in the surplus) created in the process of stimulating the economy.[32] But once the incentive effects of cutting business taxes

---

[31] The situation depicted in Figure 1 is generally consistent with that prevailing at the end of 1963: a full employment surplus of $1\frac{1}{2}$ percent of potential GNP, actual output of 95 percent of potential, and balance in the actual budget (see *Annual Report*, 1964, p. 46).

[32] This proposition is demonstrated in Musgrave, *op. cit.*, pp. 437-38. It is also implicit in the shape of the curves in Figure 1. Let t be the slope of FF' and $-m$ be the reciprocal of the slope of GG'. Tax reduction of an amount T increases income by mT and induces a rise in revenues (minus induced expenditures) of tmT. Thus the actual surplus falls by $T(1-mt)$. It appears that if t and/or $-m$ is relatively large, tm could exceed one and the actual surplus could rise. But m is $\frac{c}{1-c(1-t)}$, where c is the marginal propensity to consume out of disposable income. Thus mt can exceed one only if ct is greater than $1-c(1-t)$, which can

and the accelerator effect on investment resulting from increased output are allowed, it is entirely possible that economic activity could rise by enough to prevent any rise in the actual deficit. In terms of Figure 1, the curve GG' would move to the right, say to HH', so that output would be OA" and a surplus of A"B" would result, rather than a deficit of A'B'. In the context of the 1963 discussion, this means that the tax cut might be sufficiently stimulative to allow recoupment of the lost revenues.[33] If so, then the increase in the deficit would indeed be a temporary price for prosperity and an eventual surplus (or at least deficit reduction), and should be welcomed rather than avoided, even on the basis of budget-balancing rules.

Fiscal drag and fiscal dividends. The Council of Economic Advisers did not believe that the 1964 tax reduction would never need to be repeated. Because federal tax collections rise strongly in response to secular growth in GNP, the full employment surplus would tend to grow over time, unless the automatic growth in revenues were offset by repeated discretionary tax reductions, expanded federal expenditures, or sharing of revenues with state and local governments. In terms of figure 1, the curve FF' would tend to shift up over time. Thus, the automatic response of tax collections to increases in GNP, which is one of the economy's built-in stabilizers in a cyclical context, was seen to be a potentially ominous source of "fiscal drag" in a secular context. If the fiscal drag were allowed to develop, as it had been before 1964, economic activity would be depressed to below its potential. Thus the Council envisaged repeated "fiscal dividends" to offset this contractionary influence. Further tax reduction and revenue sharing were obvious candidates to benefit from those dividends, though Kennedy and Johnson doubtlessly saw the need for expanded expenditures as well.

Accommodative Monetary Policy. A prominent consideration in the discussions of the new economics was the role of monetary policy in stimulating expansion, or more generally, the proper mix of

---

never occur, so long as c is less than one. The problem is, of course, that high values of t imply large leakages and low values for the tax multiplier, $-m$. In the present case, $mt = .564$.

[33] It should be noted that stimulative monetary policy would also shift the GG' curve to the right, resulting in greater output and a reduced actual deficit for a given level of full employment surplus. Similarly, structural tax policy such as the investment tax credit moves curve GG' to the right and therefore has far more impact on the level of economic activity than is indicated by the change in the full employment surplus alone.

monetary and fiscal policies in meeting the nation's various economic goals. The 1964 tax cut was proposed in an environment of concern over the U.S. balance of payments. Because of the interest sensitivity of short-term capital flows, it was felt that monetary policy could not be used aggressively to stimulate the economy. Rather, fiscal policy would be the prime mover toward expansion, with monetary policy being kept sufficiently restrictive to prevent the potentially large outflows of short-term capital.[34] On the other hand, it was desired that monetary policy be sufficiently expansionary to allow the growth of output resulting from fiscal stimulus to occur without being curtailed by rising interest rates. In the words of Arthur Okun:

> Basically, monetary policy was accommodative while fiscal policy was the active partner. The Federal Reserve allowed the demands for liquidity and credit generated by a rapidly expanding economy to be met at stable interest rates. . . . The resulting increases in the quantity of money, bank credit, business loans, and total borrowing all reflected shifts in demands for funds with an essentially passive response on the supply side.[35]

This interpretation of events is discussed further below.

Econometric Forecasting and Stabilization Policy. The way in which tax reduction can be expected to affect aggregate demand is outlined briefly above. But the appropriate size of the 1964 tax cut could not be decided in such a rough and ready way, and greater precision would become essential as full employment was approached. It was to the econometric forecasters that the CEA turned in its quest for precision in managing the economy.

Stated most simply, an econometric forecast is an effort to use statistical methods to estimate the values of key economic variables

---

[34] Among the influential articles on the appropriate mix of monetary and fiscal policy was Robert A. Mundell, "The Appropriate Use of Monetary and Fiscal Policy for Internal and External Stability," *International Monetary Fund Staff Papers* (March 1962), pp. 70-79. An attempt was also made to "twist" the yield curve by shortening the average maturity of the public debt, in the hopes that short-term rates could be kept up and long-term rates down. There is sometimes uncertainty as to whether the new economists thought money really mattered. While the constraint imposed by the balance-of-payments problem makes this question rather moot, it seems certain from a balanced reading of CEA reports of the period that it was recognized that money could matter.

[35] Okun, *Political Economy of Prosperity*, p. 53. See also *Annual Report, 1964*, pp. 42-44, 47.

at some future date.[36] In most instances, attention focuses upon the estimate of gross national product (GNP), which is then compared with potential GNP. If actual output is estimated to be below (above) potential, public policy can be adjusted to bring actual GNP nearer to its potential.[37] Inherent in the econometrician's model are multipliers that relate given government policies to their expected effects on the target macroeconomic variables of the economy.[38]

The basic idea in constructing an econometric model for use in forecasting macroeconomic developments in the economy is to estimate equations explaining each of the components on the right side of the following equation:

$$Y = C + I + G + (X\text{-}M),$$

where Y is gross national product, C is consumption, I is gross investment (consisting of business fixed investment, residential construction, and inventory investment), G represents government purchases of goods and services, and (X-M) is net exports (to be ignored in what follows). Consumption, sometimes broken into three or more subcomponents, is usually specified to depend upon an estimate of personal income after taxes. If consumption adjusts mechanically to changes in net income, tax reduction could be expected to have approximately the multiplier effects on output described earlier in this section.

The theory of investment behavior was in considerably more disarray in the early 1960s than consumption theory. According to various economists, business fixed investment depended upon the flow of retained earnings and depreciation allowances, upon the expected profitability of investment, or upon the rate of change of

---

[36] For an extremely lucid explanation of econometric forecasting and its use in making policy, see Daniel B. Suits, "Forecasting with an Econometric Model," *American Economic Review* (March 1962), pp. 104-32, reprinted in Robert Aaron Gordon and Lawrence R. Klein, *Readings in Business Cycles* (Homewood, Illinois: Richard D. Irwin, Inc., for the American Economic Association, 1965), pp. 597-625.

[37] This description slurs over the potential conflict between full employment and price stability. In the discussion of the early 1960s this was a relatively unimportant qualification. Even when the conflict is taken into account, little of the brief description offered here is altered. Policy would still be aimed at bringing estimated actual GNP into line with some target level of GNP.

[38] See Suits, *op. cit.*, for an elementary explanation of the derivation of these multipliers in both a simple example and a model of the economy estimated for 1962. The values of multipliers reported in the *Annual Report* of the Council of Economic Advisers for 1963 were derived from such econometric models.

final output in the economy.[39] Residential construction was seen as depending upon the rate of family formation and credit conditions, while inventory investment was thought to depend largely upon current stocks and sales expectations. Although there might have been less agreement on the response of investment to stabilization policies than on the response of consumption, it was generally believed that the former was reliable enough to justify confidence in econometric forecasts. And, of course, it was assumed that at least the federal government's purchases could be known with considerable certainty.

One crucial complication to the use of forecasts in efforts to stabilize the economy has yet to be mentioned. This involves the time phasing of the response of the various components of aggregate demand to monetary and fiscal stimulus, or the lags, as they are generally called. Most classroom discussions of Keynesian economics and fiscal policy, at least the elementary ones, make little or no reference to the time path followed by GNP (and various other macroeconomic variables as well) as it moves from one equilibrium level to another in response to stabilization policy. Because comparative statics is the vehicle of the analysis, only equilibrium situations are examined.

Advisers to the President on macroeconomic policy cannot be satisfied with comparative statics, for a number of reasons. First, the time period that must pass before the new equilibrium is substantially achieved is of no small importance.[40] The period of adjustment depends upon how rapidly consumption responds to changes in income, the speed with which businessmen adjust inventories and the stock of fixed capital, et cetera. Second, and perhaps equally important, the adjustment process need not be a smooth one; it may involve some overshooting and subsequent falling short of the mark on the way to the new equilibrium. Again, whether or not this occurs (and the magnitude and duration of such swings as occur) depends upon the behavioral parameters and lag structure inherent in the

---

[39] For a simple explanation and an empirical test of five alternative models of investment behavior, see Charles W. Bischoff, "Business Investment in the 1970's: A Comparison of Models," *Brookings Papers on Economic Activity*, 1 (Washington: Brookings Institution, 1971), pp. 13-58. Bischoff, p. 13, quotes with approval the statement by Okun in footnote 24 above on the extent of disagreement among economists on this subject.

[40] For a clear exposition of this point, see W. L. Smith and R. L. Teigen, eds., *Readings in Money, National Income, and Stabilization Policy*, rev. ed. (Homewood, Illinois: Richard D. Irwin, Inc., 1970), pp. 25-40.

economy.[41] Only a dynamic forecasting model that incorporates these lags can be expected to predict the economy's path between equilibrium points.

Finally, it is even possible, if not likely, that the lag structure is such that poorly timed efforts to stabilize the economy could actually be destabilizing.[42] In its most elementary form, this means reacting too late to cyclical developments, and thereby accentuating them. For example, expansionary fiscal policy might be employed to bring the economy out of a recession just as recovery had begun by itself. One can imagine situations in which the fiscal stimulus would induce expansion to beyond the full employment level. Then, to complete the cycle, the expansionary policy might be reversed just as the expansion had run its course, throwing the economy into a very steep decline. Whether this would happen is, of course, uncertain, and depends upon response parameters in the economy, but it does give the fine-tuner reason for caution.[43] The Council of Economic Advisers seemed confident in 1964 that techniques of forecasting were adequate to indicate the needed directions and magnitudes of fiscal policy far enough in advance to make an active fiscal policy practicable.[44]

---

[41] The classic exposition of this point is Paul A. Samuelson, "Interactions between the Multiplier Analysis and the Principle of Acceleration," *Review of Economics and Statistics* (May 1939), pp. 75-78.

[42] For expositions of this point, see A. W. Phillips, "Stabilization Policy and the Time-Forms of Lagged Responses," *Economic Journal* (June 1957), pp. 265-77, reprinted in Gordon and Klein, *op. cit.*, pp. 666-79; Milton Friedman, "A Monetary and Fiscal Framework for Economic Stability," *American Economic Review* (June 1948), pp. 245-64, and "The Effects of a Full Employment Policy on Economic Stability," in *Essays in Positive Economics* (Chicago: University of Chicago Press, 1953), pp. 117-33; Musgrave, *op. cit.*, pp. 512-15; and William J. Baumol, "Pitfalls in Contracyclical Policies: Some Tools and Results," *Review of Economics and Statistics* (February 1961), pp. 21-26.

[43] For an analysis of the historical record before the tax cut, see Albert Ando and E. Cary Brown, "Lags in Fiscal Policy," in *Stabilization Policies* (Englewood, N.J.: Prentice-Hall, Inc., for the Commission on Money and Credit, 1963), pp. 97-163.

[44] Stein notes, *op. cit.*, p. 384, that Heller believed experience had confirmed his "guarded optimism" about forecasting. He quotes Heller, *New Dimensions in Political Economy*, p. 69:

> In part, this shift from a more passive to a more active policy has been made possible by steady advances in fact-gathering, forecasting techniques, and business practice. Our statistical net is now spread wider and brings in its catch faster. Forecasting has the benefit of not only

Price Stability in a Noncompetitive Economy. Thus far in this survey of the new economics, attention has focused primarily upon the macroeconomic analysis employed by the Council of Economic Advisers to sell the 1964 tax cut. But the new economics also contained an important element of microeconomics. It will be useful here to review very briefly several related microeconomic issues—investment, labor productivity, price behavior, and the wage-price guideposts—even though other studies in this series examine them in detail.[45]

During his first year in office, President Kennedy proposed the investment tax credit and the acceleration of depreciation allowances. Both of these measures were undertaken in 1962 in order to reduce the tax burden on business. Yet the initial proposals were met with apparent skepticism from businessmen, who doubted the President's sincerity.[46] Understandably, they asked why a liberal Democratic president was advocating tax breaks for business investment.

The answer lies in the effort to reconcile full employment and price stability. Any of a number of stimulative actions could have been taken to bring the economy to full employment. But full employment would be consistent with reasonably stable prices only if costs did not rise with output and capacity utilization. One way to prevent costs from rising would be to encourage investment in new plants and equipment. This would increase labor productivity through modernization—something that had not kept pace because of the overhang of already underutilized equipment in the 1950s. Thus, the Council of Economic Advisers argued, the tax incentives for investment were an integral part of efforts to achieve and eventually to pass the interim 4 percent unemployment goal.[47]

A second set of policies to prevent labor costs from rising can

---

more refined, computer-assisted methods but of improved surveys of consumer and investment intentions.

However, on the same page, Heller goes on to say:

So in a full employment world the economic dosage has to be much more carefully controlled, the premium on quantitative scientific knowledge becomes far greater, and the premium on speed in our fiscal machinery also rises. . . . [O]ur fiscal processes have not caught up with our advances in fiscal policy. In spite of the rapid responses to President Johnson's tax requests in 1965 and 1966, congressional tax machinery is not yet speedy enough to meet the economic needs of the times.

We will have more to say on this subject in the concluding chapter of this study.

[45] See Marten Estey, chapter 3, and Thomas Gale Moore, chapter 4, this volume.
[46] Heller, *New Dimensions of Political Economy*, pp. 80-81.
[47] *Ibid.; Annual Report*, 1962, pp. 53-56, 65-66, 132-33.

be grouped under the convenient heading of "structural policies." The CEA asserted without reservation that the bulk of the unemployment of the early 1960s was not structural, and that the interim unemployment goal of 4 percent could be reached with little pressure on prices. But it recognized the foolishness of waiting for the interim goal to be reached before attacking the bottlenecks that would occur as full employment came into sight. Thus, the Kennedy and Johnson administrations proposed a variety of manpower training, education, and relocation programs that would facilitate achieving full employment and price stability together.[48]

Without question the most famous (or, in the eyes of some, infamous) effort to improve the terms of trade between price stability and full employment by shifting the Phillips curve involved the wage-price guideposts and presidential "jaw-boning." The Council of Economic Advisers was impressed by the fact that in 1956 and 1957 prices rose appreciably in sectors of the economy where market power was great, and by the hypothesis that much of the inflation of the period could be traced to those sectors.[49] In order to prevent a recurrence of this phenomenon, the council in its 1962 *Annual Report* announced its "Guideposts for Noninflationary Wage and Price Behavior." These detailed the arithmetic of the relationship between stable prices, growth in labor productivity, and noninflationary wage increases.[50] The general guideposts, subject to qualification in particular instances, were:

> The general guide for noninflationary wage behavior is that the rate of increase in wage rates (including fringe benefits) in each industry be equal to the trend rate of over-all productivity increase. General acceptance of this guide would maintain stability of labor cost per unit of output for the economy as a whole—though not of course for individual industries. The general guide for noninflationary price behavior calls for price reduction if the industry's rate of productivity increase exceeds the over-all rate—for this

[48] See *Annual Report*, 1962 (pp. 92-96, 117-23), 1963 (pp. 41-42), 1964 (Appendix A, especially pp. 172-83), 1965 (pp. 120-31).

[49] *Annual Report*, 1962, pp. 170-76. The Council's analysis seems to have built solidly upon Otto Eckstein and Gary Fromm, *Steel and the Postwar Inflation*, and Thomas A. Wilson, *An Analysis of the Inflation in Machinery Prices*, Study Papers numbers 2 and 3, Prepared in Connection with the Study of Employment, Growth and Price Levels, Joint Economic Committee, U.S. Congress (Washington: U.S. Government Printing Office, 1959).

[50] *Annual Report*, 1962, pp. 185-90.

would mean declining unit labor costs; it calls for an appropriate increase in price if the opposite relationship prevails; and it calls for stable prices if the two rates of productivity increase are equal. These are advanced as general guideposts. To reconcile them with objectives of equity and efficiency, specific modifications must be made to adapt them to the circumstances of particular industries.[51]

It was believed that because of the direct appeal to public spiritedness and the implicit threat that uncooperative firms and unions would receive adverse publicity, the guideposts would help forestall a repetition of the 1956-57 experience and facilitate the reconciliation of full employment and price stability.[52]

Missing Components. In retrospect, we can identify several lacunae in the magnificent intellectual edifice of the new economists that were only dimly perceived in the early 1960s. These can be identified briefly as the uncertainty of effective political support for the new economics, the lack of substantial recent experience at full employment during peacetime, and uncertainty as to the role played by

---

[51] *Ibid.*, p. 189. The most important modifications were: (1) Wage rate increases would exceed the general guide rate in an industry which would otherwise be unable to attract sufficient labor; or in which wage rates are exceptionally low compared with the range of wages earned elsewhere by similar labor, because the bargaining position of workers has been weak in particular local labor markets. (2) Wage rate increases would fall short of the general guide rate in an industry which could not provide jobs for its entire labor force even in times of generally full employment; or in which wage rates are exceptionally high compared with the range of wages earned elsewhere by similar labor, because the bargaining position of workers has been especially strong. (3) Prices would rise more rapidly, or fall more slowly, than indicated by the general guide rate in an industry in which the level of profits was insufficient to attract the capital required to finance a needed expansion in capacity; or in which costs other than labor costs had risen. (4) Prices would rise more slowly, or fall more rapidly, than indicated by the general guide in an industry in which the relation of productive capacity to full employment demand shows the desirability of an outflow of capital from the industry; or in which costs other than labor costs have fallen; or in which excessive market power has resulted in rates of profit substantially higher than those earned elsewhere on investments of comparable risk.

[52] The most detailed analysis of the guidelines is John Sheahan, *The Wage-Price Guideposts* (Washington: Brookings Institution, 1967). Sheahan has noted that as time progressed and full employment was neared and finally passed, the exceptions to the general rule were played down and the general guideposts took on more the aspect of rules for wage and price behavior and less the appearance of guides for discussion.

expectations in the quest for price stability. These deserve attention at this point.

Political support: the first-best solution. There are both theoretical and practical reasons for placing the main burden of a stabilizing discretionary fiscal policy on tax policy, rather than on changes in government expenditures. Theoretically, it is desirable that the level and composition of public spending be determined by voter preferences for the use of full employment income, and not be varied to offset fluctuations in economic activity.[53] Moreover, as a practical matter, the majority of federal expenditures are more or less uncontrollable within the time span relevant for stabilization. Interest on the national debt must be paid; procurement contracts must be honored; most social security benefits, veterans pensions, and other social programs are not likely to be cut to fight inflation; and public works, once begun, often cannot economically be curtailed. Antirecessionary use of expenditure policy encounters similar difficulties. Given the magnitude of the "uncontrollables" in the budget, a flexible fiscal policy implemented through changes in expenditures would involve completely unrealistic and undesirable changes in the minority of the budget that can be varied in the short run.[54] Thus it seems that fine tuning, if it is to be implemented through fiscal policy, must be done on the tax side.[55]

The U.S. Congress, and especially the House of Representatives, is notoriously jealous of its constitutional role as initiator of revenue legislation. The House Ways and Means Committee holds extensive hearings before sending tax legislation to the House floor and to the Senate, whose Finance Committee also holds hearings.[56] The time required for the hearings is of relatively little consequence where

---

[53] See Musgrave, *op. cit.*, for the classic statement of this proposition.

[54] *The Budget for the United States Government for the Fiscal Year Ending June 30, 1971* (hereafter, *Budget* for various years) estimated (p. 42) that "built-in costs for relatively uncontrollable programs will account for an estimated 69% of total outlays." The relative merits of tax and expenditure policies for relieving the pressure of the Vietnam buildup are discussed in Okun, *Political Economy of Prosperity*, pp. 63-64.

[55] The possibility of fine tuning via monetary policy is not considered here. See Cagan, chapter 2, this volume. Whether fiscal policy should even be used for fine tuning is examined in greater detail in the last part of this section.

[56] For a brief summary and appraisal of the tax legislative process, see Joseph A. Pechman, *Federal Tax Policy*, rev. ed. (Washington: Brookings Institution, 1971), chapter 3. A more detailed political appraisal is to be found in Lawrence C. Pierce, *The Politics of Fiscal Policy Formation* (Pacific Palisades, California: Goodyear Publishing Co., Inc., 1971).

major structural reform of the tax system is concerned. Equity would be worth waiting for.

But when a simple across-the-board adjustment of rates is required for stabilization purposes, time is often of the essence. Delay in enacting the adjustment may allow a recession to become cumulative or an incipient inflation to begin to accelerate. For this reason President Kennedy requested standby authority to reduce income tax rates temporarily, within predetermined limits and subject to congressional veto.[57] But despite the widespread support of professional economists for such limited executive discretion over tax rates, the Ways and Means Committee has steadfastly refused even to consider the idea. Tax rate changes designed to stabilize the economy must follow the traditional path through the congressional maze. Thus, if the economy is to be fine-tuned, political support for fine tuning must be strong. The electorate and its representatives in Congress must understand the rationale and necessity for the frequent alteration in tax rates that an activist fiscal policy may require. Moreover, they must be content to live with budget deficits or surpluses, as the exigencies of stabilization policy dictate. They must on the one hand avoid the fear that deficits always imply fiscal irresponsibility, and on the other hand withstand the temptation to cut taxes or increase expenditures if an expected surplus is needed to prevent inflationary pressures.

Even if the new economists were to succeed in driving home the lesson that fiscal policy should be used to eliminate inflationary and deflationary gaps, a further obstacle to fine tuning might remain. Because of the lag involved in getting tax legislation through Congress and the lags with which policy actions affect the economy, fiscal policy must be geared to the future rather than to the contemporary state of the economy. This implies in turn that economic developments must be forecast sufficiently far in advance so that tax (or expenditure) legislation can be on the books and influencing aggregate demand when needed. Otherwise fiscal policy would be reacting to cold economic tracks and would be as likely to be destabilizing as

---

[57] *Economic Report of the President*, January 1962 (Washington: U.S. Government Printing Office, 1962), pp. 17-19. Kennedy also proposed standby executive authority to initiate up to $2 billion of spending for capital improvements and improvement of the unemployment compensation system. It is ironic that Kennedy requested permission only to *lower* tax rates in order to forestall recession, since the massive fiscal failure of the 1960s involved delay in *raising* taxes when needed to prevent inflation. Whether discretionary changes in rates should be applied to taxes other than income taxes is considered in the last section of this paper.

stabilizing. The difficulty is that the man in the street (and his representatives in Congress) might intellectually appreciate the need to shoot at a target that has not yet appeared on the economic horizon, but the temptation to react only to existing conditions would be great. This is especially true since acceptance of fine tuning requires a degree of faith in the predictive ability of social scientists that Americans give only with considerable skepticism.

Nor is this the end of the problem. The President and his economic and political advisers might propose tax legislation that they believe could be passed with little opposition, and therefore quickly. One approach would be to divorce tax measures intended primarily for stabilization from structural reforms (or rate adjustments within a fixed revenue total). But sometimes it is necessary for the President to accept legislation he finds unpalatable as the price of rate adjustment. For example, it became clear early in the push for tax reduction in 1963-64 that slower expenditure increases would be one of the prices politically powerful fiscal conservatives in the Congress would exact from the advocates of fiscal activism.[58] As little sense as it made from a fiscal policy standpoint, a less stimulative expenditure policy was the political *sine qua non* of stimulative tax reduction. This suggested that in the future fiscal activism might once again be held hostage by those interested in slowing the growth of federal spending. If so, the practical performance of fine tuning could fall substantially short of its theoretical potential.

In summary, only if the level of economic sophistication of American citizens, congressmen, and the President had been increased considerably by the discussion leading up to the 1964 tax cut could it have been expected that fine tuning would be successful. Even then, given existing processes of fiscal decision making, a few strategically placed politicians could scuttle the effort.

Experience at high employment. The task of an adviser on macroeconomic policy in the early 1960s was a relatively simple one. With a GNP gap of $50 billion, or even $30 billion, the need to stimulate the economy was apparent, and the precise estimate of the amount of stimulus was, within limits, a secondary matter.

The crucial test began in the second half of 1965 as the economy neared the 4 percent interim goal for the unemployment rate. The

---

[58] See Stein, *op. cit.*, pp. 451-53 for a lucid description of this episode. In *New Dimensions of Political Economy*, pp. 112-14, Walter Heller has noted that political expediency had forced Kennedy to choose tax reduction over the expenditure increases he would have preferred as a means of stimulating the economy.

interim goal had to be reappraised in the light of the tradeoff between unemployment and inflation as it appeared at the time. But knowing what the Phillips curve looked like over the relevant range was, in itself, an uncertain business.

Except during wartime, the economy had been at full employment only briefly during the 30 years preceding the inauguration of John F. Kennedy and the arrival of the new economics at the White House. For this reason there were too few observations of the price-unemployment tradeoff to be able to draw the Phillips curve with great confidence for low levels of unemployment. As noted above, the most recent approach to full employment in 1955-57 had been marred by considerable inflation, with consumer prices rising by 8 percent from May 1955 to March 1958. The Council of Economic Advisers considered the inflation during that period to be of the administered price variety, which the guideposts were intended to prevent, or at least slow down.[59]

Yet there was considerable uncertainty as to how wages and prices would react as full employment was reached in the wake of the tax cut.[60] There was, however, agreement that once full employment was neared, further reductions in the unemployment rate would be accompanied by increasing risks of inflation. This was especially true if the expansion were so rapid as to create bottlenecks in key sectors or occupational groups. In addition, it would be crucial to avoid overshooting the mark and setting off an inflationary spiral by creating excess demand. Thus the new economists urged caution in the final stages of the drive to full employment.[61]

---

[59] See *Annual Report*, 1962, pp. 170-72 for a discussion of this earlier period.

[60] It is useful to quote Okun's comments on this period:

> . . . [I]n a world of full utilization, the problem of keeping the economy close to a chosen course is compounded by the uncertainties in choosing the course. The ideal rate of utilization is necessarily a difficult compromise between the objective of maximum production and employment, on the one hand and the objective of price stability, on the other. We have had little experience historically in confronting that hard choice because the nation has so rarely remained on a reasonably satisfactory growth path. Except during wartime inflations, we have not been at full employment long enough to test, under these circumstances, the supply capabilities of the economy, its price-cost performance, or public attitudes toward price increases of various rates. (*Political Economy of Prosperity*, pp. 60-61.)

[61] Two recent chairmen of the Council of Economic Advisers have expressed this point clearly. According to Walter Heller,

> [T]he margin for error diminishes as the economy reaches the treasured but treacherous area of full employment. Big doses of expansionary

35

The role of expectations. Perhaps the biggest question mark—as revealed by hindsight, if not by foresight—was the role that expectations would play in the attempt to reconcile full employment and price stability. In their early days in Washington, the new economists clearly recognized the need to raise the expectations of businessmen with regard to the future state of the economy. Business investment seemed to be languishing in doldrums created by a long period of subpotential performance by the economy.[62] It was to break this mood of pessimism and to raise expectations, as well as to create the more objectively identifiable incentives for investment, that accelerated depreciation and the investment tax credit, and then the cut in corporate income tax rates, were proposed. Moreover, the CEA devoted a considerable portion of its lecture-circuit educational effort to the proposition that the business cycle was dead, or could be anesthetized by appropriate doses of the new economics.

Increased business confidence engendered by such prophesies would, of course, make the eulogies self-fulfilling, so long as stimulus was required. Being less afraid of being caught with excess capacity in a subsequent downturn, businessmen would invest and generate a business expansion. So long as the expansion could be continued, but contained, the business cycle would indeed be dormant.

The day of reckoning might come, however, if ever it became necessary to curtail investment in the interest of price stability. Investment might continue unabated and contribute to inflationary levels of aggregate demand, if business continued to be confident that full employment would be maintained. The problem would be magnified if inflation were allowed to get a full head of steam. If

medicine were easy—and safe—to recommend in the face of a $50 billion gap and a hesitant Congress. But at full employment, targets have to be defined more sharply, tolerances are smaller, the line between expansion and inflation becomes thinner. (*New Dimensions of Political Economy,* p. 69.)

Arthur Okun has expressed the same sentiment:

[O]nce full utilization was attained, the range of tolerance for policy error would have to shrink. Because there had been little risk of excessive demand in the early sixties, any growth performance between 4 and 6 percent could be viewed as qualitatively successful: It would be fast enough to reduce unemployment and not so rapid as to jeopardize essential price stability. Once the economy is close to target, however, there are necessarily dangers from both inadequate and excessive demand. (*Political Economy of Prosperity,* p. 60.)

[62] The council's view of the depressing effect of slack in the economy is expressed in its *Annual Report* for 1963, pp. 14-18.

businessmen expected inflation to accelerate or the costs of capital goods to rise faster than the prices of their own products, they would hasten to invest, and might be deterred very little by high nominal interest rates. A businessman who expected a 4 percent rate of inflation, for example, would be willing to pay an interest rate 3 percent higher than he would pay if he expected prices to rise at a rate of only 1 percent. This response would be shared by consumers, who would react to expected inflation by speeding up purchases of durable goods. The problem would be accentuated if the monetary authorities interpreted high nominal interest rates that merely incorporated expected inflation as signifying monetary restraint, as they would be likely to do under a rate-oriented policy.

The beginning of inflation could also cause trouble on the supply side. So long as price stability prevailed, it might be expected to continue. Such expectations would contribute to price stability by holding down negotiated wage increases. But if inflationary expectations were ever allowed to become widespread, they would make more difficult the task of arresting inflation. Wage increases would be negotiated to compensate for expected inflation, and make the expectations self-fulfilling by raising unit costs.[63] This could occur even if the economy moved out of the region of excess demand, if wage increases were negotiated to allow for catching up by those who had earlier expected price stability.

The task of stabilization policy is considerably more challenging if expectations must be reckoned with than if they can be ignored. Any deviation from an equilibrium path is more likely to be destabilizing than simple models indicate. Moreover, getting back to the equilibrium path may be a more uncertain and time-consuming process than if expectations could be ignored. In short, the effect of expectations is to raise the premium for avoiding departures from the equilibrium path.

Summary. This brief summary of the most important missing components of the new economics—a summary that has benefited considerably from hindsight—does not inspire great confidence in the possibility of fiscal fine tuning. A priori consideration of the destabilizing role of expectations suggests that the tuning must be fine indeed if large deviations to either side of the target path of output are to be avoided. Moreover, our lack of experience at full

---

[63] Recent efforts to estimate the inflation-unemployment tradeoff have emphasized the role of expectations in determining wage behavior. See, for example, Robert J. Gordon, "Inflation in Recession and Recovery," *Brookings Papers on Economic Activity*, 1 (Washington: Brookings Institution, 1971), pp. 105-58.

employment and the implied necessity to extrapolate beyond sample ranges indicate the need for caution. But potentially most devastating of all is the question of whether the President, the Congress, and the people of the United States could behave politically in such a way as to avoid slipping from the path along which full employment and price stability might be reconciled.

The New Economics at Full Employment: A Dissenting View. President Johnson's Council of Economic Advisers believed in the active use of fiscal policy to offset autonomous disturbances and keep the economy moving smoothly along its potential growth path. Taxes and expenditures would be adjusted frequently, if necessary, to offset surges and dips in the growth of private demand. Execution of such an activist stabilization policy places a high premium on economic science and political art, because it is necessary both to recognize the need for fiscal action well in advance and to gain implementation of the required action promptly.

A contrary view, associated primarily with the Committee for Economic Development, questioned the efficacy of an active fiscal policy.[64] First, it questioned the wisdom of trying to base discretionary changes in taxes and expenditures on forecasts of economic conditions. The concern was simply that forecasting was not a sufficiently precise art—or science—to serve as a sound base for major decisions of policy. Second, the CED view doubted that the requisite policy steps would be taken at the right time by the political protagonists in the activists' scenario, even if the forecasts were accurate.[65] If fiscal policy were inappropriate—even in its timing alone—either because of faulty economics or faulty politics, cyclical tendencies might be accentuated rather than dampened. Far better, according to this view, that we should occasionally stray a bit from the potential growth path than that we should risk knocking the economy far off the path by subjecting it to inappropriate stimulus or restraint.

---

[64] The classic statement of this view is contained in the Committee for Economic Development's *Taxes and the Budget: A Program for Prosperity in a Free Economy*. Though Friedman took a similar, but even firmer, position against discretionary policy in "A Monetary and Fiscal Framework for Economic Stability," the view summarized here is associated most closely with the CED. A critique of the CED position by the economist who was to become the leading exponent of the new economics had been given in Walter W. Heller, "CED's Stabilizing Budget Policy after Ten Years," *American Economic Review* (September 1957), pp. 634-51, reprinted in Gordon and Klein, *op. cit.*, pp. 696-712.
[65] In particular, the CED felt that there was an inherent inflationary bias in existing political decision-making processes.

Thus an essentially passive fiscal policy was espoused. Taxes and expenditures would be set so as to yield a small surplus at full employment.[66] They would be maintained in essentially that relationship regardless of the state of the economy, except under extreme conditions. They would not ordinarily be adjusted to offset fluctuations in aggregate demand, though monetary policy would be used for that purpose. The only fiscal stabilizers under this scheme would be the automatic stabilizers implicit in the built-in flexibility of tax collections and expenditures. In a downturn the decline in tax collections would leave relatively more disposable income in the hands of consumers and cushion the fall in corporate profits, thus buoying up private demand. Increased unemployment compensation would have an additional, if less important, tendency in the same direction. Analogous restraining effects would result from inflationary deviations from the path of potential GNP. This approach would not offset all fluctuations, or even try to. But it would avoid gross errors of fiscal policy.[67]

Failure of Fine Tuning: 1965-66

The seeds of the recent inflation were sown in the summer of 1965 when President Johnson requested a supplementary appropriation for Vietnam. Failure to raise taxes in 1966, when defense expenditures were growing rapidly and domestic Great Society programs were being initiated, allowed the seeds to germinate. One of the first fruits

[66] The surplus would supplement private savings, and therefore contribute to economic growth. A seldom asked question is whether a small surplus or even balance in the full employment budget is consistent with full employment. In terms of Figure 1, the question is whether line GG' may indicate that a perpetual (full employment) deficit is required to maintain full employment. Of course the answer may be negative, or could be made negative through structural changes or expansionary monetary policy, but the question deserves at least to be asked.

[67] Heller in "CED's Stabilizing Budget after Ten Years," p. 699, quotes Herbert Stein, one of the economists who helped to formulate the CED position as saying, "The Committee apparently felt that this plan embodied all that fiscal policy could do—in the existing state of affairs—to maintain stability. While stronger programs could be easily conceived, the Committee argued that these stronger programs are likely to be unstabilizing, because of errors of forecasting, lags, and biases in the decision-making process." Heller has also noted *(loc. cit.)* that the growth in the size of the federal sector, relative to the rest of the economy, made reliance upon built-in stabilizers a viable alternative. For a further exposition of this point, see Musgrave, *op. cit.*, pp. 505-12. Heller also notes that under the CED rule "fiscal policy could simultaneously serve two masters, i.e., economic stabilization and budgetary discipline." *(Op. cit.*, p. 697.)

of excess demand, which itself began to contribute to inflationary pressures at an early point, was an investment boom. The three villains in the inflation piece—rising federal expenditures, the failure to raise taxes, and the investment boom—are examined in greater detail in this section. But to set the stage, the situation at the end of 1965 will be reviewed.

Preconditions: The Economy in Late 1965. The 1964 tax cut and the "accommodative" monetary policy that accompanied it must be counted a major success.[68] Between February 1964 and July 1965, the unemployment rate fell from 5.4 percent to 4.4 percent, and by December it stood at 4.0 percent.[69] Expansion had reduced the GNP

---

[68] Different authors place widely differing weights on the relative importance of monetary and fiscal policy in bringing about the expansion. For a collation of the arguments on the two sides of the issue, see Milton Friedman and Walter W. Heller, *Monetary vs. Fiscal Policy* (New York: W. W. Norton & Company, Inc., 1969). Which is the correct set of weights in an issue that cannot be settled here. But it is almost certain that both extreme views are wrong. In particular, the fact that monetary policy was "accommodative" and "rate-oriented" seems to imply that otherwise interest rates would have risen and some private spending would have been "crowded out," as the monetarists claim. If so, monetary policy must be accorded some of the credit for the expansion. Okun's argument in *The Political Economy of Prosperity*, pp. 53-59, that the stability of interest rates indicates that the entire stimulative impact of public policy should be attributed to fiscal policy is completely unconvincing, as is his contention that a rate-oriented monetary policy is equivalent to a horizontal LM curve (note 30, p. 59). The accommodative monetary policy involves a sufficient shift in the LM curve to keep interest rates stable, as fiscal policy shifts the IS curve, not a movement of the IS curve along a horizontal LM curve, as Okun suggests. On the other hand, it does not appear reasonable to believe that the expansionary fiscal policy had *no* effect on the level of aggregate demand, as the monetarists sometime seem to claim. Unfortunately, this controversy involves some of the most elusive concepts in economics, as well as some of the most important ideas. An attempt to measure some of the relevant parameters is reported in Leonall C. Andersen and Jerry L. Jordan, "Monetary and Fiscal Actions: A Test of Their Relative Importance in Economic Stabilization," *Review*, Federal Reserve Bank of St. Louis (November 1968), pp. 11-24. See also the "Comment" by Frank de Leeuw and John Kalchbrenner and the "Reply" by Andersen and Jordan in the same publication (April 1969), pp. 6-16.

[69] Even if one is willing to give all the credit for expansion to fiscal policy, isolating the effect of the tax cut, even in rough terms, is an uncertain business. Though the tax cut was made effective January 1, 1964, it was not enacted until February 26, and its direct impact might not have been felt for several months. On the other hand, the expectation of the tax cut may already have stimulated the economy in 1963. Isolating the effect of the tax cut in restoring full employment is also difficult after mid-1965, because the Vietnam buildup had begun to add to aggregate demand.

gap to only about $10 billion, or 1¹/₂ percent of GNP, by the end of 1965.[70] Moreover, the advance had been achieved with only minimal adverse side effects in terms of wage and price behavior. The GNP deflator rose by 1.8 percent in 1965, compared with an annual rate of 1.3 percent during 1960-64. The consumer price index showed a similar pattern, a 1.7 percent rise in 1965 after an average increase of 1.2 percent from 1960 to 1964. On the other hand, the wholesale price index rose by 2.0 percent in 1965 after four years of stability. Moreover, unit labor costs were beginning to rise slightly more rapidly than in the previous four years.[71]

The economic advance was stronger than anticipated, however, and perhaps more exuberant than the CEA would have liked. Whereas the official government estimate of the increase in GNP in 1965 had been $38 billion, the increase reported at year's end was $47 billion.[72] Moreover, it was clear that increased defense spending would further stimulate the economy. Yet the Council of Economic Advisers remained confident that appropriate fiscal and monetary policies could hold the surging economy to a path consistent with continuation of a satisfactory price-wage performance. In its *Annual Report* for 1966 the council appraised the prospects for the year in these terms:

> [R]ising defense requirements clearly complicate the task of economic policy. The stimulative fiscal policies of recent years have achieved their mission. Consumer spending and investment demand have both been invigorated. The same logic that called for fiscal stimuli when demand was weak now argues for a degree of restraint to assure that the pace of the economy remains within safe speed limits. Measures to moderate the growth of private purchasing power are needed to offset, in part, the expansionary influence of rising defense outlays, if intensified price and wage pressures are to be avoided. . . . [T]his is a year of many uncertainties: the advance into the new territory of still lower unemployment must be made with care; meanwhile defense requirements could shift suddenly in either direction in the months ahead. Fiscal policy stands ready to meet any changing and

---

[70] *Annual Report*, 1966, p. 40.

[71] *Annual Report*, 1966, pp. 65, 76-80. For a more detailed appraisal of the state of the economy in mid-1965, see *Annual Report*, 1967, pp. 45-46.

[72] *Annual Report*, 1966, p. 38. As noted below, even this initial report fell $5¹/₂ billion short of the actual increase reported in the revised figures.

unanticipated developments, and will look to assistance from monetary policy in maintaining flexibility.[73]

The easy tests of the "experiment for prosperity" had been passed, apparently with high marks. But a more treacherous stage of the experiment was commencing. This involved holding the economy to a stable growth path by adjusting the fiscal and monetary controls. It would test the economic wisdom of the President's advisers, the political acumen of the President and his liaison men dealing with the Congress, and the economic sophistication of the voting public and the Congress. Moreover, the practice of economic activism, difficult under the best of circumstances, would be complicated by a new development, the war in Vietnam.

Defense and the Great Society. Over the period 1962-65, purchases for national defense fell from $51.6 billion to $50.1 billion, or from 9.2 to 7.3 percent of GNP. Beginning in the second quarter of 1965, the downward trend in the dollar amount of defense purchases was reversed. But, due to rapid economic expansion, defense purchases as a percent of GNP continued to fall until a low of 7.2 percent was reached in the third quarter. However, in the fourth quarter, defense purchases rose to $52.5 billion, or by almost $3½ billion above their second quarter level, and accounted for 7.4 percent of GNP. This new trend continued rapidly into 1966, and by the fourth quarter defense purchases stood at $65.6 billion, or 8.5 percent of GNP. (See Table 1.) Because the GNP gap was closed early in 1966, the rapid increases in defense expenditures created inflationary pressures that could be offset only by raising taxes, cutting other government expenditures, or practicing severe monetary restraint.[74]

Moreover, because of a technical peculiarity in the way defense expenditures enter the national income accounts, these data understate the economic impact of the rise in defense purchases.[75] The impact of defense expenditures for goods produced under contract

---

[73] *Annual Report*, 1966, pp. 31-32.

[74] See *Annual Report*, 1967, pp. 42-45, for a discussion of the closing of the GNP gap.

[75] The discussion in the subsequent paragraphs draws heavily upon Murray Weidenbaum, "Impact of Vietnam War on American Economy," *Economic Effects of Vietnam Spending*, Hearings before the Joint Economic Committee, vol. I (Washington: Government Printing Office, 1967), pp. 193-236; Harvey Galper, "The Timing of Federal Expenditure Impacts," in *Budget Concepts for Economic Analysis*, ed. Wilfred Lewis, Jr., pp. 95-109; and Kenneth L. Lay and Kent L. Jones, "Economic Impact of Defense Procurement," *Survey of Current Business* (September 1971), pp. 21-26, 31.

occurs as the work on the project is being done.[76] And in many cases progress payments are made to defense contractors. Yet, in the national accounts, purchases are recorded essentially on a delivery basis.[77] So long as defense production runs at a steady level, this poses no problem. But in a period of rapid military buildup, such as occurred in 1965-66, increased defense production is recorded in the national accounts first as an increase in private inventories, and only subsequently as defense purchases in the federal sector accounts. Two estimates have been provided, one by Harvey Galper and the other by Kenneth Lay and Kent Jones, of the amount of investment in defense goods-in-process that occurred during these years. These estimates are shown in columns 4 and 5 of Table 1.[78] If they are added to the amounts of defense purchases given in the national accounts (see columns 6 and 7), the rapidity of the Vietnam buildup can be seen more clearly. Comparing columns 6 and 7 with column 2, we see that defense purchases adjusted for inventory investment rose between the second and fourth quarters of 1965 by $4\frac{1}{2}$ to almost $6 billion, depending on the estimate used, while the unadjusted series rose by only about $3\frac{1}{2}$ billion, as noted above. This difference is, of course, reflected in columns 8 and 9, which show the rapid rise in the percentage of GNP accounted for by defense expenditures, adjusted for private investment in inventories of defense goods in process. As the buildup continued into 1966 and resulted in further private inventory investment in defense goods in process, the percentage of GNP flowing into defense purchases and inventory

---

[76] Knowing exactly when the economic impact of procurement occurs is virtually impossible, and generalization is difficult, in any case. The impact may occur when the contract is let, instead of when production occurs. Or the procurement may have little impact if it is met by drawing down excessive inventories. But defense production seems likely to be a better measure of when the impact occurs than deliveries.

[77] Weidenbaum, *op. cit.*, p. 199; Galper, *op. cit.*, p. 97; and Lay and Jones, *op. cit.*, p. 21.

[78] The figures in column 4 are the average of the two estimates presented by Galper, *op. cit.*, p. 104. Galper notes that the production assumption used is of very little consequence in the final outcome. Arthur M. Okun and Nancy H. Teeters in "The Full Employment Surplus Revisited" (*Brookings Papers on Economic Activity*, 1970, 1, pp. 89-90) note that official estimates on an annual basis by the Office of Business Economics show less fiscal stimulus from this source in 1966 than the estimates by Weidenbaum and Galper. The same is true of semiannual estimates by Barry Bosworth in "Analyzing Inventory Investment" (*Brookings Papers on Economic Activity*, 2, 1970, pp. 208-27). For 1966 the estimates by Galper and those by Lay and Jones agree quite closely. In any case, the figures reported here are indicative of the problem.

Table 1

DEFENSE PURCHASES AND INVENTORY INVESTMENT IN DEFENSE GOODS IN PROCESS, 1962-71

(seasonally adjusted at annual rates; dollar amounts in billions)

	GNP	National Defense Purchases		Defense Goods Inventory Investment		Defense Purchases Adjusted for Inventory Investment		Defense Purchases Adjusted, as Percent of GNP	
		Dollar amounts	As percent of GNP	Galper estimate	Lay and Jones estimate	Galper estimate	Lay and Jones estimate	Galper estimate	Lay and Jones estimate
	(1)	(2)	(3)	(4)	(5)	(6)	(7)	(8)	(9)
Calendar Year									
1962	560.3	51.6	9.2	1.0	*	52.6	*	9.4	*
1963	590.5	50.8	8.6	0.3	*	51.1	*	8.7	*
1964	632.4	50.0	7.9	−0.4	*	49.6	*	7.8	*
1965	684.9	50.1	7.3	0.4	1.2	50.5	51.3	7.4	7.5
1966	749.9	60.7	8.1	3.5	3.5	64.2	64.2	8.6	8.6
1967	793.9	72.3	9.1	*	2.7	*	75.1	*	9.5
1968	864.2	78.3	9.1	*	1.2	*	79.5	*	9.2
1969	929.1	78.4	8.4	*	−0.3	*	78.1	*	8.4
1970	974.1	75.4	7.7	*	−2.1	*	73.3	*	7.5
1971 I-III	1,041.6	71.9	6.9	*	*	*	*	*	*
Quarterly Data									
1964 III	638.9	49.8	7.8	−0	*	49.8	*	7.8	*
IV	645.1	48.9	7.6	−0.4	0.1	48.5	49.0	7.5	7.6
1965 I	662.8	48.6	7.3	−1.2	1.0	47.4	49.6	7.2	7.5
II	675.7	49.2	7.3	−0.4	1.0	48.8	50.2	7.2	7.4

III	691.1	50.1	7.2	1.2	0.7	51.3	50.8	7.4	7.4
IV	710.0	52.5	7.4	2.1	2.2	54.6	54.7	7.7	7.7
1966 I	729.5	55.3	7.6	2.4	2.4	57.7	57.7	7.9	7.9
II	743.3	58.5	7.9	3.2	2.6	61.7	61.1	8.3	8.2
III	755.9	63.3	8.4	4.2	3.9	67.5	67.2	8.9	8.9
IV	770.7	65.6	8.5	4.0	4.9	69.6	70.5	9.0	9.1
1967 I	774.4	69.9	9.0	*	3.3	*	73.2	*	9.5
II	784.5	71.8	9.2	*	2.5	*	74.3	*	9.5
III	800.9	73.0	9.1	*	2.1	*	75.1	*	9.4
IV	815.9	74.7	9.2	*	2.9	*	77.6	*	9.5
1968 I	834.0	76.5	9.2	*	1.7	*	78.2	*	9.4
II	857.3	78.3	9.1	*	1.2	*	79.5	*	9.3
III	875.2	79.1	9.0	*	0.4	*	79.5	*	9.1
IV	890.2	79.4	8.9	*	1.6	*	81.0	*	9.1
1969 I	906.4	78.3	8.6	*	1.7	*	80.0	*	8.8
II	921.8	77.5	8.4	*	0.9	*	78.4	*	8.5
III	940.2	79.4	8.4	*	−1.1	*	78.3	*	8.3
IV	948.0	78.4	8.3	*	−2.6	*	75.8	*	8.0
1970 I	956.0	78.9	8.3	*	−1.9	*	77.0	*	8.1
II	968.5	75.1	7.8	*	−2.2	*	72.9	*	7.5
III	983.5	74.2	7.5	*	−2.6	*	71.6	*	7.3
IV	988.4	73.2	7.4	*	−1.9	*	71.3	*	7.2
1971 I	1,020.8	73.0	7.1	*	−1.7	*	71.3	*	7.0
II	1,043.1	71.8	6.9	*	−1.3	*	70.5	*	6.8
III	1,060.8	70.8	6.7	*	*	*	*	*	*

* Not estimated.

Sources: Columns (1) and (2), *Survey of Current Business*, July of various years, *Economic Indicators*, November 1971; Column (3), Harvey Galper, "The Timing of Federal Expenditure Impacts," in *Budget Concepts for Economic Analysis*, ed. Wilfred Lewis Jr. (Washington: Brookings Institution, 1968), p. 104; Column (4), Kenneth L. Lay and Kent L. Jones, "Economic Impact of Defense Procurement," *Survey of Current Business*, September 1971, p. 24. The Galper estimate used is the average of the two presented in the source cited.

accumulation soared to 9.0 or 9.1 in the fourth quarter, almost two full percentage points above its level in the first quarter of 1965 and near its 1962 level. There was certainly considerable inflationary potential in this rapid buildup, which continued into 1967. In the first quarter of 1967 defense purchases (unadjusted) were $69.9 billion, or 9.0 percent of GNP, and they hovered at just above that proportion of GNP for the remainder of the year. Adjusted for private accumulation of inventories of defense goods in process, the percentage of GNP flowing into defense stood at 9.5 for 1967 as a whole, up from a comparable figure of 8.6 for 1966.

And the situation was worse than these figures indicate. For one thing, economists were paying altogether too little attention to the initial impact of the Vietnam buildup upon inventory investment described above.[79] Therefore, policy was not adjusted sufficiently to offset the impact of increased defense production. As Weidenbaum has said:

> *The most rapid period of expansion in military contracts to private industry occurred in 1966; so did the most rapid rate of price inflation in recent years.* But that was the period when the Nation and particularly the Administration's economists were still congratulating themselves on the success of the 1964 tax cut and little need was felt, at least officially, for greater fiscal restraint. . . . [T]he official budget and economic reports were very slow to pick up the expansionary impact of the Vietnam buildup, but very quick to take account of the deflationary impact of the expansion in revenues. *The net result is that the Federal Government, though apparently following a non-inflationary economic policy in 1966, was actually a major source of inflationary pressure in the American economy during that time.*[80]

Equally disastrous, however, was the fact that the budget presented in January 1966 underestimated defense expenditures for fiscal 1967 by nearly $10 billion.[81] Half of the underestimate is alleged to have occurred because combat operations in Vietnam were not concluded by the end of the fiscal year, as was implicit in the

---

[79] The 1966 *Annual Report* (p. 58), under the heading of "The Impact of Defense," refers to budget expenditures for defense and purchases for defense. No mention is made of the impact on inventories. Only in the 1967 *Annual Report* (pp. 46 and 52) is there explicit mention of the impact of defense production on inventory accumulation.

[80] Weidenbaum, *op. cit.*, pp. 209-10. Italics in original.

[81] *Budget* for 1967, p. 69; *Budget* for 1968, p. 74.

budget projections. The remainder has been attributed to the fact that the buildup of forces in Vietnam was more rapid and hostilities were more intense than had been expected.[82] Whatever the cause of the underestimate, little attempt was made to keep the public or professional economists abreast of the changing budget picture.[83] This severely hampered any attempt by the public, economists, and the Congress to make rational decisions on fiscal policy. In particular, the need to increase taxes to pay for the war and avoid inflationary excess aggregate demand was less apparent than it would have been if the budget picture had been known accurately throughout the year.

The rise in federal expenditures during this period was not confined only to defense. President Johnson clearly felt a strong moral and political commitment to the domestic legislation that comprised his Great Society program, and he pushed for its enactment. Thus, from their 1965 level of $73.4 billion, federal expenditures for purposes other than defense purchases rose by $29.8 billion, or 40.6 percent, by 1968. (See Table 2.) This increase represented an annual rate of growth of 12.0 percent and amounted to 16.6 percent of the growth of GNP over the period.[84] In total, federal expenditures grew by $58 billion over the three-year period, absorbing almost one-third of the entire growth of GNP.[85]

---

[82] See Weidenbaum, *op. cit.* (pp. 207-09), for comments on the testimony of administration witnesses on this question.

[83] Weidenbaum notes, *op. cit.* (p. 208), that no midyear review of the budget was issued and that the July and August issues of the Defense Department's *Monthly Report on the Status of Funds* never appeared and the September issue became available only in December.

[84] It is not quite legitimate to compare increases in expenditures in the federal sector of the national income accounts with the growth of GNP, since not all of the former represent direct federal command over resources. Nevertheless, the comparison is instructive, since most of transfer payments to households and grants-in-aid to state and local governments find their way quickly into final demand.

[85] The large increase in nondefense spending is not discussed further for a number of reasons. First, the rise in such spending as a percentage of GNP did not represent a sudden reversal of a trend, as was true of defense spending. Second, a large part of the increase was offset by increased payroll taxes levied to pay for it, and the remainder would have been financed by automatic increases in revenues generated by economic growth (see *Annual Report*, 1968, p. 69). Finally, the technical problems of estimating the increase and its impact on the economy that plagued the interpretation of the defense buildup were largely absent on the nondefense side. Thus, while dollars of fiscal stimulation and restraint cannot be neatly segregated, it does seem reasonable to attribute fiscal failure primarily to the failure to raise taxes to pay for the defense buildup. On the other hand, it is probably true that President Johnson did not push harder for a tax increase in 1966 for fear of jeopardizing his Great Society programs.

Table 2

DEFENSE PURCHASES AND NONDEFENSE EXPENDITURES, NIA, IN RELATION TO GNP, 1960-70

(dollar amounts in billions)

Year	Total Federal Expenditures		Excluding Defense Purchases		Change in Federal Expenditures as Percent of Change in GNP		
	Dollar amount	As percent of GNP	Dollar amount	As percent of GNP	Defense	Other	Total
1960	93.0	18.5	48.1	9.5	—	—	—
1961	102.1	19.6	54.3	10.4	17.7	37.8	55.5
1962	110.3	19.7	58.7	10.5	9.5	10.9	20.4
1963	113.9	19.3	63.1	10.7	−2.6	14.6	12.0
1964	118.1	18.6	68.1	10.8	−1.9	11.9	10.0
1965	123.5	18.0	73.4	10.7	0.2	10.1	10.3
1966	142.8	19.0	82.1	10.9	16.3	13.4	29.7
1967	163.6	20.6	91.2	11.5	27.2	21.2	48.4
1968	181.5	21.0	103.2	11.9	8.4	17.1	25.5
1969	189.5	20.4	111.1	12.0	0.2	12.2	12.3
1970	205.1	21.1	129.7	13.3	−6.7	41.3	34.7

Source: *Survey of Current Business,* July of various years

Failure to Raise Taxes. From 1964 to 1965 GNP rose by $52.5 billion, or 8.3 percent, and by the end of 1965 the 4 percent interim goal for the unemployment rate had been reached. But the rise in GNP had been more rapid than the Council of Economic Advisers had anticipated, so much so that it threatened to cause the economy to overheat and set off an inflationary spiral.[86] Given the state of the economy, the projected increase in federal expenditures for defense and domestic programs, and the expected strength of investment demand (discussed below), the CEA's warning in its *Annual Report* for 1966 was to be expected: "The objective of promoting balance between over-all demand and productive capacity pointed to tax cuts in recent years when demand was inadequate. The same criterion now calls for tax action to moderate the growth of private spending." [87] And, according to Arthur Okun, a member of the CEA at the time, President Johnson was advised to ask the Congress for a general increase in income taxes to prevent aggregate demand from outstripping productive capacity. Believing an income tax increase would not pass the Congress, the President did not make the request. As Okun has said, "The key fiscal decision for the January 1966 budget program was a negative one: A general tax increase was not proposed." [88] Rather, the administration offered a patchwork program consisting of graduated withholding rates for individual taxpayers, accelerated schedules of corporate tax payments and social security tax payments of the self-employed (bringing these to a more nearly current basis), and the postponement of the scheduled reduction in the excise taxes on automobiles and telephone service.[89] But the way

---

[86] To quote the *Annual Report* for 1966 (page 38): "The strength of the advance in 1965 was exceptional and surpassed expectations. The Council's *Annual Report* for 1965, which contained one of the more optimistic forecasts current at that time, estimated a gain of $38 billion in GNP for the year—the midpoint of a $33-43 billion range. In contrast the actual gain was a record $47 billion."

Even the $47 billion reported by the council understated the increase revealed by the revised GNP figures and mentioned in the text. Okun has noted in *Political Economy of Prosperity* (p. 68) that the failure of the preliminary reports of GNP to reflect accurately the rate of growth of the economy during the year contributed significantly to the difficulty of tailoring stabilization policy to the emerging situation.

[87] *Annual Report*, 1966, p. 53.

[88] Okun, *Political Economy of Prosperity*, p. 70.

[89] *Annual Report*, 1966, pp. 53-54. As has been noted elsewhere, whether a mere speed-up in tax payments is likely to restrain demand significantly is problematical. Since the *Budget* for fiscal 1967 issued at the same time expanded the sale of participation certificates, which enter the budget as offsets against expenditures rather than as borrowing, it might reasonably be assumed that

was left open for an increase in income taxes later in the year if the exuberance of the economy seemed to call for it.[90]

This piecemeal approach to fiscal restraint was quickly adopted by the Congress. It would probably have been barely adequate to forestall inflationary pressures if federal expenditures had been no larger than envisaged in the budget for fiscal 1967, since the council had estimated that the full employment budget for the fiscal year would be in approximate balance.[91] However, as noted above, defense expenditures during fiscal 1967 were approximately $10 billion greater than originally budgeted. For the 1965-66 period, the full employment budget began with a surplus of roughly $7¹/₂ billion in the first half of 1965, shifted to a deficit of about $1¹/₂ billion in the second half, due to the defense buildup plus excise tax reduction and retroactive increase in social security benefits, and then, after a pause in the second quarter of 1966, moved to a deficit of almost $7 billion by the fourth quarter.[92] (See Table 3.) Thus the decision not to ask Congress for a tax increase in 1966 virtually assured the continuation of strong inflationary pressures at least throughout that year.[93] These pressures were compounded by a strong demand for capital goods and were restrained primarily by a brutally tight monetary policy.

The Investment Boom. Spending on capital goods was spurred both directly and indirectly by the tax cut of 1964. The reduction in the

---

moving payment dates forward may have been intended largely as window dressing. For a critical analysis of the expansion of the use of participation certificates during 1966 to 1968, see "Loans, Participation Certificates, and the Financing of Budget Deficits," a staff paper prepared for the President's Commission on Budget Concepts and reproduced in Lewis, *op. cit.*, (pp. 15-36, especially pp. 20-30).

[90] *Annual Report*, 1966, p. 61.

[91] *Ibid.*, p. 54.

[92] These estimates of the full employment budget balance are from Okun and Teeters, *op. cit.*, pp. 77-116, especially pp. 104-05. In addition, the full impact of the Vietnam buildup was not reflected in budget totals, as noted above.

[93] Okun, in *Political Economy of Prosperity* (pp. 66, 73), has noted that because of the lags in the economy the strength of the advance in the second half of 1965 made some inflation during 1966 inevitable, whether taxes had been raised in January or not. The same conclusion has been drawn by Keith M. Carlson in "The Federal Budget and Economic Stabilization," *Federal Reserve Bank of St. Louis Review* (February 1967), p. 7, though he places more emphasis than Okun on the contribution of monetary ease to the strength of the advance. See also the excellent essay by Burns, in Arthur F. Burns and Paul A. Samuelson, *Full Employment, Guideposts and Economic Stability* (Washington: American Enterprise Institute, 1967).

Table 3

FULL EMPLOYMENT SURPLUS, BY QUARTERS, AND ACTUAL SURPLUS, 1960-70

(seasonally adjusted annual rates; dollar amounts in billions)

Okun and Teeters Estimates

Year	Full employment surplus, by quarters					Annual FES as % of potential GNP	CEA Estimate Annual FES	Actual Surplus
	I	II	III	IV	Year			
1960	13.8	13.4	12.4	13.3	13.2	2.5	13.0	3.5
1961	11.8	10.4	9.9	10.0	10.5	1.9	8.8	−3.8
1962	5.3	4.6	6.6	6.2	5.7	1.0	−4.4	−3.8
1963	8.1	11.0	10.4	11.7	10.3	1.7	9.0	0.7
1964	4.6	−0.1	3.0	5.9	3.3	0.5	1.8	−3.0
1965	7.8	7.5	−1.2	−1.8	3.1	0.5	1.0	1.2
1966	−2.3	−0.2	−5.7	−6.8	−3.7	−0.5	−3.6	−0.2
1967	−11.5	−12.4	−11.6	−11.5	−11.8	−1.5	−10.5	−12.4
1968	−9.9	−11.9	−5.3	−3.2	−7.6	−0.9	−6.0	−6.5
1969	7.5	12.1	8.6	10.9	9.8	1.0	11.7	7.3
1970	—	—	—	—	—	—	6.7	−13.6

Sources: Arthur M. Okun and Nancy H. Teeters, "The Full Employment Surplus Revisited," *Brookings Papers on Economic Activity,* 1970, 1, pp. 104-06; *Annual Report of the Council of Economic Advisers,* 1971, p. 73; and *Survey of Current Business,* July of various years.

income tax on business increased both the cash flow available for investment and the expected profitability of investment. In addition, the increase in consumption spending set off by reductions in the personal income tax gave further impetus to the demand for capital goods. The tax cut's effectiveness in stimulating investment is shown at least roughly by the 12.5 percent rise in business fixed investment (BFI) during 1964, to 9.7 percent of GNP. During the previous five years, the average annual increase had been 5.6 percent, and BFI had accounted for an average of 9.3 percent of national output. The investment boom continued into 1965, as shown by the 16.7 percent increase in BFI over its 1964 level and the fact that 10.4 percent of GNP consisted of investment in plant and equipment.[94]

The capital spending boom did not conveniently subside at the end of 1965 as the interim unemployment goal was approached. In 1966 business fixed investment rose by 14.4 percent over its 1965 level, to 10.9 percent of GNP. Though the source of the continued strength of the boom is subject to various interpretations, the Council of Economic Advisers was quite clear in its opinion:

> [T]he defense buildup . . . reinforced the previously planned fiscal stimuli and the forward momentum of a strong economy close to full employment. Furthermore, the expansion of defense spending contributed to a significant change in the climate of opinion. *The Vietnam buildup virtually assured American businessmen that no economic reverse would occur in the near future.*[95]

By the end of the summer it was decided that action must be taken to stem the investment boom, which was "too vigorous" and was creating unhealthy backlogs, labor shortages, and pressures on financial markets.[96] Thus on September 8 the President asked that the investment tax credit be suspended until the beginning of 1968. Suspension was granted, effective October 10, 1966. Whether caused by the suspension of the investment tax credit, tight money, or the exhaustion of investment opportunities, the ensuing slowdown in capital spending was dramatic. Though business fixed investment

---

[94] The figures reported here, like those for GNP and defense purchases, incorporate revisions to the preliminary data upon which policy decisions of necessity were based. In January 1966, the percentage increases during the two previous years were thought to have been only $11^1/_2$ and $15^1/_2$, respectively; see *Annual Report*, 1966, p. 36.

[95] *Annual Report*, 1967, p. 46 (emphasis added).

[96] *Annual Report*, 1967, p. 49.

still represented 10.5 percent of GNP in 1967, its rate of increase slowed to a bare 2.1 percent. At least for the moment, the investment boom had been throttled. In fact, because of fears that the economy was moving toward a recession, the administration asked for, and was granted, restoration of the investment tax credit early in 1967.

Monetary Conditions: The Credit Crunch.[97] The investment boom had predictable effects upon financial markets. In the second half of 1965, as the investment of nonfinancial corporations began to outrun their savings by a large margin, increasing demands for credit were felt in financial markets. Continued maintenance of stable interest rates by the Federal Reserve Board would have been disastrously inflationary under these conditions. Thus in an open break with the administration, the discount rate was raised in December 1965. This signaled the beginning of a period of monetary restraint that had as its more concrete manifestation a marked drop in the growth rate of the money supply and an increase in interest rates. Demand deposits plus currency (M_1) grew by 2.2 percent in 1966 (December to December), compared to an average of 4.4 percent over the previous two years, and the Treasury bill rate rose from 3.95 percent in 1965 to 4.88 percent in 1966.[98]

Tight monetary policy had a dramatic impact upon residential construction, due in large part to institutional restraints on interest rates. The net flow of savings to savings and loan associations fell by 63 percent between 1965 and 1966, from $9.7 billion to $3.6 billion. Mutual savings banks experienced a similar, though smaller, drop. These declines in net savings flows to important sources of mortgage financing had a direct effect on homebuilding. Private non-farm housing starts fell from 1.45 million in 1965 to 1.14 million in 1966, or by 21 percent.

The devastating effect of tight money on the housing industry underscored the need for fiscal restraint. It was demonstrated con-

---

[97] This discussion draws upon *Annual Report*, 1967, pp. 54-61; "Cycles in Mortgage Credit Availability and the 1966 Experience," prepared by the Staff of the Federal Home Loan Bank Board for *A Study of Mortgage Credit*, Committee on Banking and Currency, U.S. Senate (Washington: U.S. Government Printing Office, 1967), reprinted in Smith and Teigen, *op. cit.*, pp. 433-48; and Craig Swan, "Homebuilding: A Review of Experience," *Brookings Papers on Economic Activity*, 1 (Washington: Brookings Institution, 1970), pp. 48-70.

[98] The rate of growth (December to December) of M_1 plus time deposits fell from 8.8 percent in 1964-65 to 4.8 percent in 1966.

clusively that money does indeed matter [99]—and that it matters most to housing. The crippling effect tight money was having on housing was one strong argument for suspending the investment tax credit in September.

Concrete Results: Inflation Begins. Herbert Stein has chosen for one chapter of his *Fiscal Revolution in America* the title, "Tax Cut in Camelot." The experience beginning in the second half of 1966 suggests that indeed the Camelot phase of fiscal policy lasted only "for one brief shining moment." The nation had clearly entered a period of demand inflation by the beginning of 1966. As a result of the excess aggregate demand originating in the defense and capital goods industries, the unemployment rate hovered between 3.7 percent and 4.0 percent during 1966 and averaged 3.8 percent for the year as a whole. The implicit GNP deflator rose by 3.5 percent from the fourth quarter of 1965 to the fourth quarter of 1966, and consumer prices rose by 3.3 percent from December 1965 to December 1966. Moreover, wholesale prices rose by 1.7 percent during the year ending December 1966.

Among the first casualties of excess demand were the wage-price guideposts. During a period of inadequate aggregate demand, guideposts may be viable and they may even prevent some cost-push or administered price inflation. But once full employment is reached, they are threatened continually, and they almost surely succumb eventually in a situation of excess aggregate demand. The inevitable death blow to the guideposts came in the August 1966 settlement of the airline machinists' strike.[100] Exhortations for wage and price restraint continued to appear in the three Johnson economic reports issued after that, but they no longer rang true. The administration could hardly expect compliance with its pleas for responsibility in

---

[99] For a more detailed discussion, see Cagan, chapter 2 below. In its *Annual Report* for 1967 (p. 60), the Council of Economic Advisers estimated that "credit-financed expenditures may have been held down directly by as much as $8 billion at year-end as a result of tight money, compared with what would have happened had monetary policies continued supportive, as during 1964 and most of 1965. The direct impact of $8 billion on GNP is roughly as great as the estimated direct impact from a 10 percent surcharge on personal and corporate tax liabilities."

[100] Not only was the settlement for a 4.9 percent increase well above the guidepost figure of 3.2 percent. Equally important, President Johnson's public statement that a 4.3 percent tentative settlement would not violate the guideposts, since industry increases in productivity exceeded that amount, clearly undercut the basic rationale of the guideposts. For a summary of this episode, see Sheahan, *op. cit.*, pp. 57-60, and Moore, *op. cit.*, pp. 15-16.

wage negotiations and pricing policies, given the inflationary setting its fiscal policies had created.

Return to Fiscal Sanity: 1967-68

The first half of 1967 provided some respite from the almost frantic growth of GNP experienced during the previous year and a half—so much so that it very nearly qualified as a recession. The end of the investment boom, a massive inventory adjustment, and continued weakness in homebuilding offset a strongly expansionary fiscal policy. Thus, after six quarters in which growth in real GNP averaged about $9¹/₂ billion (1958 prices), output fell in the first quarter and, in the second, it barely regained the level reached in the fourth quarter of 1966. The slowdown was accompanied by a temporary slackening of the rate of inflation. Though the consumer price index continued to rise faster during 1967 (by 3.1 percent from December 1966 to December 1967) than might have been hoped, wholesale prices rose very little from the middle of 1966 to the end of 1967, and experienced declines during much of 1967. It seemed, as Okun has suggested, that the nation did, in fact, have a second chance to get on the noninflationary, full employment track.[101] A tax increase would be essential, however, if the recovery forecast for the second half of 1967 should exhibit the strength that was expected.

It was anticipated in January 1967 that the recovery in the second half would be fueled by a rebound in residential construction and inventory investment. On the strength of forecasts, the President's 1968 budget requested a temporary 6 percent surcharge on personal and corporate tax receipts, effective July 1.[102] However, the Congress was unwilling to raise taxes during a slowdown to prevent inflationary pressures that were only *forecast* to occur in the second half of the year. It wanted concrete evidence that the tax increase was necessary.[103]

The evidence was not long in coming. The recovery was even

---

[101] Okun, *Political Economy of Prosperity*, pp. 84-85.

[102] *Annual Report*, 1967, p. 62; *Budget*, 1968, pp. 59-61.

[103] Okun, *Political Economy of Prosperity*, pp. 86-87; Pierce, *op. cit.*, p. 149. Pierce notes (p. 152) that Congressman Mills's skepticism about forecasts was based on experience in 1962, when most economists favored a "quickie" tax cut to prevent a recession that did not materialize when taxes were not cut, and in 1966-67, when the administration requested the restoration of the investment tax credit less than six months after it had been suspended for countercyclical reasons.

stronger than initially expected and, in his tax message of August 3, President Johnson increased the requested surcharge to 10 percent. He did not, however, include any mention of cutting expenditures, which Wilbur Mills, the powerful chairman of the House Ways and Means Committee, had stated would be his price for supporting a tax increase. With virtually no chance of passing a tax bill over Mills's objection and with the President adamantly opposed to expenditure reduction, the stage was set for a vigorous legislative battle between two powerful and resourceful politicians. Eventually Mills prevailed.[104]

Because of congressional inaction on the surcharge while defense spending continued at a high level, the full employment budget remained in deficit by about $11-11$^1/_2$ billion through the second half of 1967 and the first half of 1968.[105] Moreover, the Federal Reserve system had begun to expand the money supply vigorously in the first half of 1967 on the expectation that Congress would recognize and act on the need for the tax surcharge.[106]

The combination of inaction on needed fiscal restraint and monetary relaxation had the predictable result. Real growth (at an annual rate) during the third and fourth quarters of 1967 and the first and second quarters of 1968 was $7.3, $4.7, $9.0, and $12.7 billion respectively, reflecting an average annual rate of 5.0 percent. But, during 1967, unemployment on a seasonally adjusted basis had risen only to a monthly high of 4.3 percent (in October) and by the end of the year stood at 3.7 percent. Thus, by any reasonable definition, the economy was operating at or beyond its potential and, given this rapid increase in real output, prices were bound to rise. And they did so in 1968. That year, the CPI rose at an annual rate of 4.7 percent and, more ominously, the wholesale price index rose 2.7 percent. Moreover, the GNP deflator moved up by 4.1 percent from the fourth quarter of 1967 to the fourth quarter of 1968.

It was in this atmosphere that the Revenue and Expenditure Control Act of 1968 was finally passed and signed into law by the President on June 28, 1968. The act provided a one-year 10 percent surcharge on income tax liabilities, retroactive to April 1 for individuals and to January 1 for corporations. In addition, it set a limit

---

[104] For a fascinating blow-by-blow account of this legislative "battle of the titans," see Pierce, *op. cit.*, chapter 7.

[105] Okun and Teeters, *op. cit.*, pp. 104-05. The apparent fall in the full employment deficit in early 1968 is somewhat spurious, since it reflects the retroactive tax surcharge that was not actually passed until June 28; *ibid.*, p. 88.

[106] Okun, *Political Economy of Prosperity*, pp. 85-86.

on federal expenditures for fiscal 1969 excluding those for Vietnam, veterans benefits, interest on the national debt, and social security. For the controlled expenditures, the President was required to cut $6 billion from his January budget requests.[107] As a result the full employment budget moved dramatically from a deficit of $11 billion in the first half of 1968 to a $10 billion surplus for the first half of 1969.[108] Though it was three years late in doing so, the new economics had finally delivered the restrictive counterpart of the expansionary 1964 tax cut. At this point, fearing that the sudden shift to fiscal restraint would result in "overkill," the Federal Reserve Board eased monetary conditions to cushion the impact on the economy.[109]

The fiscal impact of the tax surcharge and expenditure controls was expected to be felt in early 1969. Consumption was expected to respond strongly, though with some lag, to the surcharge, and to rise by only about $35 billion over 1968.[110] On the basis of survey data, business fixed investment was projected to rise by about $7-8 billion over its 1968 level, and residential construction was expected to continue at about the rate it had reached at the end of 1968, which was some 10 percent above the average rate for the year. Federal purchases were projected to rise by a modest $3 billion. Nonetheless, the Council of Economic Advisers believed that enough inflationary pressure would persist to necessitate extending the tax surcharge one year beyond its initial expiration date of June 30, 1969, and the President requested this extension in his budget for fiscal 1970.[111] This, it was hoped, would move the economy along a path of moderation to high employment and price stability.

When taxes were finally raised in the middle of 1968, the personal saving rate fell dramatically. For the six-quarter period in which the surcharge was applied at a 10 percent rate—from the third quarter of 1968 to the end of 1969—personal tax and nontax payments averaged 15.3 percent of personal income, or 2.1 percent more than in the previous six quarters. During the same six quarters of 1968 and 1969, personal saving averaged 5.2 percent of personal income, down 1.2 percent from the 6.4 percent average for the previous six quarters. Personal outlays as a percentage of personal income fell from 80.4 to 79.4 comparing the same two six quarter

---

[107] *Annual Report*, 1969, p. 38.

[108] Okun and Teeters, *op. cit.*, pp. 104-05.

[109] Okun, *Political Economy of Prosperity*, pp. 93-94.

[110] Consumption had increased during 1968 by about $44 billion from its 1967 level.

[111] *Annual Report*, 1969, pp. 53-58.

periods. This suggests that at least half of the increase in personal taxes took the form of reduced saving rather than reduced consumption.[112] In concrete terms, consumption rose by about $42 billion over its 1968 level, rather than the $35 billion projected in the 1969 *Annual Report*.

On the investment side, the CEA's estimates were also low. Instead of rising by $7 to $8 billion, as projected, business fixed investment increased by $10.6 billion. Inventory investment (including farm) also rose by almost $1 billion, rather than declining slightly as had been predicted. Only residential construction, by staying at its level for the fourth quarter of 1968, fulfilled the projection, though federal purchases rose by only 60 percent of the estimated $3 billion. In summary, GNP for the year was $931 billion, or $10 billion more than predicted in the 1969 *Annual Report*, and the unemployment rate averaged 3.5 percent for the year.

Price performance during 1969 was correspondingly disappointing. In the 12 months through December 1969, the consumer price index increased by 6.1 percent and, even worse, the wholesale price index increased by 4.8 percent. The GNP deflator rose by 5.2 percent from the fourth quarter of 1968 to the fourth quarter of 1969.

Gradualism: The Nixon Budgets

In January 1969, Richard Nixon replaced Lyndon Johnson in the White House and the "new economists" moved out of the Executive Office Building. But Paul McCracken, Herbert Stein, and Hendrik Houthakker, the new President's Council of Economic Advisers, relied upon the same economic toolbox that Arthur Okun, Merton Peck, and Warren Smith and their predecessors had used during their tenure on the council. There was fundamental disagreement as to the usefulness of some of the tools in the box, as is discussed below, but the new council certainly knew, understood, and appreciated what the old council had done or had tried to do. And the two groups of experts were in basic agreement as to what needed to

---

[112] This method of showing the impact of the tax surcharge on saving and consumption, only one of innumerable alternatives, is taken from William H. Branson, "The Use of Variable Tax Rates for Stabilization Purposes," mimeographed, 1971. For a similar estimate of the surcharge's effect on saving and consumption, see Arthur M. Okun, "The Personal Tax Surcharge and Consumer Demand, 1968-70," *Brookings Papers on Economic Activity*, 1 (Washington: Brookings Institution, 1971), pp. 167-204.

be done in 1969: [113] the growth of the economy should continue to be restrained so that inflationary pressures would subside.

The *Annual Report of the Council of Economic Advisers* for 1970 provides a lucid description of the gradual process by which the council expected that disinflation would be achieved. Though the scenario of gradualism may have benefited somewhat from hindsight, it merits quotation at some length:

> The growth in aggregate spending for goods and services as measured by gross national product, which was 9 percent from 1967 to 1968, would be reduced. The Federal Government's own purchases would not rise so fast, nor would its payments to State and local governments and to individuals—payments which these sectors ordinarily use to make their own purchases. By avoiding the tax reduction scheduled for mid-year, the Government would refrain from boosting private after-tax income and consequently from stimulating private spending.

> Monetary restraint and the resulting scarcity and high cost of credit would slow down spending in various ways. . . . These effects . . . would not be immediate or follow a precise formula based on the amount of the restraint, but they would come if the restraint continued.

> The slowdown in the growth of purchases would mean a slowdown in the growth of sales. . . . The most general and important response of business to a slowdown of sales would be a slowdown in the rate at which production was increasing. Initially this would involve a decline in the rate of growth and possibly some temporary decline in production itself. An absolute decline in output, however, would not be a necessary aspect of the disinflationary process. In a growing economy . . . even though output is still rising absolutely, a slowdown in the rate of growth of output reduces actual production relative to its potential and is an anti-inflationary force.

> This is part of the process that eventually builds up those back pressures which are essential to the development of a

---

[113] Okun has written in the *Political Economy of Prosperity* (p. 96) about the council's efforts in 1969: "The Nixon administration demonstrated a commitment to continued prosperity and to a gradual attack on inflation. The basic objectives and the means of attaining them reaffirm those under the Johnson administration. The general strategy of stabilization policy has become bipartisan."

new stability in the level of costs and prices.

A deceleration in the rate of growth in real output would adversely affect productivity in the short run. . . . The deterioration in productivity and increased costs per unit of output would reduce profits per unit. . . . [T]he major effect would be heavier pressure on businesses to begin actions to reduce costs. . . . [E]mployers would become more resistant to granting wage increases. At the same time, a softening labor market would lessen workers' insistence on large wage increases as a condition for employment. . . . Moreover, if business profits were less favorable, a major rationale for heavy wage demands would be removed. As a consequence, the average rate of wage increase would ultimately begin to diminish. However, in view of the momentum of past increases in wages and the cost of living, this could not be expected to happen quickly. Nor could it be expected to happen evenly in all sectors.

[M]ore sluggish market conditions would encourage businesses to pursue temperate pricing policies, especially as this influence began to be reinforced by a slowdown in the rise of wage rates and unit labor costs. The reductions in wage and price increases would tend to reinforce each other. The longer price increases moderated, the weaker would become the expectation of further inflation. In turn, business and labor would be increasingly inclined to respond to the waning inflation by making appropriate price and wage adjustments, in preference to accepting a lower volume of production and less employment. With this change the economy would be on the road to regaining full employment without setting off another round of inflation.

At the beginning of 1969 no one knew how much of this process might occur during the year. As this Council indicated in its testimony before the Joint Economic Committee in February 1969, the growth of demand would be slowed only a little in the first half of the year, because demand was strong at the outset and the turn to monetary restraint just before the year opened would not have had much time to work. A more marked slowdown of demand was likely for the second half. At first almost all of the slack in demand would probably be taken up by a slowdown of production. Price and cost trends at the beginning of the year were too strong to be deflected by the moderate deceleration expected in the first half. But it could be expected that after midyear the slower growth of real output and of employment would create sufficient excess in the supply of products and labor to begin to have visible effects on price and wage increases. By the end of the year the rate of inflation would be lower than at the beginning. The effects to that point might not be great. Still, the economy would have crossed the threshold from a state of accelerating inflation to one of decelerating inflation, and we could count on making further progress.[114]

As part of its conscious policy of disinflation, the new administration reviewed the budget Johnson had submitted for fiscal 1970 and, in April, vowed to hold expenditures for that year to $192.9 billion (unified budget basis), compared to the $195.3 billion figure in the Johnson budget. Because of growth in the uncontrollable items, this implied cuts of $7.5 billion below the Johnson budget figures. In addition, the Nixon administration initially accepted the conclusion of its predecessor that the 10 percent income tax surcharge should be continued until June 30, 1970. In April, President Nixon requested repeal of the 7 percent investment tax credit, effective immediately, on the grounds that the priorities of the 1970s did not accord with continuation of this tax subsidy to investment. At the same time, he reduced to 5 percent the rate requested for the continuation of the surcharge in the first half of 1970. Continuation of the surcharge for the second half of 1969 was approved only in early August, and the repeal of the investment tax credit and the extension of the surcharge at a 5 percent rate until June 30, 1970 were part of the tax reform act that became law on December 30.[115]

Despite the general agreement between the Johnson and Nixon economists on the proper macroeconomic policy for 1969, basic differences remained.[116] First, the Nixon administration early rejected

---

[114] *Annual Report,* 1970, pp. 25-27. A preview of this policy can be seen in Paul McCracken's comments in *Twentieth Anniversary of the Employment Act of 1946: An Economic Symposium,* Joint Economic Committee (Washington: U.S. Government Printing Office, 1966), especially p. 75.

[115] For a summary account of these developments on the fiscal front, see *Annual Report,* 1970, pp. 30-33. Because the 1969 tax reforms have primarily long run impacts, they are not discussed further here.

[116] In "The 1970 Annual Report of the Council of Economic Advisers," *Public Policy* (Summer 1970), p. 599, Lester Taylor has said: "There is a fairly widespread feeling that economic policy since the Republicans assumed control of the White House is not too much different from what it would have been had the Democrats remained in power, but this does not mean that the economists of

reinstating any variant of wage-price guideposts and jawboning. According to its economists, experience had demonstrated that such direct approaches to slowing the rate of increase in wage rates were largely ineffective and that, even if effective, they might do as much harm as good by interfering with free market forces.[117] The appropriate anti-inflation policy, the council believed, was to squeeze inflationary expectations out of the economy by slowing the rate of growth of output in the way described above. Once this was done, the economy would eventually settle down at the "natural" rate of unemployment and a rate of inflation that could be chosen as a matter of policy—within limits.[118]

The Nixon administration's announcement that the White House would not exert pressure to moderate wage and price hikes was roundly criticized by Democratic economists. There was nothing to be gained they argued, from explicitly lifting the Damocles sword of potential presidential disapproval. Even if the presidential jawbone was never to be used, they saw little reason for saying so.[119] Similarly, most of them were skeptical of the decision to base public policy in the fight against inflation upon the "acceleration hypothesis"—that is, the hypothesis that deviation from the natural rate of unemployment would result in accelerating inflation, or deflation, rather than be consistent with some steady rate of inflation. Economists who, under Kennedy and Johnson, had debated the shape of the Phillips curve showing the tradeoff between inflation and unem-

---

the two camps share the same philosophy of how economic policy ought to operate." Taylor provides a perceptive analysis of the differences between the Nixon and Johnson economists' views.

[117] Annual Report, 1970, pp. 23-25.

[118] Intellectual underpinnings for such an approach had appeared in a number of places, most prominently in Milton Friedman, "The Role of Monetary Policy," American Economic Review (March 1968), pp. 1-17.

Because they believed that inflationary expectations played an important role in the persistence of inflation, the members of the council devoted a considerable portion of their public speeches to convincing businessmen and labor leaders that inflation would soon subside and that those who bet on continued high rates of price and wage increases would be hurt. For example, McCracken entitled his remarks at a briefing for business in Washington on November 21, 1969, "The Other Side of the Valley," and Herbert Stein spoke to the downtown economists luncheon group in New York on April 1, 1970 on "The View from the Valley." The idea they were trying to instill was that recovery from the recession would find prices rising more slowly than before.

[119] Taylor, op. cit., (p. 602), has referred to the public repudiation of guideposts as "gratuitous."

ployment were not inclined to accept quickly the proposition that there was no tradeoff.[120]

Second, once inflation had been brought under control, the Nixon economists would prefer to eschew fine tuning to keep the economy on the path of full employment and price stability. Ideally, they would set the full employment surplus at the level required in the long run to meet the need for saving in the economy, and not allow it to vary much from year to year. This means that autonomous changes in federal expenditures would be offset by tax policy, but that fiscal policy would not be used to offset fluctuations in private demand. Moreover, monetary policy would not "stray widely from the steady posture that is likely on the average to be consistent with long-term economic growth. . . ." [121] This did, of course, resemble the CED position discussed in the second section above.

In the final reckoning, the council was correct in some respects and expected too much, too soon, in others. Federal outlays for fiscal 1970 were $196.6 billion on a unified budget basis, as opposed to the $192.9 billion estimated in April, largely because of growth in uncontrollable expenditures. Nevertheless, federal spending on a national accounts basis grew by only $8 billion in calendar 1969, or 4.4 percent, compared with an annual average of $19 billion or 13.7 percent in the previous three years; and the NIA budget surplus for 1969 was $7.3 billion.[122] Monetary growth slowed to 3.1 percent for the year as a whole, and by the end of the year had ceased. Fiscal and monetary restraint did slow the growth of the economy, as expected. The annual rate of growth of GNP slowed from 9.1 percent in 1968 (fourth quarter 1967 to fourth quarter 1968) to 6.5 percent in 1969, and in the fourth quarter had fallen to 3.3 percent. In real terms, GNP also grew more slowly in 1969 than in previous years, and in the fourth quarter was actually $2½ billion (1958 prices)

---

[120] Moreover, some economists concluded that nothing much would be gained from another "experiment in sadism" to squeeze inflationary expectations out of the economy. According to Gordon (op. cit., pp. 140-42, 144), "the simulations confirm the conclusion . . . that policy makers cannot 'buy' permanent price stability and full employment (when defined as a 3.8 percent unemployment rate) by engineering a recession. . . . In short, whatever the unemployment rate in the long run, the best short-run stabilization strategy is to guide the economy to it as rapidly as possible and remain there permanently."

[121] Annual Report, 1970, pp. 66-69. The quote is from p. 68. A detailed discussion of the optimal full employment surplus is contained in chapter 3. Stability of monetary policy is, of course, to be defined in terms of growth of monetary aggregates, rather than in terms of interest rates.

[122] Since the economy was at more than full employment, the actual and full employment surpluses were nearly equal; see Table 3.

below its level in the third quarter. As in 1966, much of the impact of tight money fell upon housing, though disinflationary pressures were much more widely dispersed than in the earlier period.[123]

Thus in terms of the proximate goal of reducing the rate of growth of aggregate demand and introducing some slack into the economy, the Nixon program had been successful, or even too successful. Where it had been disappointing, however, was on the price side. The reduction in the growth of real output was somewhat greater than the council felt it had reason to expect on the basis of previous experience, and the moderation in the rate of inflation somewhat less.[124] The implicit GNP deflator rose by 5.2 percent during the year as a whole and by 4.7 percent even in the fourth quarter (annual rate), more than in any year since the Korean War. Gradual indeed was the progress being made against inflation under the Nixon policy of gradualism.

Nonetheless, the CEA recognized the need to resume stimulation of the economy well before the inflation appeared to be under control. To do otherwise would throw the economy into an unnecessarily severe recession. On the other hand, a too rapid resumption in the growth of aggregate demand would cast doubt upon the administration's commitment to eliminate inflation, and thereby refuel inflationary expectations. This in turn would set off a further round of inflationary spending. In such a case the slowdown deliberately engineered for late 1969 would have been for naught, and arresting inflation might become even more difficult. In the words of the *Annual Report* for 1970, "there is a path of moderate expansion of demand which will yield both a decline of the rate of inflation and a resumption of growth of output. The task of economic policy in 1970 is to achieve that path." [125]

The Nixon game plan for 1970 was to allow considerable softness to develop during the first half of the year. This, the council hoped, would produce the back pressures described in the passage quoted earlier and lead to moderation of the rate of inflation. More rapid growth in total demand in the second half would prevent a serious rise in unemployment from developing. Though the Nixon advisers had explicitly rejected fine tuning, they were contemplating walking a very narrow path on their return to high employment with

---

[123] Private nonfarm housing starts fell by only 2.3 percent in 1969, compared to 21.3 percent in 1966. See Cagan, *op. cit.*, and Swan, *op. cit.*

[124] *Annual Report*, 1970, p. 29.

[125] *Annual Report*, 1970, p. 57.

price stability. An error in either direction could be expected to cause one of the twin goals to be forfeited.

The administration's preferred policy mix was to combine monetary ease with continued fiscal restraint. This approach, spelled out in the *Annual Report* for 1970, would allow easing of the pressure on capital markets and some recovery of residential construction. In budgetary terms, it translated into an expected slight drop in federal purchases from their 1969 level. Though no official estimate was published of the full employment budget for 1970, Okun and Teeters estimated that the budget for fiscal 1971 implied a full employment surplus for calendar 1970 of roughly $10 billion, about equal to the figure for 1969.[126]

No explicit statement of the inflation or unemployment rates expected during 1970 was made in the economic documents issued in January 1970. However, reading between the lines suggests that the GNP deflator was expected to rise by about 4.4 percent during the year.[127] In testimony before the Joint Economic Committee, CEA Chairman Paul McCracken estimated that the unemployment rate would average no more than 4.3 percent for the year as a whole.[128]

The economy's performance in 1970 could only be termed disappointing. Real GNP fell by six-tenths of one percent, whereas it had been expected to advance by roughly one percent. On the other hand, the rise in the GNP deflator of 5.3 percent was faster than had been anticipated. This translated into an unemployment rate for the year of 4.9 percent, substantially above the 4.3 percent McCracken had foreseen. Even worse, the unemployment rate at the end of the

---

[126] Okun and Teeters, *op. cit.*, p. 108.

[127] GNP was expected to reach $985 billion in 1970. Yet, it was expected to be but $944 billion in 1969 prices (*Annual Report*, 1970, p. 79). This implies a rate of growth of the GNP deflator from its 1969 level of roughly 4.4 percent. Lester Taylor, *op. cit.*, places the implicit rate of inflation at 3½-4 percent. The 1971 *Annual Report*, p. 28, indicates a projected inflation rate of 4.4 percent for 1970.

[128] It is worth noting something here that has been missed in many post-mortems of this period that have decried this and other official statements as unrealistic. The Nixon council was convinced of the crucial role inflationary expectations played in sustaining inflation. This being the case, since any pronouncements on the expected rate of inflation would probably be widely interpreted as the *minimum* that could be expected, the council was more or less constrained to understate the expected rate of price increase, if it offered any estimate at all. At a later date understatement of the expected rate of unemployment would seem advisable if lack of consumer confidence was the problem. By the nature of things, realistic public estimates by the council might turn out to be destabilizing. On the other hand, overly optimistic estimates might be ignored as being unrealistic. Apparently, public statements must be fine tuned to a path of realistic optimism!

year stood at 6.2 percent. Although this rate was certainly raised artificially by the General Motors strike, it stood well above the 4.6 percent figure implicit in McCracken's February testimony. Thus inflation was proving to be particularly stubborn in the face of rather severe increases in unemployment. The back pressures had simply failed to produce the effects on the rate of increase of wages and prices that had been prophesied. Instead, wage increases were being negotiated that virtually assured the persistence of inflation because of their impact on unit costs of production.

A good measure of the performance of GNP and its components during 1970 is the change from third quarter 1969 to third quarter 1970, because this period largely eliminates the effect of the General Motors strike. The gain in output during this year was $43.3 billion, or roughly two-thirds as much as in the year ending with the third quarter 1969, just before the recession. (See Table 4.) The weakness in demand can be attributed to the $4.2 billion fall in federal purchases, the large ($5.3 billion) drop in inventory investment, the $2.0 billion decline in residential construction, and the small increase of $4.1 billion in business fixed investment. Together, the decline in the growth of these four components more than equaled the decline in the growth of GNP during the year. Consumption spending, spurred by increased transfer payments and reduced personal taxes, rose fairly strongly, despite the general weakness of the economy, and served to buoy up aggregate demand. But in the last three quarters of 1970, the savings rate out of personal income stood at over 8 percent, well above the historical average, suggesting that consumers had become cautious.[129]

It seems likely that the recession might have been deeper or longer if fiscal policy had not turned out to be less restrictive than budgeted in February 1970. Okun and Teeters estimated in April 1970 that the full employment surplus for the first half of 1970 would be $8.8 billion and that for the first and second halves of fiscal 1971 it would be $11.4 billion and $18.7 billion, respectively; they warned that the budgetary stance projected for the first half of calendar 1971 was considerably more restrictive than either 1969-70

---

[129] See the *Annual Report*, 1971, pp. 28-34, for a more detailed analysis of the movements of the various components of demand during the first three quarters of 1970. Note that consumption rose by $3.3 billion less in the period covered than in the comparable period a year earlier, contrary to the preliminary indication that it had risen by $1.7 billion more.

Table 4

CHANGES IN GROSS NATIONAL PRODUCT, BY COMPONENT, 1967 III–1971 III

(change in seasonally adjusted annual rates; dollar amounts in billions)

Component	1967 III to 1968 III	1968 III to 1969 III	1969 III to 1970 III	1970 III to 1971 III	1969 III to 1970 I	1970 I to 1970 III	1970 III to 1971 I	1971 I to 1971 III
Total GNP	74.3	65.0	43.3	77.3	15.8	27.5	37.3	40.0
Federal purchases	8.4	0.5	−4.2	1.3	−0.1	−4.1	0.6	0.7
Personal consumption	48.5	40.1	36.8	51.6	19.9	16.9	23.7	27.9
Nonresidential fixed investment	5.5	11.9	4.1	4.5	0.1	4.0	−0.5	5.0
Change in business inventories	−1.0	2.7	−5.3	−4.0	−1.1	3.8	−1.9	−2.1
Residential structures	3.1	1.0	−2.0	14.6	−0.7	−1.3	7.7	6.9
Net exports	−2.2	−0.6	1.2	−3.5	0.7	0.5	0.2	−3.7
State and local purchases	11.9	9.4	12.8	12.8	5.9	6.9	7.5	5.3

Source: *Survey of Current Business*, July 1971, p. 13, and *Business Statistics*, November 26, 1971, p. 2.

or historical experience.[130] Such a budgetary development would have been particularly dangerous in the context of the de-escalation of the war in Vietnam. The percentage of GNP represented by purchases for national defense had fallen from 9.2 in the first quarter of 1968 to 8.3 in early 1970, and by the second half of fiscal 1971 stood at 7.0, below the comparable figure for calendar 1965. Moreover, just as the national income accounts understated the defense buildup in 1966 through 1968, in 1969 they began to understate the reduction in defense production. Table 1 shows that, according to estimates by Lay and Jones, inventories of defense goods in process fell by close to $2 billion in each of fiscal years 1970 and 1971, contributing to the fall in inventory investment in 1970 and 1971 noted above and below.

The full employment surplus actually realized for calendar 1970 was $6.7 billion, $3.4 billion below the originally predicted level of $10.1 billion. The shortfall is more than accounted for by expenditure increases of $3.9 billion over the February budget levels.[131] Moreover, by the end of 1970, the full employment surplus figure that was projected for calendar 1971 had been lowered to $4.0 billion, dramatically below the $15 to $19 billion first-half surplus projected in April and September of 1970 on the basis of revised budget figures for fiscal 1971.[132] A $4 billion full employment surplus would equal about 0.6 percent of potential GNP, and therefore would represent slightly less than average fiscal restraint.

In its *Annual Report* for 1971 the Council of Economic Advisers predicted that GNP for the year would reach $1,065 billion. This level, it stated, would be roughly consistent with a gradual reduction of the unemployment rate to about $4^{1}/_{2}$ percent and a fall in the rate of inflation to the 3 percent range, both by mid-1972.[133] The $88 billion increase in GNP in current dollars would represent an increase of 9 percent over the 1970 level of output. It would probably be translated into roughly equal increases in real output and the GNP deflator for the year as a whole. Most private forecasters thought

[130] Okun and Teeters, *op. cit.*, pp. 108-10. The May revision of the budget resulted in a reduction of about $3 billion in the estimated full employment surplus for the first half of fiscal 1971.

[131] *Annual Report*, 1971, pp. 70-74; Okun and Teeters, *op. cit.*, p. 100.

[132] Okun and Teeters, *op. cit.*; and Nancy Teeters, "Budgetary Outlook at Mid-Year 1970," *Brookings Papers on Economic Activity*, 2 (Washington: Brookings Institution, 1970), pp. 303-12, and "The 1972 Budget: Where It Stands and Where It Might Go," *Brookings Papers on Economic Activity*, 1 (Washington: Brookings Institution, 1971), pp. 226-33.

[133] *Annual Report*, 1971, pp. 75-85.

that the council's projection involved an overly optimistic assessment of the likely path of recovery of real output.

By the third quarter, GNP stood at only $1,060.8 billion, and for the first three quarters it was only $1,041.6 billion (at an annual rate). It was therefore destined to fall far short of the $1,065 billion target for the year as a whole. Growth in the fourth quarter of $20 billion, the average for the second and third quarters, would put GNP for 1971 at just above the $1,050 billion mark. This would represent a gain of only 8 percent over the level of 1970.

Though business fixed investment rose slightly more than in the same period a year earlier, it continued to be weak in the year ending with the third quarter of 1971. Moreover, inventory investment fell by $4.0 billion during this period, and in the third quarter was barely positive. Finally, net exports fell by $3.5 billion during the period and federal purchases rose by a scant $1.3 billion. Sources of strength were (1) consumption, which rose by $51.6 billion, after average annual increases of only $38.5 billion in the previous two years, (2) residential construction, which rose by $14.6 billion, after falling by $2.0 billion in the comparable period a year earlier, and (3) state and local purchases, which matched their $12.8 billion increase of a year earlier.

Percentage gains for the year ending with the third quarter of 1971 were split evenly between the first and second halves of that year, but the composition of the gains in the two halves differed substantially in several important respects. Business fixed investment fell by $0.5 billion from the third quarter of 1970 to the first quarter of 1971, but rose strongly—by $5 billion at an annual rate—in the next two quarters. This strength in the second half of the year was largely offset by the $3.7 billion fall in net exports. Personal consumption rose by 7.6 percent and 8.6 percent, at an annual rate, during the first and second halves respectively of the 12 months ending with the third quarter of 1971. This growth suggested some revival of consumer confidence, as the savings rate fell by 0.5 percent between the two half years, to 7.7 percent in the second and third quarters of 1971.

As had been true throughout the Nixon years, inflation was again proving to be more stubborn than the council had expected. In the year since the third quarter of 1970, the GNP deflator had risen by 4.7 percent, so that real growth over the period was a modest 3.8 percent. On the other hand, between the first and second quarters of 1971, inflation, as measured by the GNP deflator had moderated to an annual rate of 4.0 percent, so that real output grew at an impressive 4.8 percent. But then real output grew by only 3.8 percent between the second and third quarters, although the freeze that occurred midway in the third quarter makes suspect the fall in the deflator's rate of increase to 2.9 percent.

These developments translated into little solid change in the unemployment rate. From its May high for 1971 of 6.2 percent, the unemployment rate fell dramatically to 5.6 percent in June, but rose to 5.8 percent in July. While the administration seemed confident that progress was being made, the progress was painfully slow, as it had been so often in the previous 2¹/₂ years. Neither the rate of inflation nor the unemployment rate showed any strong tendencies to behave as predicted.[134]

It seems likely that the Nixon administration would have continued at least until the end of the year to apply the conventional medicine to the underemployment inflation gripping the economy. In the early signs of revival of business fixed investment, residential construction, and consumer confidence there could be found reason to believe that the recovery would continue to strengthen, and the administration was repeatedly on record as disavowing the use of price and wage controls to halt inflation. But political conditions changed in the late summer of 1971. Economic advisers more sympathetic to controls seemed increasingly to have gained the President's confidence. Moreover, Chairman of the Federal Reserve Board Arthur Burns must have been applying increased pressure for intervention in major wage and price decisions, a course he had advocated for some time. As the 1972 elections neared, President Nixon may have become more inclined to this initially abhorrent approach to the dilemma of high employment and reasonable price stability, especially since he may have felt that the voters' views on intentionally engineered unemployment had been made abundantly clear in the 1970 congressional elections. But the deciding factor must surely have been the pressure on the dollar during the second week of August. Whatever the precise mixture of pressures, the administration decided to suspend the convertibility of the dollar into gold and to impose a 10 percent surcharge on imports. Coupled with this was a 90-day freeze on all wages and prices and proposals to reinstate the investment tax credit, this time at a 10 percent rate, and to speed up the increases in personal income tax exemptions included in the 1969 tax reform act. After 2¹/₂ years of almost religious avoidance of direct intervention in wage and price decisions, the Nixon administration

[134] The unemployment rate returned to 6.1 percent and 6.0 percent for August and September after its brief fall.

had assumed a markedly activist stance. And it was clear that this stance might not soften appreciably at the end of the 90-day period. Having once entered the field of wage and price controls, the administration could not gracefully retreat quickly. Thus it seemed likely that the American economy would be subjected to wage and price controls of some kind for a long time.

Appraisal and Conclusions

The detailed examination of the fiscal failure of the late 1960s suggests several policy conclusions. The first part of this concluding chapter appraises the fiscal experience of the period in an attempt to determine whether bad economics or bad politics should be held responsible for it. The second part reexamines the controversy over "rules versus discretion" in fiscal policy in the light of the experience of the late 1960s. Then the possibility of employing a new fiscal device to control swings in aggregate demand is explored.

Appraisal of Fiscal Failure. Americans' esteem for economists paralleled the rise in GNP, but only until it became obvious that the nation was on a severe inflationary binge. As inflation built and finally was slowed only at the cost of recession and substantial unemployment, the feeling may have grown that the new economics of the 1960s was not so new after all: deficit spending can stimulate the economy, but carried too far, it will be severely inflationary. Not surprisingly, by the time they left the Executive Office Building, the new economists were being blamed for the fiscal errors of the 1960s, and the new economics had fallen somewhat into public disrepute.[135]

There can be little doubt that inappropriate fiscal policy was the primary reason that the economy departed from the path of full employment and price stability during the late 1960s. The failure to raise taxes in the face of rising defense production, first in 1966 and again as the economy regained strength after the mini-recession of 1967, allowed inflationary pressures to build. In addition, the expectation that fiscal policy would not be tightened as needed has been blamed by CEA economists of that period for much of the ensuing strength of investment demand. Moreover, the abdication of fiscal

---

[135] The zenith of popular acclaim for the new economics, new economists, and economists in general can conveniently be dated with reference to the appearance of John Maynard Keynes on the cover of *Time* magazine in December 1965. At that time the unemployment rate stood at 4.0 percent and consumer prices had risen by only 2.0 percent during the year.

policy meant that monetary policy, and therefore housing, would bear the brunt of stabilization efforts in 1966 and 1969.[136] Finally, it can reasonably be argued that the extent of the readjustment necessary to unwind the inflationary spiral can be attributed in large part to the earlier errors of omission and commission in fiscal policy.

The blame for the failure to raise taxes in 1966 must fall jointly, but not equally, upon politicians and economists. The lion's share of the blame, it seems, must be awarded to the politicians. Though the economists advising the President underestimated the exuberance of the economy in late 1965 and 1966, they correctly saw the need for a tax increase. President Johnson refused to request the increase, apparently not wishing to damage his political image and power by requesting an increase he thought he could not get.

One widely accepted normative view of political processes in a democratic society would interpret congressional reluctance to raise taxes to finance the war as a sign that the war was not sufficiently popular with the electorate to deserve the budgetary support it received. President Johnson apparently did not share this view.[137] He believed the war was worth fighting, and since taxes could not be raised, he attempted to suppress inflationary pressures through a patchwork fiscal approach. Perhaps he thought that the war would be so brief and limited that it would pose little inflationary threat, or that the war should continue even at the cost of inflation. At any rate, the Vietnam buildup proceeded rapidly, with devastating effects on price stability.

It could be argued that by endorsing the President's actions in Vietnam and yet not pushing for higher taxes, the Congress deliberately chose to finance the war through inflation.[138] But this is unrealistic. It seems more accurate to say that the Congress failed to consider carefully and explicitly the expected costs and benefits of

---

[136] In addition, the premature monetary expansions of 1967 and 1968 can be blamed upon the mistaken expectation that fiscal action would be taken in the first case and for the failure of fiscal policy to be as effective as expected in the second.

[137] One vital question about which only speculation is possible is whether Johnson could have gained popular support for a tax increase by linking it to the war. The author believes that he could have. But such an approach would have stiffened the opposition to the war that became telling only several years later. Moreover, it might have created a backlash against war dissenters that would have been even more divisive than what actually happened.

[138] Given the uproar over the tightening of monetary policy in 1966, it does not seem likely that the Congress would have explicitly accepted high interest rates and the implied reduction in residential construction as a cost of fighting the war.

the war before deciding whether to support the war and how to finance it.

In defense of the politicians, it could be claimed that the economists did not provide sufficiently accurate forecasts of the war's economic impact. There is, of course, some merit to this claim, since the impact of the defense buildup was understated by budget figures and therefore probably did not figure importantly enough in the advice of economists. But the fact that the economic advisers were not kept apprised of defense plans and developments is probably at least as much to blame for the understatement, and *that* must be laid at the feet of the politicians. Besides, taxes could have been adjusted repeatedly, as needed, under the ground rules of the new economics. All in all, Okun's description of the failure to raise taxes in 1966 as "the first defeat of the new economics by the old politics" seems just.[139]

The scenario for the second delay in raising taxes, which occurred after President Johnson finally asked for a tax increase effective July 1, 1967, is different from the scenario in 1966, but the judgment is similar. The Council of Economic Advisers correctly saw that a tax increase was needed, but the congressional leadership refused to act. Instead, the tax increase was held hostage for a year by those who sought a slower rate of growth in expenditures and by those who refused to raise taxes without clear evidence that contractionary policy was needed. The 1967-68 experience is an even clearer case of political failure causing fiscal failure.

An important question is whether the 1967-68 political failure should be attributed to the executive or the legislative branch. Under one interpretation, the Congress was at fault for not raising taxes enough to pay for the war it was endorsing. Under another, the President was to blame for refusing to accept the expenditure cuts the Congress was demanding. In the final analysis the judgment depends upon which branch read correctly the desires of the public. If the war and domestic programs were popular enough to deserve to be carried on, then Congress is to blame for not raising the taxes to pay for them. But if the congressional view that expenditures should be curtailed was correct, one must conclude that the President acted irresponsibly in refusing to cut expenditures. The desires of the public are, of course, difficult to ascertain, even now.

When taxes were increased in 1968, the right fiscal policies were

---

[139] Okun, *Political Economy of Prosperity*, p. 71. We might add that the understatement in the preliminary GNP figures for 1965 did not facilitate fiscal decision making.

finally in place, at least for the moment, but the period of fiscal failure had not ended. Private spending continued to be much stronger than might have been expected in the wake of the tax increase. This may have been in part the result of the premature and excessive expansion of the money supply that resulted from fear of "overkill." In any event, it now seems that overkill was not a serious threat, but the fear of it was. Thus, economists must receive low marks for 1968.[140]

The excessive monetary expansion that continued through 1968 meant that improvement on the inflationary front was not likely in 1969, and in fact the 3.5 percent unemployment rate for December 1969 equaled its average for the year. But when restrictive measures took hold, they produced a far greater increase in unemployment than was expected or desired. Business fixed investment rose little between the third quarters of 1969 and 1970, inventory investment fell substantially, and residential construction fell marginally. It seems likely that the lagged impact of the income tax surcharge, the reduction of defense production, and the turn to monetary restraint in 1969 combined to create a far greater contractionary force than was planned. Thus the emphasis in the 1971 budget on holding down expenditures was probably misplaced. Whether the economists or the politicians should be blamed for the overly tight policy is unclear. Both groups within the administration probably favored holding back expenditures and over emphasized budget balancing.[141] But the economists must bear the blame for underestimating the cost of such a policy in terms of unemployment and for the failure to foresee the slow pace of relief on the inflation side.

It does, however, seem unfair to judge the politicians' failure of 1966-68 and the economists' failure of 1969-71 by the same standards. Most obviously, the economists would never have faced the

---

[140] Okun, who was chairman of the Council of Economic Advisers at the time has written: "[T]he boom proved remarkably stubborn, and the experience was a sobering one for many economic diagnosticians, forecasters, and policy planners. . . . The height of the patient's fever was misdiagnosed in the spring of 1968, and consequently the dose of medicine administered to bring it down was inadequate. . . . [T]he Federal Reserve celebrated the enactment of the fiscal program with some easing, supporting and following bullish developments in financial markets. This turned out to be the wrong policy because it was the right policy for what turned out to be the wrong forecast. And in believing that erroneous forecast, the Federal Reserve had lots of company—at the Council and among other government forecasters and business economists." (*Political Economy of Prosperity*, pp. 92-94.)

[141] It must be noted that budgetary tightness was to be combined with monetary ease in order to make more funds available to housing.

task in 1969 of unwinding the inflation satisfactorily if the politicians had performed more responsibly in 1966 or 1967. More importantly, the task of unwinding the inflation was substantially more difficult than the task of preventing it would have been. In 1966, economists knew in broad terms both what should be done and what to expect from what actually was done.[142] On the other hand, they were far less certain of the optimal policy response in 1969. Not very much is known about the process of unwinding an inflation of three years duration without creating substantial unemployment.[143]

In summary, it is probably fair to say that failure at the political level of fiscal policy formulation was largely responsible for the advent of the inflationary excesses of recent years, but that, once inflation got underway, economists became increasingly less able to predict accurately the appropriate policy response. An attractive conclusion for an economist to draw, therefore, is that the whole episode should be attributed to faulty politics, rather than to faulty economics. This may even be an accurate, if not very useful, judgment. More to the point, however, is the conclusion that macroeconomics, of whatever vintage, is probably more beneficial as a preventative than as a corrective. Stated differently, it is crucial that inflation not be allowed to gain a foothold, since our knowledge of how to unwind it without inflicting severe costs is as yet quite rudimentary. Whether some variant of "incomes policy" is the way out remains to be seen.

Budgetary Practices: Rules vs. Discretion Again. As the 1960s began, economists were split over whether or not discretionary fiscal policy should be used to try to stabilize the economy. One group argued that an active fiscal policy should be pursued. Another, represented perhaps most prominently by the Committee for Economic Development and Milton Friedman, thought that forecasting errors, lags, and political intransigences would make discretionary fiscal policy as likely to be destabilizing as stabilizing. Given these difficulties, the latter group advocated that ordinarily primary reliance should be

---

[142] We certainly knew that inflation would result from following highly expansionary policies during a period of full employment. We were, of course, less confident of our ability to walk the tightrope of full employment with price stability.

[143] In addition, there is evidence that changes in the composition of unemployment have resulted in a worsening of the inflation—unemployment tradeoff, if indeed the tradeoff exists. Essentially the Phillips curve has shifted to the right according to this hypothesis. See George L. Perry, "Changing Labor Markets and Inflation," *Brookings Papers on Economic Activity*, 3 (Washington: Brookings Institution, 1970), pp. 411-41, and William Fellner, chapter 5, this volume.

placed on built-in stabilizers, with the budget being set to yield a small surplus at full employment and not altered to offset cyclical fluctuations.[144] It was, of course, those who favored the activist position who advised Presidents Kennedy and Johnson on economic policy.

Looking back over the period beginning with mid-1965 one can only conclude that discretionary fiscal policy failed miserably to live up to its advance billing. It had been implied, if not stated explicitly, that judicious use of discretionary fiscal policy, with an assist from the wage-price guideposts and presidential jawboning, would permit fine tuning the economy so as to achieve prolonged prosperity without significant inflation. But fiscal policy was not used judiciously, as has been documented in the previous parts of this essay.

A number of eminent economists suggest that discretionary fiscal policy is to blame for our recent macroeconomic woes. Herbert Stein, a member of the Nixon council and an architect of the CED position, has written: "The net effect of fiscal policy in the postwar period, aside from the automatic effect of having a relatively large budget, has been destabilizing." [145] G. L. Bach, in his recent examination of experience in the stabilization field, has concluded in a similar vein: "Merely to eliminate destabilizing policies would mark a major advance in fiscal policymaking." [146] Finally, Otto Eckstein, a CEA member under Johnson, has written that "the record of the 1960's seems to repeat the verdict of the 1950's. Discretionary policy did harm as well as good. The policy proposed by the Committee for

---

[144] See pages 38-39, for a more complete description of the CED view. Musgrave, *op. cit.*, pp. 515-17 contains an excellent short discussion of rules vs. discretion controversy, including the following quote from G. B. Shaw's *Man and Superman*:

> *The Devil:* What is the use of knowing?
> *Don Juan:* Why, to be able to choose the line of greatest advantage instead of yielding in the direction of the least resistance. Does a ship sail to its destination no better than a log drifts nowhither? The philosopher is Nature's pilot. And there you have our difference: to be in hell is to drift; to be in heaven is to steer.
> *The Devil:* On the rocks, most likely.
> *Don Juan:* Pooh! Which ship goes oftenest on the rocks or to the bottom? The drifting ship or the ship with a pilot on board?

[145] Herbert Stein, "Where Stands the New Fiscal Policy," *Journal of Money, Credit and Banking* (September 1968), p. 469.

[146] G. L. Bach, *Making Monetary and Fiscal Policy* (Washington: Brookings Institution, 1971), p. 157.

Economic Development in 1947, if it had been followed, would have done better."[147]

As Eckstein notes, the necessary simulations have not been run, but it is almost certain that the CED rule (that a small full employment surplus be maintained and more ambitious stabilization policies be avoided) would have produced a more desirable path of output, prices, and employment than actually developed. Under the rule, the Vietnam war and the Great Society programs would have been financed, whether via higher taxes or lower expenditures on other programs, or they would have been forgone.[148] Attitudes might have been less bullish, and the investment boom might, therefore, have been more restrained. The credit crunch and its effects on housing would probably have been avoided, at least in large part. Moreover, the post-Vietnam economic adjustments would have been easier to digest, as they would probably have occurred in a situation of substantially lower rates of unemployment and inflation. And, to carry this reasoning to its ultimate conclusion, the wage-price freeze and its successors might never have been necessary.

But having engaged in this brief journey into what might have been if the CED rule had been followed, we must ask whether it might, in fact, have been. A realistic answer seems to be that it would not, and perhaps could not, have been. First, the discussion of section three above suggests that a substantial portion of the early inflationary pressures came from inventory investment in defense goods in process. This inventory investment can be traced directly to the budget. But would the CED rule have called for contemporaneously higher taxes to offset it? Probably not, so ·long as defense is treated in the budget on a delivery basis. Even under the CED rule, taxes would probably have been raised only as the goods were delivered and recorded in the budget. If anything, the balance might be in favor of discretionary fiscal policy unless the budget is placed on an accrual basis. Now it may be that the slight delay in raising taxes would have been of little practical consequence, especially compared to what actually happened. But it should be noted that the CED rule is easier to announce than to implement.[149]

---

[147] Otto Eckstein, "The Economics of the 1960's—a Backward Look," *Public Interest* (Spring 1970), p. 91.

[148] *Ibid.* Eckstein also notes that under the CED rule the excessively tight budgets of the late 1950s and early 1960s would never have been allowed to develop.

[149] Moreover, tax policy may affect private spending with such a lag that the primary impact would have been felt just as business was slowing in 1967. But then, under a different set of fiscal rules, the slowdown might not have occurred,

The difficulty in implementing the rule is further accented if we recall that defense expenditures during fiscal 1967 were underestimated by $10 billion in the January 1966 budget. Presumably the rule would have called for increases in taxes as the underestimate was corrected. But it is not really clear that the rule could have been followed, since at times those responsible for the framing of economic policy seem not to have been privy to the Pentagon's plans. The CED rule, like discretionary fiscal policy, requires that all the budgetary cards be on the table.

Finally, analysis of political processes does not provide much reason for optimism that even the CED rule could have prevented the inflationary excesses of the late 1960s. In this regard it is instructive to quote Eckstein once again: "Even if the government had abandoned discretionary policy altogether . . . the same political difficulties would have gotten in the way. Taxes would have had to be raised. It is likely that the political process would have failed to execute the CED policy, just as it failed to carry out a rational discretionary policy." [150] Unless it were institutionalized in the form of a mandatory legal requirement on the President and the Congress, the CED rule would probably have been largely ineffective precisely when needed most.

Herbert Stein has recently written in a darkly pessimistic tone about the possibility of such a rule being adopted:

> Whatever its merits might be if it were imposed, the concept of the balanced high-employment budget does not exist as a rule and there is no visible way to bring it to life as one. Those who initially proposed it hoped it would inherit the potency of what they believed to be the rule of the annually balanced budget. But the old rule is dead and had in any case, nothing to bequeath. Any new rule would have to be established *ab ovo*, a very difficult procedure. This is especially true in view of the fact that it would have to be proposed and ratified by the President and Congress, the very parties it would be designed to restrain. Although Congress can lay down a monetary rule for the Federal

---

or might not have occurred then. Trying to second-guess policy making in this way illustrates the value of running the simulations Eckstein mentions. For a more comprehensive list of possible failures of the CED rule, see Heller, "CED's Stabilizing Policy after Ten Years."

[150] Eckstein, *loc. cit.*

Reserve, no institution has the power to impose a fiscal rule on the President and Congress.[151]

Perhaps more surprising, Stein argues that adoption of such a rule might not even be wise.

> To tie fiscal policy down with a rule would be unwise amid the present uncertainty and disagreement about the effectiveness of monetary policy in stabilizing the economy. Furthermore, it would probably be impossible, starting, as we do, with no rules at all for fiscal policy. If steady growth of the money supply proves to be as effective an instrument of stabilization as many expect, fiscal policy will not in fact have to be bent much to the achievement of stability. But preserving the freedom of fiscal policy will provide a safeguard if that expectation is mistaken.[152]

Thus at the same time that some new economists are becoming disenchanted with discretionary fiscal policy, those who entered the 1960s strongly supporting a rule for fiscal policy seem to be less sure of either the possibility or the wisdom of adopting such a rule. The best approach, then, may be to aim for approximate budgetary balance at full employment, without legislating it.[153] A strong pre-

---

[151] Herbert Stein, "Unemployment, Inflation, and Economic Stability," *Agenda for the Nation*, ed. Kermit Gordon (Washington: Brookings Institution, 1968), pp. 298-99. Bach has made the same point, *op. cit.*, p. 170: "Nor has anyone explained how Congress and the President could be persuaded to yield to a 'rule' their prized powers over taxes and expenditures."

[152] "Unemployment, Inflation, and Economic Stability," p. 300.

[153] This statement ignores the nagging possibility that a balanced budget at full employment might not be consistent with the achievement of full employment. Two comments can be made on this score. First, other tools, such as monetary policy and tax structure can be used to guarantee consistency. Second, since we have never operated for long with such a rule, it seems worthwhile at least to try the rule. There is nothing inconsistent with the proposal offered here and that in the 1970 *Annual Report* that would base the target full employment surplus on the savings needs of the nation and private saving flows.

A further potential danger is that if a presumptive rule were adopted, overzealous adherence to it could hamper the flexible use of fiscal policy when the economy is far from the desired path of output growth. An example is the 1972 budget. President Nixon's acceptance of the merit of gauging the restraint or stimulus of fiscal policy with reference to the full-employment budget, rather than the actual budget, is laudable. But in the January budget message and more recent statements, Nixon has emphasized keeping the unified budget at least in balance, on a full employment basis, except in emergency. While this new orthodoxy might be appropriate if deviations from the desired path of GNP were slight, it was probably inappropriate when it was announced, and it will probably be inappropriate again. The economy was simply too far from

sumption that the full employment budget should ordinarily be roughly in balance is common to both the CED position and those who favor a more active fiscal policy. It would not in principle preclude discretionary use of fiscal policy to offset expected developments in private spending. It would, however, spotlight blatant deviations from the budgetary norm of approximate balance at full employment such as occurred in 1966-68.

Whether or not future budgetary policy will be constrained by a presumptive norm of approximate balance in the full employment budget can not be predicted with any confidence. Experience does not elicit much optimism. We did not, after all, discover only in 1966-68 that large deficits at full employment are likely to lead to inflation. We knew, at least in general terms, what to do, but did not do it. But one thing seems fairly certain: given present institutional arrangements, the primary fiscal responsibility for the avoidance of excess aggregate demand must lie with the President.[154]

The recent mistakes of fiscal policy almost certainly have left a wiser public and wiser Congress. Important lessons were learned (or relearned) about balancing receipts and expenditures at full employment. Yet we can not be sure that the Congress will always pass taxes or reject expenditure increases if price stability is threatened by excess demand created by deficit spending at full employment. Thus it seems reasonable to believe that we can expect a satisfactorily noninflationary macroeconomic performance only if

---

the optimal path for the new orthodoxy to make sense. The full employment surplus is probably the best single *measure* of the stance of fiscal policy. But requiring at least balance in the full employment budget, more or less without regard to the state of the economy, may be to succumb unnecessarily to a slower than desirable recovery. This point, ironically enough, has been made forcefully by men associated with the CED. See, for example, Emilio G. Collado, "Statement to the Joint Economic Committee on the 1971 Economic Report of the President," March 10, 1971. In a personal statement before the American Academy of Political and Social Science in Philadelphia on April 3, 1971, Frank Schiff, the chief economist for the CED, made similar observations. They also noted that balance in the unified budget, the object of Nixon's concern, implied a surplus of about $7 billion in the national accounts budget.

[154] This ignores the role of monetary policy, the failure of expenditures to correspond closely to budget impact, as in 1966, et cetera. Moreover, only demand-pull inflation is considered in this statement, since that seems to be the most useful context for a discussion of avoiding a repetition of the fiscal policy mistakes of the late 1960s.

the President submits fiscally sound budgets.[155] In this regard Herbert Stein has drawn the following conclusions from the experience of the '60s:

> No immediate alternative exists to a discretionary fiscal policy which reflects the weights Congress and the President place on numerous objectives from time to time. Still, the President might promote the idea that overall economic considerations, including stability and balance-of-payments equilibrium, should have a more significant role in fiscal decisions. The President bears main responsibility for these objectives, is more limited by them than Congress is, and has every incentive to try to get them accepted by Congress. To do this, he will have to demonstrate his acceptance of the limitations these objectives place on his own freedom. If Congress suspects that the President's concern with overall economic objectives is turned on and off as he finds convenient to support policies he wants on other grounds, it is not likely to be guided by those objectives. Moreover, if Congress thinks that the President is asking it to take strong, and often distasteful, action on the basis of weak forecasts of the economy, it will also be reluctant to accede.[156]

Effectiveness of Temporary Taxes. The income tax surcharge of 1968 seems to have had substantially less impact on private spending for consumption and investment than was expected. Robert Eisner, among others, has argued that this small impact is exactly what should have been expected.[157] That consumption should not respond strongly to a temporary tax on income is a direct implication of the

---

[155] It should be noted that this is a necessary, but not sufficient, condition for price stability. Moreover, it may be worth emphasizing, that "fiscally sound budgets" refers to approximate balance in the full employment budget. It decidedly does not mean that the actual budget should be balanced at all times.

[156] Stein, "Unemployment, Inflation, and Economic Stability," p. 299.

[157] Robert Eisner, "Fiscal and Monetary Policy Reconsidered," *American Economic Review* (December 1969), pp. 897-905, and "What Went Wrong," *Journal of Political Economy* (May-June 1971), pp. 629-41. It should be noted that although the failure of the 1968 surcharge to affect final demand as strongly as expected is sometimes interpreted as a victory of the "monetarists" over the "fiscalists" Eisner also holds out little hope for monetary policy as an offset to large increases in government purchases. For comments and a reply by Eisner, see the *American Economic Review* (June 1971), pp. 444-58.

permanent income and life-cycle hypotheses of consumer behavior.[158] Unless the tax changes were to alter greatly the levels of income expected to prevail over a longer period, which seems unlikely, they should have relatively little impact on consumption. Instead, their primary effect should be on saving.

Even if temporary tax increases affect private spending by households exactly as permanent taxes do, as Okun suggests is very nearly the case, the lags may be sufficiently long and unpredictable to make them an unreliable tool of fiscal policy. In defending the 1968 surcharge, Okun notes that "a year after an income change has begun, only 50 to 60 percent of it is expected to show up in consumption. The models teach the important general lesson that it takes time for tax changes—whether permanent or temporary—to build up their complete direct impact on consumption." [159] But the important corollary to this lesson, which Okun seems reluctant to draw, is that the lags may mean that extremely accurate forecasts and expert political manipulation may be essential—though perhaps not sufficient—if this rather blunt instrument is to be used aggressively for countercyclical purposes.

A similar argument can be made with regard to tax effects on investment. To the extent that investment is determined by the (near-term) flow of internal funds, even temporary tax increases can be expected to deter investment. But if profitability (or longer term flows of internal funds) is the key to investment demand, the situation is different. Tax increases known to be temporary should leave long-run expectations of profits (and flows of funds) largely unchanged, and thus they should have little negative impact on investment. Moreover, they could even have a perversely stimulative impact on business spending. Firms may be willing, or even anxious, to incur costs during a period of high tax rates that will produce gross revenues after tax rates have reverted to their normal levels. The temporarily high rates increase the tax saving from a given dollar of expense. Finally, if consumption is not restrained appreciably by

---

[158] See Franco Modigliani and Richard Brumberg, "Utility Analysis and the Consumption Function: An Interpretation of Cross-Section Data," in *Post Keynesian Economics*, ed. Kenneth K. Kurihara (New Brunswick: Rutgers University Press, 1954), and Milton Friedman, *A Theory of the Consumption Function* (Princeton: Princeton University Press, for the National Bureau of Economic Research, 1957). For further discussion and other references to the relevant literature on this subject, see Eisner, *op. cit.*, and Okun, "The Personal Tax Surcharge and Consumer Demand, 1968-70," *op. cit.*

[159] "The Personal Tax Surcharge and Consumer Demand, 1968-70," pp. 199-200.

the surcharge on the personal income tax, an acceleration theory of investment would suggest little induced reduction in investment.[160]

These theoretical arguments and recent experience with the surcharge raise serious doubts about the countercyclical use of discretionary changes in income tax rates. The short-term restraint provided by temporary rate increases may be too weak to be of much use in reducing inflationary pressures. Moreover, a sizeable portion of the impact on private spending may occur with such a long lag as to be destabilizing. Unless discretionary tax policy is to be abandoned as a tool of stabilization policy, it may be necessary to look beyond the income tax.

The obvious alternative would be to vary taxes on consumption, if only the United States made sufficient use of indirect taxes at the federal level for this to be practicable. Whereas saving can be expected to adjust to soften the impact on consumption of a temporary income tax, a tax increase of the same magnitude tied to consumption, if it is known to be temporary, can be expected to induce some postponement of consumption.[161] This postponement effect is a potentially important plus for U.S. adoption of a value added tax or a retail sales tax.[162] The tax could be varied for countercyclical purposes, presumably to greater advantage than the personal income tax.

There are, however, several strong arguments against adopting a broad-based consumption tax for this reason. Most fundamentally, the tax would involve an unacceptable increase in the regressivity of the tax system.[163] But more important in the present context, such a

---

[160] These arguments are made forcefully in Eisner, *op. cit.* It might be added with regard to both arguments that inflationary expectations can only accentuate the likelihood that tax increases will be ineffective. Needed fiscal action can itself reinforce attitudes that purchases should be made before prices rise even further.

[161] Branson has noted, *op. cit.*, that a temporary tax on consumption has important intertemporal substitution effects not shared by a temporary income tax of equal magnitude.

[162] This and other aspects of value added taxation are discussed in Charles E. McLure, Jr., "Economic Effects of Taxing Value Added," mimeographed, 1970.

[163] This could, of course, be overcome with some combination of income tax credits, low income relief, or (as a last resort) exemptions. Alternatively, the tax could be used only for countercyclical purposes, and not as a net source of revenue over the cycle. In such a case the rates would move about a basic rate of zero, depending on the state of the economy. In an inflationary situation rates would be positive, but if unemployment threatened, they would be negative, i.e., consumption would be subsidized. In principle such a scheme would not be regressive over the cycle. But one might reasonably doubt the wisdom of establishing the administrative machinery necessary to administer a federal tax on value added or retail sales if the basic tax rate were to be zero! Moreover, it is virtually certain that the basic rate would not long remain zero.

wholesale change in the U.S. tax system simply is not necessary to achieve the desired intertemporal substitution effects. A broad-based consumption tax is likely to induce postponement of purchases primarily of durable goods, but to have relatively little impact on the timing of purchases of nondurables and services. This being the case, most of the postponement effect could be obtained by applying the variable-rate tax only to durables. Moreover, the large swings in revenues that would be involved if the rates were varied on all consumption would be avoided if the rates were varied only on durables.[164] Thus monetary policy would not need to be varied so drastically to offset the monetary effects of cyclical variations in needs for treasury debt issue. Finally, if indirect (and even direct) taxes have serious cost-inflationary implications, as has recently been strongly suggested,[165] it may be advisable to use the taxes with the strongest deflationary impact for a given cost-push effect. Thus it is proposed here that attention be devoted to the possibility of using a variable-rate tax/subsidy with a zero "normal" rate applied to durable consumer goods in the effort to stabilize the economy.

Extending this reasoning one step further suggests that the variable rates might also be applied to business fixed investment.[166] Modest tax (subsidy) rates applied for fairly short periods of time create incentives for postponing (accelerating) purchases that could be matched by tight (expansionary) monetary policy and higher (lower) interest rates only at the risk of devastating effects on the homebuilding industry.[167]

The idea of varying rates of taxation on durable consumer goods and business fixed investment about a basically zero rate may appear

---

Rising expenditure needs plus pressures to reduce income taxes would probably quickly result in positive net revenues over the cycle.

[164] This point has been stressed by Branson, *op. cit.*

[165] See, for example, G. Brennan and D. A. L. Auld, "The Tax Cut as an Anti-Inflationary Device," *Economic Record* (December 1968), pp. 520-25, and John H. Hotson, "Adverse Effects of Tax and Interest Hikes as Strengthening the Case for Income Policies—or a Part of the Elephant," *Canadian Journal of Economics* (May 1971), pp. 164-81.

[166] It seems unreasonable to apply the tax to inventory investment, though this question should be examined further. Moreover, given the extent to which housing has borne the brunt of recent efforts to stem inflation via monetary policy, it may be desirable not to apply the tax to residential construction. On this point see Branson, *op. cit.* Given the purpose of the scheme, it should be applied only to domestically produced goods. Schemes such as this have also been suggested by Eisner, "Fiscal and Monetary Policy Reconsidered."

[167] Branson, *op. cit.*, stresses this point and gives illustrations of interest rate equivalents of temporary purchase taxes applied for various lengths of time.

novel, especially insofar as the tax rate would need to be negative if stimulus were required. Yet the negative rate portion of such a scheme was precisely what was in effect involved in the investment tax credit. Under the investment tax credit, a subsidy was paid on all qualifying investments. The administrative difficulties involved in applying positive rates to investment when needed to restrain the growth of aggregate demand would seem to be minimal, since the definitions and legal rulings developed for the investment tax credit could be carried over intact.[168] On the consumer-durable side, the tax/subsidy would probably be most effectively administered if it were collected from (or paid to) manufacturers, though it might conceivably be enacted as an add-on or credit against the personal income tax.[169] In any case, specific items to be made subject to the variable-rate tax/subsidy would need to be listed.

It might be argued that this scheme would impose an undesirable share of the burden of stabilization on the selected industries. But this seems to miss a basic point. If the rate averaged out to zero over the cycle, there would be no net fiscal burden on the target industries. And since the industries that would be most affected by the tax/subsidy scheme are precisely those now subject to the most extreme cyclical swings in output, the scheme would probably smooth production within the industries, rather than destabilizing it.[170] Thus the scheme should contribute to economic efficiency as well as stability.

The discussion to this point has been in the context of a variable-rate tax/subsidy scheme, with the variation centered about a zero basic rate. There is, however, no reason to presume that the basic rate should be zero, especially for the portion on business fixed investment. For example, if investment were felt to be chronically depressed, the basic rate might be set to subsidize investment in

---

[168] Of course, the incentives for reporting investment would be reversed. This seems to be a secondary problem, especially as investment would need to be reported before depreciation could be taken for income tax purposes.

[169] In this case, the credit would be fairly easy to police, but the tax would not. The necessity of reporting the purchase in order to take depreciation later does not exist in the case of consumer durables. It might also be argued that a temporary tax or subsidy stated explicitly in the purchase price would have a greater "announcement effect" than if it were collected or credited under a personal income tax.

[170] This is not to imply that the investment and durable consumer goods sectors are the source of most fluctuations in economic activity. But they do have a strong cyclical element. Some thought would need to be given to the possibility that this scheme would cause troublesome fluctuations in the bases of state and local sales taxes, though at first glance this seems to be a remote possibility.

"normal" times.[171] The rate of subsidy could be increased or decreased (or converted to a tax) relative to the normal level as the state of the economy demanded.[172] It is, after all, the countercyclical *change* in the rate of tax or subsidy, rather than the *level*, per se that acts to stimulate or depress spending in the affected industries.

In order for the scheme to have maximum effect, the rate of tax or subsidy (within preset limits) should be a matter of presidential discretion, subject to congressional veto. Otherwise the uncertainty of the outcome of legislative action would rob the measure of much of its impact. Moreover, if the tax/subsidy on consumer durables were collected or paid on purchases, rather than via the personal income tax, the scheme could not easily be made retroactive to the date of its announcement, as the investment tax credit can be. Finally, if changes in rates could not be imposed administratively, requests for rate changes would have perverse effects on stability. Announcement of a request for an increase in rates would set off anticipatory buying and accentuate inflationary pressures.

This approach might seem extreme. It might, of course, reasonably be argued that the maintenance of economic stability is worthy of extreme solutions. But more to the point, this proposal is not very extreme. On the investment side, its obvious precursor is the investment tax credit, which was removed in 1966 and restored in 1967 for countercyclical reasons, and then formed part of President Nixon's economic package of August 15, 1971, after having been removed "permanently" by the Tax Reform Act of 1969. On the durable goods side, there are also precedents, though imperfect ones. Controls on installment credit are, for example, a clumsy way of raising the price of consumer durables. Moreover, they hit only those who must borrow to make purchases. The tax scheme would impinge uniformly upon all buyers of selected items. Moreover, it could be applied more easily than other schemes to stimulate household investment in consumer durables if stimulation were the appropriate policy stance.

Though much research remains to be done on the specific items to be subjected to the countercyclical tax/subsidy on purchases, the administrative details of implementing the scheme, the variation in tax rates that would be necessary to evoke a given response, and the

---

[171] Such an approach could be used as in the early 1960s to stimulate investment in the face of a constraint on monetary policy posed by interest sensitive international flows of short-term capital.

[172] This implies, of course, that the rates of tax or subsidy need not be the same on the consumer durable and business investment components.

dynamics of the induced response, it does not seem premature to propose serious consideration of the scheme. Temporary changes in income tax policy seem not to affect spending strongly enough, and they may have lags that render them destabilizing. Monetary policy can affect spending, but recently its impacts have been concentrated too narrowly on housing. Taxing postponable purchases, on the other hand, should affect spending significantly, is likely to have short lags, and helps to spread the burden of stabilization.

2
MONETARY POLICY

Phillip Cagan

Introduction

In 1965, after having experienced relative price stability since the
late 1950s, the U.S. economy entered a period of accelerating inflation. The recovery from the business contraction of 1961 had been
slow and the economy did not approach full employment until 1965.
At that point, when restraint would have been in order, no change
in policy was made, and the economic expansion continued into the
zone of increasing prices. The GNP price deflator rose 22 percent
from 1965 to 1970 and continued rising in 1971.

As with other major inflations in U.S. history, this one was
accompanied by an expansion of war expenditures. But it differed
from other wartime inflations in that nonmonetary influences had a
smaller effect on prices. Armament expenditures did not require the
gigantic diversion of resources that had been necessary in World
Wars I and II, and consumers did not go on a buying spree in anticipation of shortages as they had after the outbreak of war in Korea.
While the conjuncture of war and inflation supported the popular
view that inflation follows inevitably from an increase in war expenditures, the sequence was certainly not inevitable in this instance.
The current inflation conforms to a classic example of overexpansion
of the money supply. The growth rate of the money supply gradually
increased from its low point in the 1961 recession, and continued to
increase until 1966, instead of becoming restrictive during 1965 when
the first signs of inflation appeared. Without continued monetary
support, the inflation would have withered.

Monetary policy lives in controversy. This was true of its role
in the slow recovery of the economy during the early 1960s and in

the beginning of inflation in 1965. Controversy also surrounded the question of whether monetary restraint would be effective in combatting the growing inflation. Monetary restraint was nevertheless applied in 1966 and again in 1969, producing two revealing experiments in its powers and problems. In each of those years the monetary authorities undertook to curb the inflation by contracting the growth in the money supply for two to three quarters. There can be no doubt that these contractions of monetary growth were deliberate steps of policy, rather than the feedback from a slowdown in the economy, which in past mild cyclical contractions had obscured the direction of influence between money and economic activity.

This essay recounts the story of the inflation and the policies to combat it up to the imposition of the wage-price freeze in August 1971. The first section describes the purposes and steps of policy, leaving to the remaining two sections an analysis of the results and problems. A final section surveys the lessons to be learned from this experience.

Formulation of Policy

Background of Price Stability: The Years up to 1965. During the Eisenhower administration, economic policy fought and finally conquered inflation. Following the sharp price increases of the Korean War, prices advanced broadly in the business boom of 1955-56. The deterioration of the balance of payments after 1957 and the continuing outflow of gold made it appear imperative that price stability be quickly achieved and maintained. Inflationary tendencies subsided during the second half of the 1950s, but slowly. By the late 1950s pressures to increase prices had finally been eradicated from the economy, as evidenced by the virtual stability in the wholesale price index and an average rise in consumer prices of only 1.2 percent per year from 1958 through 1964. The cost of achieving stability was several bouts of monetary restraint, which kept the economy below full employment and led to several recessions. The fourth of these since World War II occurred in 1961, during which unemployment reached 7 percent.

In the presidential campaign of 1960, John F. Kennedy promised "to get this country moving again." Ironical as it appears today, the overriding domestic concern of his administration was to speed up economic growth. Public opinion then ignored, as today it overplays, the problems of pollution aggravated by growth. Slogans are very much a sign of the times and, in 1961, sluggish business activity and high unemployment headed the list of public issues. To dramatize the issue, many critics of the performance of the U.S. economy pointed to the alleged rapid growth and technological advances of the Russian economy. The first Sputnik had startled the world in 1957. There were alarming charges that the U.S. was losing its technological and military superiority. The earlier concern with inflation faded, and the nation set its sights on growing as fast as possible.

The Kennedy administration's goals, however, were not immediately translated into a fundamental change in macroeconomic policy. The economy recovered from the 1961 recession at a steady pace, which was moderate rather than rapid, and unemployment did not reach the interim target of 4 percent until the end of 1965. Both fiscal and monetary policy were blamed for the slowness of the expansion.

Fiscal policy was faulted because the expansion in federal expenditures did not keep pace with the natural growth in tax revenues. The government tended to absorb more of expanding incomes through taxes than it replaced by increased expenditures. This drain slowed down the expansion and kept the economy from catching up with the natural growth in the labor force and thus from attaining full employment. The Treasury was running a deficit, to be sure, but this reflected the less than full-employment level of income. To reduce this "fiscal drag," as it was called, tax rates had to be lowered, or federal expenditures raised, continually along with growth in the economy at large. This extended the theory of a stable full-employment budget, discussed in the 1940s, to the idea that without changes the budget could also hold back economic growth. The objective was to maintain tax rates and expenditures in such a relation to each other that the budget would be balanced only when the economy was at full employment. At lower levels of employment, income and tax revenues would be lower and the budget would be in deficit, thus contributing to a needed increase in aggregate demand.

Newspaper accounts of the effects of fiscal policy usually assume that a change in government expenditures has a dollar for dollar effect on aggregate expenditures, and give no consideration to the offsetting effects on private expenditures. When the government runs a larger deficit and has to borrow more, however, it absorbs credit which might otherwise have gone into private investment. With the offsetting reduction in private investment, there will be a net increase in aggregate demand only to the extent that higher interest rates produced by government borrowing reduce the public's demand for money balances. This is equivalent to an increase in the supply of money and will increase aggregate expenditures.

The multiplier effects of a budget deficit are much greater if the money stock expands at the same time. Then the deficit is indirectly financed by new money, and there is no tightening of credit supplies to offset the deficit's expansionary effects. In such a combined monetary and fiscal operation, the results cannot be attributed to fiscal policy alone. The proposals in the early 1960s to cut taxes generally did not specify a cooperative expansion of the money supply, but the sizable effects often claimed for fiscal actions suggest that an accommodating monetary policy was implicitly assumed.

At the urging of his economic advisers, President Kennedy proposed a tax cut in June 1962 to take effect at the beginning of 1963. The proposal languished in Congress, in part because it was packaged with tax reform but also because many congressmen were opposed to reducing taxes at a time when the budget was in deficit. The theory of "fiscal drag" had not yet made much impression on the public. When the tax cut was finally enacted under President Johnson in early 1964, the economy had recovered considerably from the 1961 recession, though unemployment still remained around 5¹/₂ percent. Following the tax cut, unemployment fell—to 5 percent by the end of 1964 and to 4 percent in another year. The tax cut was acclaimed a great success. However, since monetary policy had become more expansive in 1963 and 1964, this did not demonstrate the power of fiscal policy acting by itself.

In the early 1960s, administration economists did not pay much attention to monetary policy, but it too, like fiscal policy, was open to criticism for holding back economic growth. On average, the money supply (excluding time deposits) grew slowly during that period (see Figure 1). Its annual growth rate did not exceed 3 percent for any six-month period during 1961-62 and even declined to zero in mid-1962. It rose to an annual rate of 4 percent for the six months centered at the end of 1962 and fluctuated narrowly around that rate during 1963. GNP grew during those years, but by barely more, after allowing for increases in prices, than the growth in potential output of 3¹/₂ percent per year. Consequently, even though unemployment had recovered from the 1961 recession in short order, it remained around 5¹/₂ percent during 1962 and 1963.

The low monetary growth of these years was not viewed by the monetary authorities as overly tight or inappropriate. The reason was that they did not attach special significance to the money supply at that time and therefore were not trying to produce any particular

Figure 1

GNP, MONETARY GROWTH AND FEDERAL BUDGET
SURPLUS OR DEFICIT, 1961-71

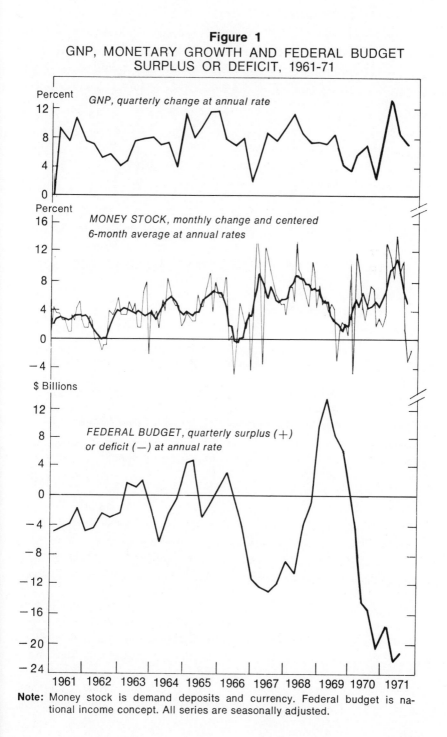

Note: Money stock is demand deposits and currency. Federal budget is national income concept. All series are seasonally adjusted.

rate of monetary growth. Their main attention was directed to "credit market conditions," such as interest rates and the availability of credit. These indicators seemed to suggest that credit was readily available, and that monetary policy was therefore providing the conditions for economic expansion and should attempt no more: First, high-grade corporate bond yields trended downward during 1960-62 from a peak of over 5 percent at the end of 1959 and, although they rose in 1963-64, remained around $4^1/2$ percent until mid-1965. Second, free reserves of member banks (excess reserves minus borrowings from the Federal Reserve), though falling during 1961-63, remained substantially positive during those years. This, in the Federal Reserve's view, was indicative of easy conditions. And third, total bank credit was growing much more rapidly in the early 1960s than demand deposits, because of more rapid growth in time deposits. Another reason for not easing credit further was the adverse balance of foreign payments. The U.S. payments deficit had not improved since deteriorating in 1958, and it continued to cause great concern in financial circles.

A slack economy and a large deficit in the balance of payments posed a dilemma for policymakers and led to consideration of sophisticated methods of improving the balance of payments and domestic business simultaneously. One scheme was to raise short-term interest rates, as a means of attracting capital inflows from abroad, and to lower long-term rates, as a means of stimulating domestic activity. A proposal to accomplish this so-called "twist of the yield curve" by selling Treasury bills and buying bonds was discussed in early 1961. Under prodding from the new administration, the Federal Reserve gave lip service to it. But the purchase of bonds went against the Federal Reserve's "bills preferably" policy of the time, and they did not in fact attempt this twist aggressively. Yields did move in the desired direction, but largely because of market developments rather than Federal Reserve actions.

The summary of meetings of the Federal Reserve Open Market Committee, as reported in each *Annual Report of the Federal Reserve System*, does not disclose a sharp change in view during 1962 and the first half of 1963. Some members of the committee continued to be concerned over the deficit in the balance of payments, and others were equally concerned over the failure of unemployment to decline. The committee was clearly in a quandary over the appropriate policy. After each discussion a majority opted for a compromise of moderate expansion in activity. So long as the balance of payments did not deteriorate further, policy was directed toward producing a slow decline in unemployment. The committee was boxed into this decision during 1962 and the first half of 1963, as no basic change occurred either in the balance of payments or the level of unemployment. The lack of change despite the appearance of easy money markets fostered the view that monetary policy was not very important and that the unemployment problem required a fiscal stimulus.

Despite the absence of change in the Open Market Committee's directives, monetary policy was not in fact static over this period. Growth of the money stock, either including or excluding time deposits, declined during the first half of 1962. Business indicators weakened in the second quarter, and the year-old recovery from the 1961 recession faltered. (The accompanying decline in common stocks was dubbed the "Kennedy bear market" because the administration's angry attack on a rise in steel prices was widely interpreted as revealing an anti-business bias and precipitated a wave of selling. But the faltering pace of the business expansion produced a basic weakness in stocks and underlay the decline.) Then, in September 1962, monetary growth spurted sharply and maintained an average rate of growth of about 4 percent through the first half of 1964. The spurt coincided with a general improvement in business conditions. Business loans expanded and the monetary authorities allowed the expansion of bank credit to increase monetary growth. The increase in turn supported the renewed business expansion.[1]

During the second half of 1963 policy directives continued unchanged, but the committee viewed the money market as taking on a "firmer" tone, and members were not dissatisfied with that development. They approved the sharp rise in Treasury bill rates and the decline in free reserves of member banks. Nevertheless, policy had in fact become easier; the market was firmer owing to the rise in business activity.

An important reason for not taking steps toward restraint at this time was that the balance of payments improved markedly in the second half of 1963 and first quarter of 1964, due partly to introduction of an interest equalization tax and partly to an increase in the payments balance on goods and services. Though the improvements did not last, they made the balance of payments a less imperative issue for a while. Moreover, there was a growing conviction

[1] This description of the actual policy is based on figures for the money supply which have been revised several times since then and which do not necessarily agree closely with the data available to the committee at the time. But in general, and for this period in particular, the revisions have not altered the general picture of monetary developments.

that the balance would be adverse on average for some time and could not be allowed to override domestic economic goals. This view was reinforced by a widely publicized report of the Brookings Institution [2] in 1963 which forecast that a gradual attainment of balance in U.S. payments was underway but would not be fully achieved for five years.

The year 1964 was the economic turning point of the decade. After two years of little change, the unemployment rate (seasonally adjusted) fell fairly steadily during the year, from $5^1/_2$ percent at the beginning to around 5 percent in the fourth quarter. This was clear evidence of a pickup in the rate of expansion of economic activity. Sentiment grew in the Federal Reserve Open Market Committee for imposing restraint. Nothing was done during the first half, however, since the economy, though expanding, gave little cause for alarm. The tax cut, which began to take effect in the first quarter of 1964, was immediately reflected in increased consumer expenditures (though it was partly absorbed by a higher personal saving rate in the last three quarters of the year). While the balance of payments began to deteriorate again during 1964, this was due to capital outflows; the balance on goods and services remained strong. Scattered price increases broke the calm surface of general price stability, but they were moderate during the first half and did not at first seem to be spreading.

By August 1964, with the economy continuing to expand and with capital outflows rising rapidly, a majority of the committee finally voted for a "firmer" money market, though not without strong dissents. The growth rate of the money stock, which had risen during the first half from 3 to above 5 percent per year, now began to decline and, from December 1964 through May 1965, averaged only $2^1/_2$ percent, despite a willingness by the Federal Reserve to accommodate Treasury financing in January and February. This tightening of policy appears to have been an appropriate response to the prevailing conditions, though perhaps too severe to be maintained very long. In any event, unemployment continued to decline, and the reduction in monetary growth promised to restrain the expansion without immediately halting it.

Outbreak of Inflation: 1965. In June 1965, the monetary growth rate suddenly doubled and for the next eleven months averaged more than 6 percent per year. Why was restraint abandoned in the midst

---

[2] Walter S. Salant *et al.*, *The United States Balance of Payments of 1968* (Washington: The Brookings Institution, 1963).

of a vigorous business expansion and numerous signs of spreading inflation?

Surprisingly, the Open Market Committee issued no directive for easier monetary conditions during 1965. Several directives early in the year called for "firmer" conditions, and one, on October 12, called ambiguously for achieving a "firm tone." The increase in the rate of monetary growth was simply not viewed by the committee as indicative of a shift to an easier policy. Here was a classic conflict between monetary growth and credit market conditions as indicators of the direction of policy. Free reserves of member banks turned negative in early 1965, after being positive for many years, and remained negative for most of the year. Interest rates of all maturities rose substantially during the second half. These were indications, in the Federal Reserve's view, of a tighter money market and a "firmer" monetary policy.

But the demand for credit was increasing, and the higher monetary growth helped fuel an expansion of aggregate expenditures. In that sense monetary policy was expansionary and not "firm" as directed.

This was not a case of monetary policy being forced by circumstances to underwrite heavy Treasury borrowing. As Vietnam expenditures rose, federal receipts initially rose just as fast. Budget deficits did not get out of hand until the end of 1966. Interest rates rose sharply in 1965, in response to expanded business activity and anticipations of heavy Treasury borrowing to come. Monetary growth increased because the Federal Reserve was trying to moderate the rise in interest rates, which required them to supply part of the expanding demand for credit. The President and top administration officials were adamantly opposed to a tightening of credit until "full employment" was reached. An indication of administration and congressional attitude toward restraint at this time was the reaction in December when the Federal Reserve felt compelled to raise the discount rate from 4 to $4^{1}/_{2}$ percent. This modest step touched off a furor of criticism, marked by barely concealed indications of presidential outrage and congressional hearings on the breach between the administration and Federal Reserve.

Inflation did not suddenly emerge in 1965 as a surprise. Wholesale prices of crude materials rose all during 1964, while other wholesale prices began to rise in late 1964. Their rise during 1965 was unmistakable and gave no sign of slackening as the year wore on. This did not go unnoticed; many people outside the government called for restraint.

Because it was gradual, however, the emergence of inflation did not suddenly demand the attention of policymakers in contrast to the Korean and 1955 episodes. Most of the accelerated increase in consumer prices during 1965 was due to foods, which reflected short-run supply conditions and which government economists dismissed as temporary. Labor costs per unit of output did not rise significantly until 1966. The human inclination of policymakers here, preoccupied for over half a decade with unemployment and now in sight of the cherished goal of 4 percent, was to ignore minor price increases as not justifying the imposition of restraint. They no doubt thought that a slow rise in prices could be easily stopped later by adjustments of policy—a judgment not widely criticized until later experience revealed the momentum which was developing behind the price increases.

In hindsight, the major mistake of policy was to disregard the first stage of inflation and to drive the economy full speed toward full employment in 1965 with a foot on the accelerator rather than the brake.

First Attempt at Curbing the Inflation: 1966. By early 1966 it was clear that the prevailing Federal Reserve policy of fostering "firm" monetary conditions was failing to curb rising prices. More drastic steps had to be taken. The authorities now slammed on the brakes and produced a rare experiment in the efficacy of severe monetary restraint. Seldom have the monetary authorities deliberately produced so sharp a break in monetary growth. In the past such breaks usually accompanied panics or speculative collapses, and cause and effect were hard to distinguish. Here the Federal Reserve clearly engineered the whole episode.

On February 8 the Open Market Committee unanimously called for a gradual reduction in bank reserves. (An important constraint on monetary policy was removed in the preceding month when the seasonally adjusted unemployment rate reached the administration's "interim" target of 4 percent for the first time since early 1957.) This directive to restrain credit was unchanged during March and April. While free reserves became increasingly negative, however, the effect on monetary growth was initially moderate. The annual growth rate of the money stock excluding time deposits remained above 5 percent in February and March and then jumped to almost 10 percent in April. Time deposits also continued to grow, though less rapidly; the maximum interest rate payable on large denomination certificates of deposit had been raised from $4^1/_2$ to $5^1/_2$ percent in the preceding December and exceeded the offering rate until July.

The money market appeared to tighten in early 1966 as judged by the sharp rise in most interest rates, particularly bond yields. In the largest movement in many years, high-grade corporate bond yields rose from 5 to almost 6 percent in the first half and municipal bond yields, which started the year at $3^1/_2$, rose to 4 percent by August (see Figure 2). But bank reserves did not decline as policy had prescribed. On a seasonally adjusted basis, member-bank reserves available for private demand deposits were virtually unchanged in January and February and even rose in March and April.

Accordingly, on May 10 the committee called again for gradual reduction in bank reserves and added, for the first time, a proviso that further restraint should be imposed if growth in required reserves (hence also net deposits) did not moderate substantially. The results were dramatic. The seasonally adjusted money stock excluding time deposits actually declined in May and, apart from monthly fluctuations, did not expand for the rest of the year.

There can be no doubt that this policy slowly curtailed economic activity. Although the growth of aggregate expenditures did not decrease until the first quarter of 1967, when real GNP actually declined slightly, the seasonally adjusted index of industrial production gradually leveled off during 1966 and then declined through the first half of 1967. In general, however, the slowdown in the economy was quite mild. It does not qualify as a conventional business recession, even though home building contracted severely.

The federal budget on a national income basis had run a surplus in the first half of 1966. The surplus was too small and occurred too far beforehand to account for the slowdown in the economy in the fourth quarter. In the second half of the year federal expenditures continued to rise fairly steadily while the growth of receipts began to level off, and the budget began a steep descent into deficit. This was also true of the full-employment budget. Despite the easing of the budget, the economy slowed down at the end of 1966. Fiscal changes, therefore, reflected the slowdown and did not produce it.

The deficits did add strain to the money market, coming as they did on top of severe monetary restraint. But Treasury borrowing was to be much higher during 1967 than it was in 1966, while a tightening of financial markets became severe in August of 1966, reached its peak in September, and subsided appreciably by the end of the year. The supply of credit slowly contracted and could not satisfy the growing demand. Increasingly, normally acceptable borrowers had to be disappointed, even though banks stretched their resources. During these months interest rates soared, and many corporations

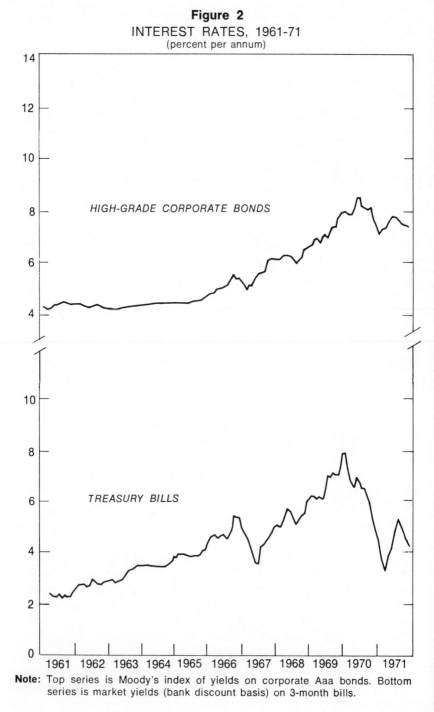

Figure 2
INTEREST RATES, 1961-71
(percent per annum)

Note: Top series is Moody's index of yields on corporate Aaa bonds. Bottom series is market yields (bank discount basis) on 3-month bills.

that borrow short-term funds on a regular basis began to doubt whether they would be able to meet upcoming financial commitments. The financial and business community developed a severe case of the jitters. Few had ever experienced a general financial stringency.

Many people felt that the Federal Reserve was carrying restraint too far and might blunder into a liquidity crisis. This would involve the wholesale dumping of securities on the market by businesses short of cash and cause widespread bankruptcies. Such a crisis did not occur, but the "credit crunch" imposed hardship on many, particularly small businesses and home building. The credit crunch is discussed further, below.

The widespread complaints produced by monetary restraint alerted the Open Market Committee in September to the desirability of easing the pressure. This followed by one week a presidential announcement of a planned reduction in the rate of growth of federal expenditures and a suspension of tax incentives for corporate investment. The anticipated effects of thus reducing credit demands helped relieve financial markets. After the September tax and dividend payments were out of the way, financial strains subsided. In October new bond offerings fell. Signs of declining growth in business activity also began to appear. By November, weakness in the economy had spread, wholesale prices appeared to be stabilizing, and the committee voted for easier monetary conditions.

Renewal of Monetary Expansion and Inflation: 1967-68. For a while, the seven months of no monetary growth during 1966 appeared to have been successful. It slowed the economic expansion and brought the rate of change of wholesale industrial prices down appreciably, while unemployment remained below 4 percent. A milder restraint might have accomplished just as much and jolted money markets less, but, overall, the policy achieved its purpose. The change to ease at the end of 1966 was also appropriate, though it probably should have come sooner.

The fault of policy was in the magnitude of the turnaround. In the first three quarters of 1967 the money stock excluding time deposits grew at an average annual rate of 8.2 percent, faster than in the three quarters preceding the second quarter of 1966. A comparable increase in growth rate occurred for money including time deposits. Why so sharp a reversal?

The major reason was a failure to foresee the strong recovery that high monetary growth during 1967 would provide for the mild slowdown in the economy. Real GNP was practically unchanged in the first quarter, but then jumped to a 3 percent annual rate of growth in the second quarter. The strength of this recovery was not sensed by the committee until May, and then uncertainly. Clear signs of the recovery were slow to appear. The index of industrial production declined until midyear, and the index of twelve leading indicators, a barometer of economic change, did not begin to rise until the second quarter. Moreover, it must be remembered that these indexes only become available with a lag of a month or more, and even then cyclical changes of direction often cannot be discerned for several more months. The Federal Reserve Board has a good record of recognizing economic developments once they occur, but it has done no better than most forecasters in foreseeing changes in direction of the economy. The period since 1965 has had its full share of forecasting blunders.

Despite the recognition by midyear of a resumption of economic expansion in the second quarter of 1967, no change in policy was made until November. The reports of the Open Market Committee indicate several reasons for the delay. Uncertainty continued to exist over the strength of the upturn in activity. And in August the President repeated his January proposal to add a surcharge to the income tax, now to be 10 percent, to begin in October for individuals and retroactively in July for corporations. This tax was expected, if enacted soon, to obviate the need for further monetary restraint. The proposal induced a wait-and-see attitude on the part of the monetary authorities. Finally, bond yields rose sharply during most of 1967 to levels much higher than the peaks of 1966, which had exceeded yields experienced since the early 1930s. Such high yields created the impression that somehow monetary policy must be tight. More tightening would raise interest rates even higher and complicate further the financing of the coming Treasury deficits and the revival of home building.

The second two reasons were related. The high and rising interest rates were not welcome to the populist-minded President Johnson, and he must have suggested to the Federal Reserve that it forego further monetary restraint and instead let the tax surcharge dampen the economic expansion and the rise in interest rates. The Open Market Committee could in good conscience go along with this suggestion, because most forecasters in and out of government expected the surcharge when enacted to be very effective. Later on many even shuddered at the possibility of "overkill."

Unfortunately for this strategy, the committee had to wait until the middle of 1968 for the passage of the tax surcharge, and then more months to discover that this fiscal bomb was a dud. Meanwhile, the economy continued to expand and interest rates continued to rise. There was practically no recognition at this time that interest rates were high because of anticipated inflation and that, in real terms, they were not unusually high. To that extent the inflation—and not solely tight money—was contributing to financial disintermediation and the difficulties of mortgage financing.

As it became clear during 1967 that Congress would not pass the tax surcharge that year, sentiment in the committee gradually swung in favor of greater monetary restraint. A significant change in policy could not be made in November because of negotiations to provide assistance to Britain to shore up the pound—though the turbulence in international exchange markets following devaluation of the pound on November 18 led to an increase in the discount rate on the 19th. Finally, in December, with a menacing increase in speculation against the dollar in foreign gold markets, the committee called for "slightly firmer" monetary conditions on the 12th and voted on the 27th to increase reserve requirements effective the middle of January.

Actually, monetary growth had declined slightly the preceding August. From a $7^1/_4$ percent average annual rate during the first eight months of the year, it fluctuated narrowly around a $5^1/_2$ percent rate until April 1968. Then for the rest of the year the growth rate became volatile again and grew on average at the higher annual rate of $8^1/_2$ percent, despite another directive on March 5th, unchanged until December, calling for firmer conditions.

This discrepancy between stated policy and actual monetary growth again illustrates the contrast between "credit market conditions" and monetary growth as indicators of policy. The failure of credit market conditions to indicate the true degree of monetary restraint during 1968 had become evident, and the Open Market Committee started to pay more attention to "monetary aggregates," meaning the money supply and bank credit. Nevertheless, while the May 28th report of the Open Market Committee notes that "the money supply continued to grow rapidly in May . . ." it concluded that

> a considerable degree of monetary restraint had . . . been achieved; the banking system was being subjected to increasing liquidity pressures; over-all expansion of bank credit appeared to have halted in April and May; and market rates of interest had advanced sharply to levels that could give rise to a substantial amount of disintermediation.

The disinclination to tighten further was supported, after mid-year, by the turn in fiscal policy. With the new tax surcharge in effect, the budget deficit on a national income basis fell from an $11 billion annual rate in the second quarter of 1968 to $3.5 billion in the third quarter. Yet economic activity did not slow down during the third quarter, and inflationary forces even gained strength. By autumn the evidence of these developments would normally have led the committee to conclude that monetary restraint should be intensified no matter how "firm" it was thought to be. But faith in the power of the surcharge died slowly, and the majority still hesitated, expecting the surcharge eventually to provide all the restraint necessary. The report of September 10th concluded that:

> greater restraint was not considered desirable in view of the outlook for slowing in over-all economic activity, although it was noted that firm evidence was lacking thus far on the amount of slowing in prospect.

In preceding years Federal Reserve Board officials had often lectured the administration and the Congress on the necessity of fiscal restraint to avoid overburdening the "limited" powers of monetary policy. In 1968 the request was granted, but ironically the monetary authorities paid dearly. Monetary policy was disastrously expansionary at a time of accelerating inflation for 17 months from mid-1967, when the need for effective restraint was first recognized, to December 1968.

Second Attempt at Curbing the Inflation: 1969. The Nixon administration took office in early 1969 with the announced objective of curbing the inflation, though as gently as possible. The concept of a "tradeoff" between inflation and employment had been widely discussed and was very much in the minds of policymakers. There was general agreement that any success in slowing inflation would produce a higher rate of unemployment. The unemployment would reflect a gap between potential and actual output, and this pressure of excess capacity in commodity and labor markets would bring down the rate of inflation. The policymakers thus had a choice: Larger excess capacity would bring inflation under control faster, but would also require a higher peak level of unemployment. The challenge to policy was to follow a thin line, bringing about reasonable if not spectacular reductions in inflation at the cost of moderate unemployment in the short run.

The new administration therefore faced the politically unappealing prospect of temporarily condoning unemployment in order to curb inflation. Yet it saw no choice; continued inflation was unacceptable. This distasteful necessity was sweetened by the hope that the short-run trade-off would not be too harsh and would allow a reduction in inflation without raising unemployment too high in the process and that, in any event, the worst would be over before the congressional elections of November 1970.

The election of the new administration was promptly reflected in the posture of the Open Market Committee. At its meeting on December 17, 1968, the members were "unanimously of the view that greater monetary restraint was required at this time in light of the unexpected strength of current economic activity." The reported shift to restraint was left basically unchanged in the directives during 1969. There ensued a precipitous decline in the growth of the money stock including time deposits. From a rate of growth over the two preceding years of 11 percent per year, this stock actually declined 1 percent during 1969 because of a $10 billion reduction in time deposits. The reduction reflected mainly a runoff of certificates of deposit; their ceiling interest rates remained at $5^1/_2$ to $6^1/_2$ percent depending upon maturity, while the competitive commercial paper and Eurodollar rates soared.

The money stock excluding time deposits told a different story. Revised figures, first published in December 1970, show a small decline in the annual growth rate of this stock to 5 percent from January to July 1969 compared with a rate of over 8 percent in the preceding nine months (April-December 1968). But the figures available at the time showed a 2 percent rate of growth for the January-July period, down from $6^1/_2$ percent during 1968. (This revision in the money data was unusually large, because a heavy volume of Eurodollar borrowing by banks considerably overstated cash items in the process of collection in the unrevised figures.) While monetary policy was viewed at the time as becoming increasingly tight during the first half of 1969, the degree of tightening as noted was moderate. According to the revised figures, commercial banks managed to acquire sufficient reserves to keep expanding demand deposits until July. Monetary policy appeared at the time to be tightening because interest rates were rising sharply and free reserves and time deposits were declining. But the shift by time depositors to commercial paper and Eurodollars did not reduce the total supply of credit; one asset was simply substituted for the other because of the change in relative rates of return.

The standard economic forecast made at the beginning of 1969 was for a slowdown in the first half of the year and an acceleration in the second half. This revealed an optimistic confidence in the ability of fiscal and monetary policy to attain their stated objectives. In large part these forecasts were wishful thinking, and they soon had to be revised upward. The new Council of Economic Advisers, testifying in February 1969, expressed doubt that the economy would slow down much before the end of the year. On that schedule, the acceleration previously slated for the second half could not be expected until early 1970.

Further indication of a stronger-than-expected first half of 1969 came from the Commerce-SEC survey taken in February. The survey indicated a planned increase in expenditures on plant and equipment of 14 percent in 1969 (a projection that was subsequently scaled down to 12½ percent in the April-May survey). This led many to doubt whether the economy would ever slow down, given the tendency to view corporate investment as the key to changes in GNP.[3]

At the meeting of the Open Market Committee on April 1, its staff's previous GNP projections of a slowdown in 1969 were accordingly revised upward. The staff noted that the recent declines in bank credit gave a misleading picture of monetary tightness, because banks had developed unconventional means of raising and supplying credit in response to the runoff of their certificates of deposit. The magnitude of these new sources of financing had not previously been fully recognized. Moreover, funds that normally traveled through banks were finding their way to ultimate borrowers through an expansion of the commercial paper market and other channels, so that total credit was not declining despite the decline in bank credit.

The committee decided that the tightening effect of two coming policy steps—an increase in the discount rate in early April and an increase in reserve requirements in mid-April—should not be offset by open market operations. The language of this policy change reads like a minor adjustment. Combined with the policy directives issued since mid-December, however, the effect was dramatic. The growth in the monetary base slowed sharply after May, and the money stock excluding time deposits grew hardly at all from July to December.[4] This shift in monetary growth provides a second revealing test, along with 1966, of the power of monetary policy.

Unlike 1966, fiscal policy was not wholly passive in 1969. As noted, the tax surcharge of mid-1968 reduced the federal deficit

---

[3] The actual increase was 11½ percent, and all of this came in the first three quarters.

[4] This statement is based on revised (1970) figures. Unrevised (1969) figures show the money stock virtually unchanged from April to December.

sharply. The new administration also put a lid on the expansion in federal expenditures and produced a surplus, on a national income basis, of $9¹/₂ billion (annual rate) in the first quarter of 1969 and $13¹/₂ billion in the second quarter. Thereafter, the budget eased. The surplus slid to $6 billion (annual rate) by the fourth quarter, and then the budget fell into deficit. As with the tax surcharge in 1968, the effect on aggregate activity of the 1969 swing to a budget surplus is difficult to detect. The growth in GNP (in both dollar and real terms) remained fairly steady through the third quarter of 1969 and fell sharply only in the fourth quarter, three quarters after the shift of the budget to surplus. We expect a lag of that length for monetary policy but not for federal expenditures. What happened in this case was that private expenditures took up the slack in the growth of federal expenditures. Although the 7 percent investment tax credit was repealed in April 1969, business investment continued to expand. With the budget shift from deficit to surplus, the Treasury no longer raised funds in financial markets but became a net supplier of funds. The strong private demand for credit absorbed these funds and channeled them back into the stream of expenditures. The Treasury surplus in 1969 no doubt helped to moderate the rise in interest rates and to that extent made monetary velocity lower than it otherwise would have been. But that contribution to dampening the boom was inconsequential, and the economy finally slowed down only after monetary restraint began to contract aggregate spending.

The continued expansion of the economy in the first three quarters of 1969, which contradicted the earlier forecasts of a slowdown, confused the public as well as many professional forecasters. The switch to a budget surplus had failed to produce the expected effects, and monetary restraint appeared to have failed too. It was, of course, not known at the time, as later data revealed, that the rate of growth in the money supply (excluding time deposits) had declined only moderately during the first half. A belief that no downturn was coming, or that if it came it would be extremely mild, gained wide currency in the business community during the summer and autumn and hardened the anticipations of continuing inflation. A survey of corporations by the Federal Reserve Bank of Philadelphia [5] in October found that 80 percent expected their after-tax profits in 1970 to increase over 1969, in the aggregate, by 8¹/₂ percent. (Actually, corporate after-tax profits *declined* 8¹/₂ percent in 1970!)

Financial markets tightened severely in the second half of 1969, and the public expectations of strong business activity were not con-

[5] *Business Review*, September 1969.

sidered inconsistent with widespread fears of another "credit crunch" as in 1966. Interest rates rose at a speed and to such high levels as to recall the financial panics of pre-1914 days. Funds bypassed or flowed out of savings institutions—which were no longer competitive due to deposit-rate ceilings—to be invested directly in security markets, thus drying up a major source of mortgage financing. Municipal bond yields rose above statutory rate ceilings in many states and prevented new issues. The growth of bank loans declined during the year despite the strong demand for credit. Many borrowers, especially many small businesses dependent upon bank loans, could not be accommodated. These developments are discussed further below.

Despite the turmoil, financial markets continued to handle a heavy volume of new security issues at rising interest rates during 1969. Many in Wall Street feared that monetary restraint would make credit tighter and tighter without ever restraining business activity. While the Open Market Committee was confident that business activity would eventually slacken, it shared the general uncertainty as to when this would occur. Around midyear the Federal Reserve staff began to report signs of slower economic activity, but the committee insisted upon waiting for concrete results before allowing policy to ease.

This flagrant disregard of the much-discussed lag in monetary policy can be explained by the committee's fear of repeating the policy mistake of 1966-67. At that time, the inflation was weakened by monetary restraint, only to resurge as soon as policy relaxed. Another such failure would surely harden public anticipations of inflation and magnify the degree of restraint which would then be required in the next attempt. There was even some sentiment for waiting until inflation was completely under control. But evidence of such control remained scanty, whereas multiplying signs of a downturn in general activity by year-end made the urgency of easing policy increasingly clear.

The consequence of such a "hardline" monetary policy was that restraint was maintained too long, thus leading to a larger decline in economic activity than was originally contemplated or intended. This raised the danger that the Federal Reserve Board might later over-react to the larger-than-expected decline in the economy with a rapid monetary stimulation which would refuel the inflation. Policy in 1966-67 was pointed to as having mistakenly fallen into such a stop-go pattern.

While both the Federal Reserve and its critics (which included

108

some high in the administration) could accuse the other of interpreting the lesson of 1966-67 incorrectly, the events of 1969-70 disappointed both sides. The downturn in activity was considerably greater than that in 1967, despite not much more monetary restraint, but then took far longer to affect prices.

Economic Slowdown and Easing of Monetary Policy: 1970. By the start of 1970 the earlier buoyant optimism of the business community had swung around to pessimism, and sentiment in the Open Market Committee for a change in policy had grown. The January 15th directive called for moderate growth in money and bank credit, but ambiguously specified that the growth should be consistent with the continuation of the prevailing conditions of firm credit. In February, Arthur F. Burns replaced William McChesney Martin as chairman of the Board of Governors and, at the first meeting in February, the new policy was modified, though not without dissents. The directive called for less restraint "implemented cautiously." At the next meeting, on March 10th, the qualification was dropped and the directive called simply for "moderate growth in money and bank credit."

The money stock (excluding time deposits) had spurted in the last week of December 1969, but most of this reflected the unexpected effects of international transactions. The spurt largely disappeared during January, and not until the stock increased in March was it clear that monetary growth had resumed. For 1970 as a whole the stock grew $5^{1}/_{2}$ percent, though less in the latter than in the earlier part of the year.[6]

Statements of policy now gave full recognition to the lag in monetary effects. Real GNP had declined slightly in the fourth quarter of 1969, and was expected to show no growth in the first quarter because of past monetary restraint. The resumption of monetary growth in the first quarter was expected to initiate an upturn in activity in the second and subsequent quarters.

Paul W. McCracken, chairman of the Council of Economic Advisers, testified to the Joint Economic Committee in February 1970 that the administration foresaw a rise and then a decline in unemployment during the year, with a maximum of less than 5 percent of the labor force. This proved to be optimistic. Real GNP declined 3 percent (annual rate) in the first quarter, considerably more than expected, and increased only slightly in the "recovery" of the second

---

[6] Pre-December (unrevised) data had suggested that money was growing at a somewhat slower rate.

and third quarters. The fourth quarter registered a 4 percent (annual rate) decline because of the strike at General Motors. (Without the strike there would have been little or no decline.) Industrial production continued on a contractionary course throughout the year and reached a trough in November. The unemployment rate climbed steadily to a peak of 6.2 percent by December.

Both the administration and the Federal Reserve stressed monetary policy as the key to economic developments during 1970, but differed on the appropriate rate of growth of the money supply. Administration officials wanted a growth rate higher than the 5 to 6 percent rate implied by Federal Reserve pronouncements of its intentions. They reasoned that a 5 to 6 percent rate would not permit real output to expand fast enough to keep unemployment around 5 percent, an unemployment rate that was considered sufficient to maintain pressure on prices and slowly unwind the inflation. Monetary growth of 5 to 6 percent might be adequate to hold the economy on the desired growth path once attained, but not to get back to it. Curbing inflation was going to take a long time, and little could be gained in the short run by accepting an excessively high unemployment rate. If the fight against inflation became too unpopular, political forces might force its abandonment. This was underscored by the November elections in which the Republican Party suffered setbacks partly because of unemployment.

Another argument given in favor of the higher growth rate target for 1970 was that, for two decades, money balances held by the public had been falling relative to national income while the economy expanded. If the desired ratio of money balances to national income stopped falling or even rose in 1970 as the economy slowed and interest rates fell, which was all to be expected, monetary growth would have to be stepped up to offset the drag that the increased demand for balances would exert on the expansion of aggregate expenditures. The monetary growth rate suggested by these arguments was 8 to 10 percent or more per year until economic activity returned to the desired path.

On its part the Federal Reserve was reluctant to pursue such a policy for fear of the effect on anticipations. A vigorous expansion in the economy, even though only for a few quarters, might convince the public that the fight against inflation had been abandoned, no matter how the policy might be explained publicly. In that event, anticipations of inflation would intensify and the long labor of policy to slow down economic activity and to begin controlling inflation would have been lost, as had happened in 1967. The adverse balance of payments also counseled restraint. To be sure, tight money had brought capital inflows which produced temporary surpluses on a liquidity basis during 1969, and abandonment of support of the private gold market in 1969 took pressure off the gold stock. But the Federal Reserve continued to be concerned over the continued deterioration in the balance on goods and services.

Although Federal Reserve officials were dismayed at the continued weakness in the economy as the year unfolded, they maintained monetary growth at an average rate of $5^1/_2$ percent, as noted. This represented a standoff between those who wanted more growth and those who wanted less. The argument for less was based mainly on three developments during 1970: the large decline in short-term interest rates mainly in the second half of the year; the phenomenal growth in certificates of deposit following the February increase in the ceiling rates and the June removal of any ceiling on the large denomination, short maturities; and the meager progress in curbing inflation. The first two developments had uncertain significance, however. The decline in interest rates reflected in large part a fall in demand for credit, and did not indicate that monetary policy was overly easy. Moreover, such a decline might tend to raise the demand for money balances and, if the supply did not rise commensurately, would work to reduce aggregate expenditures. The growth of CDs, like their runoff in 1969, reflected a switching among similar financial assets; at the time the large growth seemed likely to subside after several months. A much stronger argument against further easing was the third development—the meager progress in curbing inflation.

The persistence of inflation during 1970 was generally unexpected and a major disappointment to policymakers. A key indicator was the index of wholesale industrial commodities. During 1970 its annual rate of increase fluctuated around an average of 3.6 percent, down only one-half percentage point from 1969, and gave no clear indication that it would continue to decline. The consumer price index and the GNP deflator rose about 5 percent and showed virtually no deceleration compared with 1969. Econometric studies predicted that the annual rate of increase in prices would decline only about 1 percentage point in 1971-72. Union wage settlements and nonunion wage adjustments were higher in 1970 than in 1969 and showed little tendency to moderate. Inflation was cooling at an excruciatingly slow pace.

The problem facing policymakers in this instance was not the traditional trade-off dilemma in which a permanently lower level of unemployment required a permanently higher rate of inflation. In

1970 the economy was in flux, and the permanent trade-off was far off and largely unknown. With excess industrial capacity, both inflation and unemployment could decline for a while. The problem was that inflation was coming down slowly and unemployment would remain high for some time unless policy took the risk of stimulating the economy much more vigorously.

Different prescriptions emerged from this dilemma. The administration view, as noted, was to take the risk. Another view was to bring political pressure against "excessive" wage and price increases. If the pressure worked, a given expansion in aggregate demand would result in more increase in output and less in prices. Federal Reserve Board Chairman Burns wanted the administration to establish a wage-price review board to intensify such pressure, particularly in certain areas like construction, and to take various other steps to increase competition in labor and commodity markets. The administration, originally skeptical of the value of such measures and opposed to the philosophy of governmental intervention in private markets which some of these measures implied, was persuaded to intervene in a few special cases during 1970. These are discussed further below. Outside of general price and wage controls, which the administration at this time did not seriously consider, such measures are not capable of having a decisive influence on the rate of price increases in the short run.

Any near-term progress against inflation would therefore have to depend upon the usual pressure on prices of a reduction in aggregate demand. This orthodox method of curbing inflation would produce either lower profit margins, smaller increases in wages, or greater labor productivity (as measured by output per man-hour). Profit margins in general were already very low, however, and wages as noted gave no sign of slowing their rate of advance. Although wages could be expected to respond eventually to an extended period of less than full employment, the response might be slight as long as anticipations of inflation remained strong. At the time, it seemed that anticipations themselves were following the actual rate of inflation and were likely to continue doing so, barring a massive increase in unemployment. These two avenues of reducing inflation therefore promised little immediate progress. The key to success appeared to require increases in labor productivity. Output per manhour had been virtually constant during 1969 and rose only $1^1/2$ percent in 1970, well below its trend rate of $3^1/2$ percent per year. Yet business was under strong pressure to reduce costs in 1970, and trimming the number of workers is a time-honored method of doing so. A delay in realizing the benefits of such trimming would be consistent with past cyclical behavior. Normally, such benefits do not show up until output recovers, at which time the ability to produce more with fewer workers cuts costs per unit of output. On this reasoning the benefits of economic restraint would not be revealed until the economy recovered, which was confidently expected to occur in 1971.

Economic Recovery: The First Half of 1971. Economic activity rebounded in the first quarter of 1971. While some of the quarter-to-quarter increase in real GNP of $6^{1}/_{2}$ percent (annual rate) was attributable to the end of the General Motors strike, a normal cyclical recovery was clearly underway. Typically cyclical recoveries produce a vigorous expansion in the first year. In its annual report issued in February, the Council of Economic Advisers set a target GNP of $1065 billion for the year, which implied an increase of a little over 12 percent from fourth quarter 1970 to fourth quarter 1971. If allowance is made for the General Motors strike by adding $10 billion to GNP for the fourth quarter of 1970, the implied increase would be about 11 percent. That figure equals the gain recorded in the strongest of the previous three first-year cyclical recoveries (those beginning in 1954, 1958 and 1961), which ranged from 8.8 to 11.1 percent. But those previous cycles were deeper than the 1970 cycle and so could be expected to have had stronger recoveries. To most private forecasters, the council appeared too optimistic.

The council's target reflected its desire to reduce both inflation and unemployment. That was feasible on the argument that price increases depended upon the gap between actual and potential output. According to this view, it was possible to reduce this gap, thereby producing less unemployment, and still maintain pressure on prices to decelerate.

An estimate of the increase in GNP required to achieve this goal could be obtained by adding up for 1971 the components of projected GNP growth on the supply side: (1) the projected increase in the labor force was $1^{3}/_{4}$ percent; (2) hours per worker for the whole economy could be expected to increase about $1^{1}/_{4}$ percent; (3) output per manhour probably had to rise at least $3^{3}/_{4}$ percent for the whole economy [7] if unit labor costs (subject to likely wage increases averaging over 7 percent and supplemented by some improvement in profit margins) were to allow (4) a deceleration of inflation to 4 percent; and, finally, (5) a drop in the unemployment

---

[7] Based on the experience of past cycles, an increase in productivity of this amount was not out of line.

rate of about one percentage point to 5 percent was desired. These components of GNP add to a total nominal growth of nearly 12 percent for the year,[8] or approximately 11 percent adjusted for the General Motors strike, about the same as the council's target. Any less growth in GNP appeared insufficient to reduce unemployment to 5 percent by the end of the year.

The Council of Economic Advisers called for a monetary policy which would produce this growth in GNP. (Fiscal policy was to play a supporting role: initial plans called for approximate balance in the full-employment budget, so that the actual budget would run a deficit.) The required growth in the money stock was 8 percent or more for the year, dependent upon reasonable assumptions about the behavior of monetary velocity.[9] With such a sizable expansion in real output in the first year, the remaining excess capacity would allow a much smaller expansion in the second year of recovery; monetary growth would need to be correspondingly less for 1972. The policy proposed by the council thus assumed that monetary growth of 8 percent in 1971 would not carry the expansion in GNP into 1972 at so rapid a rate that it would revive the inflation later.

The Federal Reserve Board indicated in February [10] that it intended to continue the moderate stimulation applied to the economy during the previous year of recession, when monetary growth had totaled $5^1/_2$ percent. This was well below the growth needed to achieve the administration's 1971 target, which the Federal Reserve considered unrealistic. (Indeed, it was clear by the end of the first quarter of 1971 that real GNP would not attain the council's target.) By taking a middle-of-the-road position, the Federal Reserve was again seeking—as it had in 1970—a compromise in the trade-off between inflation and unemployment.

However, beginning in February, the month in which this policy was announced, the monetary growth rate jumped to a high annual rate, averaging 11 percent from February to June (based on November 1971 revision). This spurt could be attributed initially to a desire to make up for a slackening of monetary growth in the second half of 1970. (The growth rate appeared to be 4.8 percent per year compared with 5.9 percent in the first half, though the later 1971 revision

---

[8] For further explanation of these figures and a comparison with previous post-World War II cycles, see my article "Monetary Policy Choices in 1971 Recovery Year," *The Commercial and Financial Chronicle*, May 6, 1971.

[9] This is my estimate (see *ibid.*). The Council of Economic Advisers did not publish a desired monetary growth rate.

[10] See testimony of Chairman Burns before the Joint Economic Committee, *Federal Reserve Bulletin*, March 1971.

of the data gave figures of 5.2 and 5.6, respectively.) But the make-up was accomplished by the end of the first quarter. The continued high growth rate in the second quarter appeared to reflect a concern over the moderate pace of the business recovery (in which the second-quarter increase in real GNP was 4.8 percent at an annual rate) and the sharp cyclical recovery in interest rates from the lows reached in February and March.

The decline in interest rates during the second half of 1970 and the first quarter of 1971 had been a welcome relief from the tight financial markets of 1969 and early 1970. Rates on prime commercial paper and Treasury bills plunged over 4 percentage points, falling to less than half their peak levels; and most of this fall occurred after mid-1970, even though the actual deficit in the federal budget rose from an annual rate of $3 billion in the first quarter of 1970 to $13¹/₂ billion in the second and third quarters and then to $22 billion in the fourth. The drop in open-market interest rates spurred the growth of CDs during 1970 and of other time deposits during 1971. The money stock including time deposits grew at a 14 percent annual rate from February to December 1970 and at a 17 percent rate in the first half of 1971. An important result of these developments was that increased credit flows through banks and savings institutions aided municipal and mortgage financing, which relieved the distress imposed upon them in 1969 by monetary restraint.

While the sizable decline in interest rates was welcome for the domestic economy, it aggravated the adverse balance of payments. Just as rising domestic interest rates in 1969 drew massive short-term capital flows from abroad, the declining rates of 1970-71 reversed the flows. In 1969 capital movements on the official settlements basis showed a small net inflow of $700 million, while in 1970 the net outflow was $14.3 billion. Dollars continued to flood European capital markets in early 1971 as well, to the increasing alarm of foreign central bankers. In May 1971, several European countries led by Germany allowed the value of their currencies to rise relative to the dollar. This stopped the capital outflows from the United States for the time being.

Interest rates had nevertheless recovered roughly half of their preceding cyclical decline by midyear, despite the massive growth of money and credit. It was feared that the increasing credit demands of the business expansion would carry interest rates higher. Monetary policy could not continue to fight rising rates without accelerating the inflation. Faced with this prospect at midyear, the Federal Reserve took steps to reduce the monetary growth rate.

Resort to Controls: The Second Half of 1971. Although monetary growth dropped to an annual rate of 6.8 percent in July and August and then fell slightly below zero in September and October, interest rates stopped rising in July and fell in subsequent months. This behavior of interest rates reflected the moderate pace of the recovery. After the spurt in the first quarter, nominal GNP grew at an annual rate of 9 percent in the second quarter and 7 percent in the third quarter. Although the lack of vigor reflected in part a rundown of steel inventories built up in anticipation of a strike and a sharp rise in foreign imports, the recovery was on the mild side even allowing for the fact that shallow cyclical contractions like 1970 usually give rise to weak recoveries. Unemployment remained around the 6 percent rate.

Yet, as could be expected, the recovery initially strengthened some prices. While consumer prices slowed their advance mainly because of a decline in mortgage interest rates included in the index, wholesale prices speeded up. The policy of curbing inflation by maintaining slack in the economy was making progress too slowly to still the critics. The administration's patience gave out shortly after mid-year and, on August 15th, the President announced a dramatic change of policy. He instituted a 90-day freeze of prices and wages, invited a depreciation of the dollar relative to foreign currencies by discontinuing the Treasury's purchase and sale of gold, imposed a 10 percent surcharge on imports and, in order to stimulate economic activity, asked Congress to enact a one-year investment tax credit and other tax reductions. These measures had apparently been under discussion within the administration for some months as a needed response to growing public dissatisfaction with the imperceptible progress in reducing unemployment and curbing inflation. But the imposition of the new policy was speeded up in order to counter alarming increases in speculation against the dollar on world currency exchanges resulting from a large fall in the U.S. export surplus in the second quarter. Something had to be done about the growing imbalance of foreign payments, since the domestic gold stock was dwindling and would not last indefinitely. The dollar was overvalued in world trade, and devaluation was the logical solution.

The three months of the wage-price freeze resulted in zero increase in the industrial component of the wholesale price index. With this apparent initial success, the administration's program moved into a second phase in November. A Pay Board and a Price Commission were established to monitor and limit wage and price increases. The announced guidelines, with room intended for exceptions, were $5^{1}/_{2}$ percent per year for wages and $2^{1}/_{2}$ percent for prices. In the initial public satisfaction that the administration was now actually "doing something" about inflation, little attention was paid to the likely effectiveness of the controls. But it soon became apparent that the administration, in apprehension over the difficulties of running a massive control apparatus, had leaned the other way and created weak regulatory bodies. The Pay Board, in its initial decisions, permitted substantial increases above the guidelines on the grounds that some special situations justified a "catch up" with past inflation. As the year 1971 ended, it was still not clear how fast wages and prices would continue to rise under the Phase II program.

Effects of Monetary Restraint on Financial Markets and Housing

The monetary experiments of 1966 and 1969 unsettled financial markets and produced deep contractions in residential construction. These effects raised anew the complaint that monetary restraint falls unfairly upon particular sectors of the economy. To achieve broad effects on the economy, it was widely proposed—after the experience of 1966—that major reliance be placed on fiscal policy. However, this strategy was undercut by the failure of the 1968 tax surcharge to restrain the economy. Therefore, at the start of 1969, monetary restraint was generally accepted as bitter but necessary medicine which had been tested and certified by an initial success in 1966, but then too quickly reversed.

As 1969 progressed, however, the afflicted sectors did not quietly accept the treatment. Financial markets experienced a ferocious competition for credit, and widespread sentiment developed behind proposals to distribute credit "more equitably" (which usually meant more for small businesses and homebuyers) by putting credit controls on some other form of borrowing. Some congressional and public opinion favored restraining installment loans. That consumer loans should be asked to shoulder the main burden of restraint was ironical. It is true that they had been controlled during previous wars and were somewhat easier to restrict by regulation than other kinds of loans. But consumer durable purchases were a weak spot in the economy during 1969, and consumer credit controls would, in effect, have the shoe of monetary restraint pinch a lame foot. The strong demand for credit came from business fixed investment, and controls on corporate borrowing made more sense and were proposed by the

Joint Economic Committee.[11] But corporate credit controls involve difficult problems of enforcement. Although the Congress authorized the President to control credit, this authorization was not used.

The pressure that monetary restraint inflicts upon financial markets can be explained in part by the fact that it has a lagged effect on aggregate expenditures. Reductions in monetary growth in 1966 and 1969 worked to reduce the supply of credit, but for a while business activity remained strong and the demand for credit continued to expand. The resulting rise in interest rates attracted funds from existing money balances, which were pared down in relation to the volume of transactions. The process of paring balances occurred in one form through the purchase of newly issued financial assets, but this addition to the supply of credit could not be maintained without continual increases in interest rates which took them beyond the reach of more and more borrowers. The so-called "credit crunches" of 1966 and 1969-70 largely represented a pricing of many borrowers out of the market. And many of those who were still willing and able to pay the high price found regular sources of funds no longer available, because financial institutions rationed credit in favor of long-standing, low risk customers.

These crunches differed from the financial panics of an earlier era in which there were runs on banks and "bank holidays." In those cases, depositors rushed to exchange deposits for currency because of the risk of bank failures. In 1966 and 1969-70, by contrast, the banks were relatively safe, thanks to federal deposit insurance and to their ability to obtain large amounts of currency from the Federal Reserve. A crunch developed because the supply of credit did not expand as fast as the demand for it, reflecting in turn the curtailed growth in the total stock of money. This led to a squeeze on business liquidity.

The strain on financial markets was most severe during two periods, the third quarter of 1966 and again during the first half of 1970. In each case, when credit demand weakened after a quarter or two, the markets eased considerably and short-term rates fell sharply. At the height of the pressure while demand was strong, the amount of credit supplied actually declined, sending interest rates up sharply. Total funds raised in credit markets fell in the second half of 1966 and in the second half of 1969 and first quarter of 1970 (see Table 1).

---

[11] See Joint Economic Committee, *Report on the January 1970 Economic Report of the President*, March 25, 1970, pp. 19-20.

Table 1

TOTAL FUNDS RAISED BY NONFINANCIAL SECTORS, 1966-67
AND 1969-70, SEASONALLY ADJUSTED ANNUAL RATES
(billions of dollars)

	1966				1967			
	I	II	III	IV	I	II	III	IV
TOTAL	84.1	83.2	62.6	49.9	74.3	44.3	104.6	108.9
U.S. Gov't	10.8	6.7	4.9	2.9	8.0	−21.3	34.7	29.2
State & Local Gov't	6.6	7.5	6.1	6.9	10.5	11.8	8.1	11.4
Business	38.7	43.3	30.9	21.1	34.7	35.8	36.9	41.4
Households	25.1	23.1	21.0	17.7	15.6	14.2	21.1	24.1
Foreigners	2.7	2.5	−.4	1.2	5.5	3.7	3.9	2.8

	1969				1970			
	I	II	III	IV	I	II	III	IV
TOTAL	92.5	93.6	88.4	86.8	80.9	102.9	92.2	105.7
U.S. Gov't	−5.4	−9.5	−.7	1.2	2.7	16.2	12.3	19.6
State & Local Gov't	13.4	9.7	5.8	5.1	9.4	10.4	9.2	19.7
Business	47.4	51.3	49.4	49.9	41.6	54.1	45.4	44.4
Households	33.0	36.0	31.5	28.2	24.5	20.6	22.7	17.5
Foreigners	4.0	6.0	2.3	2.4	2.6	1.7	2.6	4.5

Source: *Federal Reserve Bulletin*, May 1968; "Flow of Funds, Revised Data for 1967-70," Board of Governors of the Federal Reserve System, February 22, 1971.
Note: Figures may not add to totals because of rounding.

The decline was more severe in 1966, when it affected all borrowing sectors. Although the cutback in monetary growth was as great in 1969 as it had been in 1966, the decline in loanable funds was smaller, in part because credit demand was apparently stronger, and interest rates temporarily had to rise much farther in order to induce holders of money balances to purchase more securities. The 1969 rise in interest rates lifted rates above statutory ceilings in many states and hampered the borrowing of state and local governments,[12] while business corporations borrowed heavily and obtained an unusually large share of the available funds.

Many businesses nevertheless suffered delay or loss of investment opportunities, with hardship or even bankruptcy for some. Especially hard hit were the borrowers of depository institutions. Not only did the growth of demand deposits (seasonally adjusted) stop in the second half of 1969, but so did the growth of time and savings deposits as market interest rates rose far above the ceiling rates

---

[12] According to a Federal Reserve survey, state and local governments were forced to cut back desired long-term borrowing by $5.2 billion from mid-1969 to mid-1970, a reduction of 28 percent. See John E. Petersen, "Response of State and Local Governments to Varying Credit Conditions," *Federal Reserve Bulletin*, March 1971, pp. 209-32.

allowed on those deposits (see Figure 3). These funds flowed into security markets to absorb the heavy issue of corporate bonds. Non-corporate businesses and small corporations normally cannot market bonds, however, and for a time equity issues of small risky enterprises could not be sold. Banks could not satisfy the heavy demand of these customers for loans. Dollar liabilities of business failures rose sharply in the closing months of 1969 and the first half of 1970. This all added to the anguish instilled by the severe decline in prices of common stocks during 1969 and the first half of 1970, which also created severe financial difficulties for many brokerage firms. Despair and anger shook the public's earlier staunch support for monetary restraint.

Then the collapse of the giant Penn Central Railroad in June 1970 precipitated a crisis of several weeks duration in the commercial paper market. That troubled company had seemed bound to go under sooner or later, but tight money hastened the debacle. Because of the large losses to holders of its commercial paper, lenders now held back from that market, and many regular borrowers could not raise funds there. The Federal Reserve rushed to reinstate banks in their traditional role as the major suppliers of commercial credit. This was done by the simple step of removing the rate ceiling from large denomination CDs of short maturity, which allowed banks to increase the rate paid on such CDs to competitive levels and raise funds again in large volume. Also, during the first weeks of this crisis in the commercial paper market, the Federal Reserve lent freely to banks with the understanding that they should lend freely to companies in need of short-term funds. This they did, preventing further serious difficulties.

In 1966 and 1969, when the rates available on Treasury bills and commercial paper rose sharply, the authorities kept deposit rate ceilings down, despite the temporary but disturbing decline in savings deposit flows and mortgage financing. One reason was to prevent banks and savings institutions from competing with each other for deposits. But this reason does not explain the maintenance of low ceilings for large denomination CDs in 1966 and 1969. These are purchased by large corporations and do not compete with savings deposits. The main explanation is that the authorities also wanted to restrict bank credit. Yet the ceilings served mainly to redistribute credit rather than reduce the total. If such interferences with the flow of funds are avoided in the future, monetary restraint need not disrupt financial markets so severely.

There is another reason why monetary restraint may not produce

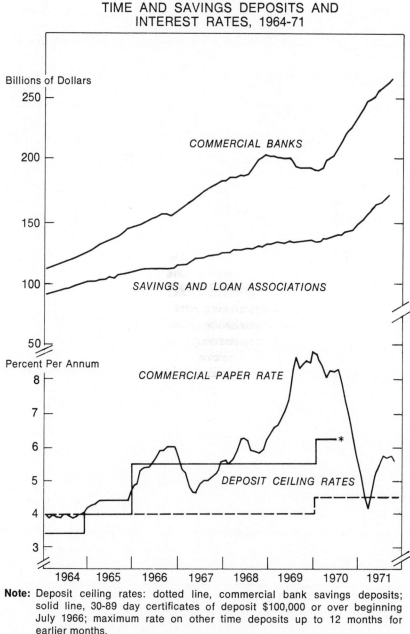

Figure 3
TIME AND SAVINGS DEPOSITS AND
INTEREST RATES, 1964-71

Billions of Dollars

COMMERCIAL BANKS

SAVINGS AND LOAN ASSOCIATIONS

Percent Per Annum

COMMERCIAL PAPER RATE

DEPOSIT CEILING RATES

Note: Deposit ceiling rates: dotted line, commercial bank savings deposits; solid line, 30-89 day certificates of deposit $100,000 or over beginning July 1966; maximum rate on other time deposits up to 12 months for earlier months.
Commercial bank time deposits are seasonally adjusted; other series are not. Commercial paper rate is for dealers' 4-6 month prime paper.
* Ceiling suspended June 24, 1970.

121

financial "crunches" in the future. Businesses reduced their liquidity to low levels in 1966 and 1969, partly in the belief that monetary restraint would not be carried so far. An examination of "Corporate Liquidity in 1969 and 1970" in the 1971 *Annual Report of the Council of Economic Advisers* reveals that most large manufacturing corporations had a decline in liquidity by standard measures during 1969 and 1970. Few corporations reached a dangerously low level of liquidity. The general decline appears to have reflected planned responses to market incentives rather than involuntary adjustments to a deterioration in financial position. Nevertheless, the large issue of bonds in the first half of 1970, which kept bond yields from declining despite the contraction in economic activity, was required to refund previous short-term borrowing and to rebuild liquidity. This reversed actions taken during 1969 to avoid the high cost of long-term funds then mistakenly expected to decline in early 1970. Thus, gross private domestic investment fell $4 billion in 1970 while the net issue of securities by non-financial businesses rose 11^{1}/_{2}$ billion. These businesses raised $22.8 billion net in 1969 from bank and other loans, compared with $15.4 billion in 1968, but in 1970 they raised only $7.8 billion, indicating that many firms were reducing short-term borrowing. The costly heavy borrowing and investment in 1969, when financial markets were extremely tight, was a miscalculation based on anticipations of continued economic expansion and of a reduction in interest rates. The experience will not soon be forgotten.

But a dose of monetary restraint comparable to that administered in 1969, no matter how smoothly the economy adjusts to it, will always produce large fluctuations in interest rates. The steep rise in nominal bond yields in 1969 partly reflected heightened anticipations of inflation. However, the rise in short-term rates and the equally steep decline later in 1970 and early 1971 are typical responses to changes in monetary growth, though in magnitude they are more characteristic of the pre-1914 period than recent decades.

Because of this accompanying large rise in interest rates, monetary restraint will continue to have a sizable effect on housing in the future, as it did in 1966 and 1969. From the first to the second half of 1966, housing starts declined 28 percent. For 1969 the first- to second-half decline was only 14 percent due to federal mortgage loans discussed below. Complaints of "discrimination" against housing failed to mention that curtailment of long-term investments like housing is natural when financial markets are tight. The rise in interest rates was a signal to postpone some investment in view of the excessive demand on total resources; long-term investments like housing could be expected to decline the most, other things the same, since part of the rise in interest rates appeared to be temporary. While the sharp contraction of mortgage credit during 1969 had elicited dire warnings of the collapse of the home building industry, they proved totally inaccurate. The industry revived dramatically after monetary policy eased in 1970. Housing starts, after hitting a low in January 1970 of 1.1 million units at a seasonally adjusted annual rate, recovered by July to the $1^{1}/_{2}$ million rate of 1968 and then rose to 2 million units by December.

The dependence of mortgage financing on savings and loan associations helps explain why the decline in housing was so sharp while commercial construction remained about the same. The associations have financed about half of home mortgages in recent decades. Since their deposits can be withdrawn on demand, they can attract a steady inflow of funds only by paying an interest rate on deposits competitive with other short-term financial assets. They are unable to do so, however, when interest rates rise rapidly. The average return on association portfolios rises slowly, despite higher yields on new mortgages, because most home mortgages, though extinguished long before maturity, still remain outstanding over five years.

Indeed, the associations avoided a disastrous outflow of funds in 1966 and 1969 only because the government, concerned for their solvency, maintained the ceilings on deposit rates paid by commercial and mutual savings banks (as noted above), refrained from paying a competitive return on U.S. savings bonds, and (in March 1970) upped the minimum denomination of Treasury bills after they started to become popular with small savers. The small saver has benefited over the years from government protection of savings and loan associations, but he paid a price in terms of restricted investment options during the recent periods of financial tightness.

Although the savings and loan associations avoided widespread failures in 1966 and 1969, their sudden decline in growth was transmitted to the residential mortgage market. Their deposit growth of $8.1 billion in the fourth quarter of 1965 at a seasonally adjusted annual rate fell to $1.4 billion by the third quarter of 1966. The net annual rate of increase in their home mortgages fell from $7.6 to $0.1 billion in the same period (seasonally adjusted). In 1969, on a comparable basis, deposit growth of $8.0 billion in the first quarter fell to $0.7 billion in the fourth quarter, and the net annual rate of increase in their home mortgages declined from $9.1 billion in the first quarter of 1969 to $3.0 billion in the first quarter of 1970.

The basic problem here was the use of short-term funds to finance long-term mortgages, a development which public policy had long fostered. The federal government has taken various steps over the years to make sure that housing can be financed on easy terms. Among other actions it enhanced the attractiveness of savings and loan deposits in federal associations in 1950 by providing insurance virtually identical to that for commercial and mutual savings banks. The charters of the associations required that they invest the bulk of their funds in mortgages. Since mortgage yields generally exceeded short-term interest rates during the 1950s and early 1960s, the associations paid an attractive rate of interest, and their growth was phenomenal. In the period from mid-1950 to mid-1965 their savings capital (deposits) increased from $13 to $105 billion, an average rate of growth of 15 percent per year.

At first, little thought was given to the weaknesses of such an arrangement. Even during the 1950s, however, cyclical swings in home building became more and more pronounced as fluctuations in interest rates grew larger and affected the differential return on savings deposits and their rate of growth. Deposit-rate ceilings on commercial and mutual savings banks protected associations from severe competition, however, and the industry prospered without making important structural changes. Finally, in 1966 and again in 1969, as interest rates rose steeply, the flaw in this regulated cartel arrangement came to the fore: open-market securities became extremely attractive to small savers, and major outflows from depository institutions could not be prevented.

The Housing Act of 1968 had set an ambitious goal of 26 million new dwelling units by 1978. With the 1966 and 1969 declines in construction, that goal began to slip out of reach, though the rapid growth in mobile homes (413,000 were produced in 1969) brightened the prospects. Among the government's myriad programs to help housing, the largest recent contribution in dollar terms has come from the Federal National Mortgage Association, which finances purchases of mortgages by selling bonds guaranteed by the Treasury. The net increase in its mortgage holdings was $1.9 billion in 1966 and $3.8 billion in 1969. All together the federal government and federally sponsored agencies poured $3.6 billion into the residential mortgage market in 1966 and $8.6 billion in 1969 (including the borrowing of savings and loan associations from Federal Home Loan Banks). This was one-third of total home mortgage loans in 1966 and over one-half in 1969.

Since these programs prevented mortgage yields from rising

even higher and thus encouraged some private funds to go elsewhere, the net increase in mortgage financing so produced is unclear. The effect probably was not inconsequential, however, because housing declined much less in 1969 than in 1966 as noted, consistent with the larger government support.

Despite the assistance of federal programs, the fluctuations in the availability of mortgage funds in 1966 and 1969 have made financial reforms imperative, and a Presidential Commission on Financial Institutions was appointed in 1970. Its report, issued early in 1972, endorsed many previously made proposals to reverse the proliferation of financial regulations and allow the institutions to adapt more freely to changing market conditions. In particular, the government needs to extricate itself from past attempts to help housing by artificial constraints on credit flows. Savings and loan associations have to be allowed more flexibility to compete in tight money markets. This means freedom to alter the form of their investments and liabilities, and a removal of deposit-rate ceilings. In place of this regulatory support of mortgage financing, other sources and forms of financing have to be developed. Reducing the dependence of the mortgage market on narrow institutional channels of funds would help to moderate the fluctuations in housing produced by changes in monetary policy. But the key to long-lasting reform is to bring the maturity of mortgages into line with the instruments used to finance them. Thus, long-term funds could be raised by mortgage-backed bonds, which the federal government helped to start in 1970, and mortgages might be written for five years instead of 25, as Canada had long been doing.

It will take time to make the mortgage market flexible and to free depository institutions from regulations which have accumulated over many decades and which have distorted the flow of funds. But it is desirable to take some immediate steps, such as relaxation of deposit-rate ceilings, to remove the more severe distortions which hamper the operation of monetary policy.

Mistakes and Problems of Policy

The inflation that began in 1965 can be attributed largely to the mistakes of monetary policy. Excessive expansion of the money supply allowed inflation to gain a foothold in 1965 and to gather momentum in 1967-68. The accompanying expansion of war expenditures contributed to the inflation indirectly through an influence on monetary growth and on the speed with which new money affected the economy. By themselves federal expenditures were not critical, however. For example, monetary restraint still slowed the economy in 1966 at a time when those expenditures were rising rapidly.

Errors of forecasting will always occur, but errors of judgment based on a faulty analysis of events can be avoided by learning from past mistakes. This section discusses the lag in monetary policy, the role of bank credit, the effect of fiscal policy, the behavior of interest rates, the behavior of prices, and direct controls.

Lag in Monetary Policy. During 1969, monetary restraint appeared to most of the public to be pushing up interest rates—creating havoc for residential construction and small business—but not to be working to curtail aggregate activity. And it is true that the anti-inflationary monetary policy that was announced in early 1969 took almost a year before a perceptible slackening in general business activity occurred. But a change in monetary growth impinges on the public's money balances and induces adjustments in lending and spending which affect aggregate activity, all with a lag. Furthermore, several months can elapse before a stated shift in policy takes hold of monetary growth, because the Federal Reserve has trouble controlling the money supply in the short run and, until 1970, did not even view the money supply as a major indicator of policy. Finally, it takes a few months to recognize a change in business activity.

Even so, by historical experience the lags in 1966 and 1969 were not of unusual length.

1966 peak. The Open Market Committee voted to impose restraint in February 1966. A sharp reduction in monetary growth occurred in May, and economic activity turned down near the end of the year. For the turning points in economic activity, we may rely on Fabricant's dates.[13] He selected November as the peak. The lag from the monetary step peak in April to November is seven months.

1967 trough. The committee voted to lift the restraint in November 1966, and monetary growth resumed the following February. Economic activity recovered around late spring or early summer 1967. The exact date is unclear, because real GNP rose in the second quarter while other measures of output declined until later. Fabricant puts the trough in May. From the January monetary step trough to May is four months.

1969 peak. The committee voted for a second round of restraint in December 1968. Monetary growth declined moderately during the

---

[13] Solomon Fabricant, "Recent Economic Changes and the Agenda of Business-Cycle Research," *National Bureau Report 8*, Supplement, May 1971.

first half of 1969 and then sharply around midyear. The accuracy of the money series for this period is questionable because of a large volume of foreign bank transactions which falsified the figures for cash items in the process of collection. The series as noted has been revised twice, first in late 1969 and then again in late 1970. The original series showed a gradual though sizable reduction in monetary growth during the early months of 1969. The first revision indicated a sharp step to a lower rate in May. The second revision, now the official version, moved the step to August. It is not clear that this second revision is more accurate. Because of the problems of separating domestic and foreign transactions in banking data, it is conceivable that a better procedure is not to deduct cash items in the process of collection from gross demand deposits at all. This question will have to be examined by future research.

For the present it seems best to rely on the 1970 revision, showing a step peak in July. Fabricant selected November 1969 as the peak in activity. The lag from July to November was four months.

1970 trough. The committee voted in January 1970 to ease monetary restraint. Monetary growth spurted in March according to the data then available (or in January, according to the later revision). Fabricant selected November as the trough in activity. The lag was therefore 11 months measured by the revised series. (The General Motors strike in the fourth quarter may have made this downturn longer than it would otherwise have been; the second and third quarters showed a slight recovery before the strike brought a slump in the fourth quarter.)

These lags seemed longer at the time, because the turning points in activity became apparent only several months after they had occurred.

How do these lags compare with previous experience? Milton Friedman and Anna J. Schwartz examined the monetary lag in 21 cyclical movements from 1870 to 1961 and reported their findings in the *45th Annual Report of the National Bureau of Economic Research.* One of their measures of the lag corresponds to that used above, namely, a comparison between the date of a step in monetary growth to a higher or lower average rate for at least several months and the corresponding peak or trough in the level of economic activity.[14]

---

[14] Their figures pertain to money including time deposits, whereas the lags reported above are for the narrow definition of money excluding time deposits. The choice of definition influences the results somewhat, but the mixing of two different definitions here seems appropriate. Time deposits were not clearly distinguished from demand deposits in banking data before the 1930s and should

(Using the rate of change of economic activity gives much shorter lags.) They found a median lag at peaks of seven months with an interquartile range from zero to 13 months. The median lag at troughs was four months with an interquartile range from zero to nine months. The wide range indicates that the lags have varied appreciably in length.

The 1966-67 lags equal the historical medians exactly. The 1969-70 lags differ from the medians but lie within the interquartile range. At the 1969 peak, the lag was three months shorter than the median, and at the 1970 trough, seven months longer.

The short lag at the 1969 peak is full of irony, because the elapsed time from the announced change in monetary policy in January 1969 to the peak of activity in November was 10 months, which overran the public's expectation based on the 1966 episode and proved exasperating to administration officials anxious for some tangible effect of their unpopular anti-inflation policy. According to the revised money figures, however, most of this lag was the inside lag of changing the policy; for many months, the talk of restraint exceeded the bite.

There was considerable confusion during 1969, not only over how long it would take monetary policy to work, but also over where its effects would fall. Ordinarily monetary restraint curtails investment expenditures. But surveys of business investment plans showed surprising strength all during 1969, notwithstanding the highest interest rates in a century. This did not mean, as was widely thought, that monetary restraint would not affect aggregate expenditures. A reduction in monetary growth forces some money-using sectors of the economy to make adjustments which require holding down expenditures. In reality, not all the plans for business investment could be financed, and actual expenditures were less than anticipated in the surveys. Even so, business investment was still high, which forced restraint upon other expenditures, not only for residential construction but also for consumer durable goods, state and local capital projects, and business inventory investment.

The lesson of this experience is that the sectoral effects of

---

not be excluded for that earlier period. In recent years, however, time deposits have undergone large fluctuations as a result of the ceilings on interest payable on deposits; time certificates of deposit, which have expanded rapidly since 1960, are particularly close substitutes for Treasury bills and commercial paper and therefore are highly affected by changes in interest-rate differentials. For the recent period the inclusion of time deposits would introduce a misleading source of fluctuation.

monetary restraint are hard to foresee. A strong demand for funds in one sector transmits the pressure of a limited supply to other sectors which are hard to identify ahead of time. Forecasts of GNP made in mid-1969 and based on elaborate models specifying fixed channels of monetary effects generally underestimated the decline in growth of GNP in the fourth quarter of 1969 and the first quarter of 1970. Thus, the regular panel of forecasters surveyed by the American Statistical Association [15] in August 1969 missed the decline in growth in those quarters. The median forecast was for a rise in nominal GNP of $13 billion in the third quarter of 1969 and of $12 billion in each of the next two quarters, whereas the actual pattern of increases was $19, $9, and $8 billion, respectively. Predictions in mid-1969 by the Federal Reserve Bank of St. Louis, which were based on conditional forecasts of changes in the money stock, caught the slowdown more accurately—though one had to correctly assume little change in the money stock for the rest of the year. Even then, these predictions erred by anticipating a slight slowdown in the third quarter of 1969 when actually GNP continued expanding until the fourth quarter.

A monetary model of the economy developed by two economists in the Office of Management and Budget,[16] which was widely publicized in early 1971, claimed to show that the effects of money had virtually no lag. Their results can be questioned, however, as being inconsistent with all other evidence on monetary effects. The unfavorable response which this model received both in and out of the government indicated that lags in the effect of monetary policy had finally been widely accepted.

Whether fiscal policy had much effect on the length of the lag at the 1969 peak is unclear. The full-employment federal budget (NIA basis) ran a deficit of $6 billion in 1968 and a surplus of $11.7 billion in 1969,[17] a change of $18 billion, largely through a slowing in expenditure growth. In terms of quarterly budget figures, all of the increase in the surplus occurred in the first two quarters of the year. This cannot account for the downturn in activity in the fourth quarter of 1969 unless fiscal policy has a longer lag than monetary policy does, which—for a change largely on the expenditure side,

---

[15] The American Statistical Association, "Third Quarter Survey of the Economic Outlook," mimeographed, 1969.

[16] Arthur B. Laffer and R. David Ranson, "A Formal Model of the Economy," *Journal of Business*, July 1971, pp. 247-68.

[17] From the 1971 *Annual Report of the Council of Economic Advisers*, pp. 24 and 73.

such as here—is implausible on theoretical grounds. But the continuing budget surplus during the second half of 1969 could have reinforced the monetary restraint which came at that time and thus may help explain the fairly short lag observed for monetary policy.

The long lag in monetary policy in producing the upturn in economic activity in 1970 cannot be explained by perverse fiscal policy; the full-employment surplus declined moderately in 1970. The contraction in activity was both longer and deeper than that in 1967, though the decline in the average rate of monetary growth was about the same, roughly five percentage points. However, the six-month moving average of monetary growth (Figure 1) brings out two differences: Compared with 1966-67, the period of declining monetary growth in 1968-69 lasted twice as long, and the subsequent easing in 1970 was not as sharp. After allowance for the General Motors strike at the end of 1970, these differences appear to account for the greater effect on the economy of the second round of monetary restraint.

Role of Bank Credit. Much evidence, including the 1969-70 episode, indicates that monetary restraint initially affects postponable spending, which means a decline, not only in housing and capital equipment, but also in consumer durables and luxury items. This evidence is consistent with the theory that changes in monetary growth disturb the desired distribution of assets in portfolios, thus producing adjustments which in the first instance affect purchases of assets and their prices. A popular—and narrow—view of this process stresses the first-round effect of monetary change via bank credit. In this view monetary restraint curtails investment because it affects the supply of bank credit (that is, loans and investments of commercial banks). The Federal Reserve has traditionally framed its policy directives in terms of bank credit rather than the money supply, though the emphasis shifted to include money for the first time in 1970. Sometimes the rates of growth of bank credit and the money supply (excluding time deposits) are approximately equal, but generally not.

The important difference between money and bank credit was dramatically highlighted by the events of 1969 noted earlier. Interest rates climbed, but the maximum rates that banks could pay on time deposits were not raised during the year, and these deposits declined drastically. Deposits were withdrawn to purchase commercial paper and corporate bonds, thus supplying funds directly to the market that had previously been channeled through banks. The decline in credit supplied by banks did not reduce the total supply of credit but resulted in a different distribution among potential borrowers—

home and municipal financing suffered while corporate investment benefited (see Table 1). When banks began to tap non-deposit sources of funds in large volume during 1969 as a substitute for the loss of time deposits, the Federal Reserve took steps to block these too. For example, the Eurodollar borrowing of commercial banks was made prohibitively expensive in September 1969 when the amounts in excess of May levels were made subject to reserve requirements. Before that, this borrowing tapped foreign as well as U.S. funds, thereby increasing the supply of money and credit to the U.S. market—which ironically required the Federal Reserve to tighten even further to offset the inflow from abroad.

These restrictions on banks reflected a basic confusion over the appropriate indicator of monetary policy.[18] The Federal Reserve was intent upon restricting the growth of bank credit. But bank credit gives a misleading picture of monetary effects on aggregate demand, because radical shifts in the channels of credit flows do not necessarily imply anything about the total supply of credit. For example, while total bank credit grew less rapidly during 1969, it nevertheless continued to grow through most of the year, which seemed to suggest that policy was not achieving the intense restraint desired; but the lack of growth in the money stock after midyear meant that the policy was in fact succeeding. During the second half of 1970, on the other hand, bank credit expanded at an annual rate of 13 percent due to the explosive growth of CDs, whereas the money stock excluding time deposits grew at 5 percent per year. The poor per-formance of the economy in the second half of 1970 was a clear indication that the rapid expansion in bank credit was not producing a comparable expansion in the aggregate use of credit.

Fluctuations of time deposits and of financial intermediation in general hamper the interpretation of monetary policy and make growth of the money supply a less than perfect indicator of policy. But bank credit has much more serious conceptual drawbacks as an indicator and has declined in favor.

Effect of Fiscal Policy.[19] Misjudgments of policy also occurred with respect to fiscal policy, especially the tax surcharge of 1968. The effect of government deficits and surpluses is often exaggerated because of the implicit assumption of a cooperative monetary policy.

---

[18] A similar confusion characterized Canadian monetary policy too. See Thomas J. Courchene, "Recent Canadian Monetary Policy," *Journal of Money, Credit and Banking,* February 1971, pp. 35-56.

[19] See also discussion of fiscal policy by McLure, this volume, chapter 1.

Little was said about monetary policy when the tax surcharge was enacted in mid-1968. The surcharge was supposed to restrain the economy by itself, but it did not do the job. Although the rate of expansion of current dollar GNP fell from 11½ percent per year in the second quarter of 1968 to around 8 percent in the third and fourth quarters, the reduced rate still almost matched the fastest growing quarters of 1966-67.

No government estimates of the expected effect of the tax surcharge at the time of its enactment were published, but the text-book theory of fiscal effects suggested that the surcharge would reduce GNP by at least $20 billion. This can be derived as follows: The actual increase in annual federal revenues from the surcharge, as reported in the 1969 *Annual Report of the Council of Economic Advisers*, was $10½ billion. The surcharge legislation also required a $6 billion cut in federal expenditures—though the cut pertained to the budgeted level for fiscal year 1969 rather than the actual level of spending at the time of enactment. When signing the new tax measure in June 1968, President Johnson boasted that it would reduce the federal deficit by $20 billion. While that was an exaggeration, the $10½ billion figure given by the CEA was probably less than the total effect on the deficit from the change in fiscal policy. Although the actual budget deficit in the national income accounts fell only $9 billion from the second to the fourth quarter of 1968, the high-employment budget deficit, as estimated by the Federal Reserve Bank of St. Louis, fell $15 billion.

According to the standard procedure, the decline in the deficit should be multiplied by the fiscal multiplier to give the sum of the initial and all subsequent effects on aggregate expenditures. One typical estimate of this multiplier is about two.[20] Using a range of

---

[20] From Ronald L. Teigen; see Teigen and Warren L. Smith, *Readings in Money, National Income and Stabilization Policy*, Irwin, 1970, p. 102. See also 1963 *Annual Report of the Council of Economic Advisers*, p. 48.

The Federal Reserve-MIT econometric model indicated that a 10 percent tax increase would raise revenues $4 billion initially and decrease GNP by $10 billion in three quarters and $15 billion in six quarters. For a $10 billion increase in revenue, the corresponding effect on GNP would be $25 and $37½ billion, respectively. These calculations do not hold the money stock completely constant, however, and so are somewhat overstated for present purposes. See Frank de Leeuw and Edward Gramlich, "The Federal Reserve-MIT Econometric Model," *Federal Reserve Bulletin*, January 1968, pp. 11-40.

This model has an unusually large multiplier. For a personal tax cut, its multiplier after three years is 4.2. For the Brookings model the corresponding multiplier is 1.2, for the Wharton model 2.4, and for the Michigan model 1.7. See *ibid.*, Table 6, p. 28.

$10 to $15 billion for the effect of the tax measure on the deficit, this multiplier gives a range of $20 to $30 billion for the reduction in GNP. Little wonder that fears of "overkill" arose, leading the Federal Reserve to hold back in imposing monetary restraint.

It is difficult to measure the actual effect of the surcharge on GNP, since we do not know for sure what would have happened without it. One estimate is provided by comparing the increase in GNP in the second half of 1968 with that in the first half. GNP at an annual rate rose $42 billion in the first half of 1968 and $33 billion in the second half, or $9 billion less. This suggests that fiscal restraint had just about half the minimum effect of $20 billion it was expected to have. (Probably even less, because monetary growth slightly declined on average during the second half of 1968, which contributed to the lower GNP growth.)

An estimate more favorable to the power of fiscal restraint in 1968 can be obtained by projecting the second quarter increase in GNP rather than the increase for the entire first half. The second quarter increase was $23 billion and, if continued, would have raised GNP by $46 billion in the second half, or $13 billion more than it actually rose. If all this is attributed to fiscal restraint, the shortfall is 65 percent of the anticipated minimum effect of $20 billion derived above.

These estimates assume that the effect of the surcharge built up to a maximum in two quarters and remained at that level. Quite a different time path, as well as a different final effect, is given by estimates of the Federal Reserve Bank of St. Louis, which take account of both monetary and fiscal effects on GNP. The fiscal multiplier reaches a maximum in two quarters of about unity, most of which then fades away in the next two quarters, leaving a permanent effect of only about 20 percent.[21] By this estimate the reduction in the high-employment deficit of $15 billion reduced GNP by that amount in the second half of 1968, but thereafter GNP partly recovered and remained only $3 billion lower than it would otherwise have been.

A rationale for such a time path is that the surcharge has both direct and indirect effects, which in the long run tend to offset each other but do not occur simultaneously. The direct effect on GNP results from immediate changes in federal expenditures and in personal consumption when new tax rates change disposable income. The indirect effect results from the financing of the Treasury deficit

---

[21] Federal Reserve Bank of St. Louis, *Review*, April 1970.

or surplus, which changes the supply of credit available to private borrowers and affects investment expenditures with a lag. In 1968 the surcharge reduced disposable income and consumption,[22] but the resulting reduction in the deficit also meant less Treasury borrowing and freed credit for a subsequent increase in private investment (including consumer investment in homes and automobiles).

The surcharge of 1968 was supposed to repeat the policy success—in the other direction—of the tax cut of 1964, which was given credit for the subsequent decline in unemployment. In dollar effect on tax revenues, the 1968 surcharge was the larger of the two. But a comparison of effects on revenues is misleading. While the economy expanded following the 1964 tax cut, credit for the expansion must be shared with the accompanying increase in monetary growth. In 1968, although the monetary growth declined over the second half, the money stock continued to grow rapidly and to be very stimulative, counteracting the surcharge. Even aside from the differing role of monetary policy in 1964 and 1968, however, other explanations have been offered as to why the surcharge appeared weaker than the tax cut.

The first explanation starts from the fact that the economy was at virtual full employment in 1968, with a strong demand for credit straining financial markets. This was quite unlike the situation in 1964 when the economy was below full employment. The funds not borrowed by the Treasury in 1968 found other eager borrowers, whereas in 1964 the Treasury borrowed funds not all of which would have found other takers right away. Therefore, in 1964 aggregate expenditures increased because Treasury borrowing raised interest rates and induced a rise in monetary velocity, while in 1968 the Treasury surplus did not have a comparable effect on monetary velocity. The reason given for this difference is that the effect on velocity of a given change in interest rates was large in 1964 at low interest rates and low in 1968 at high rates.[23] That the relation between monetary velocity and interest rates has this particular form is an old idea, but so far no statistical evidence has confirmed it.

A second explanation for overestimating the power of the tax surcharge is that it was originally scheduled to expire in six months and, even though later extended, was viewed as temporary. As a

---

[22] Arthur M. Okun, in "The Income Tax Surcharge and Consumer Demands, 1968-70" (*Brookings Papers on Economic Activity*, June 1971), concludes that the effect on consumption was in line with the consumption functions of the major econometric models.

[23] This explanation is given by Henry C. Wallich, "Fiscalists vs. Monetarists," *Financial Analysts Journal*, September-October 1970.

result, households simply saved less and kept spending at near previous levels, at least for a while, in the expectation that an undesired temporary reduction of consumption could be avoided. Personal saving as a fraction of disposable income fell from an average of 7.3 percent in the first half of 1968 to 6.5 percent in the second half. As a fraction of prevailing income levels, this reduction in saving amounted to $6 billion at an annual rate. The increased federal revenue due to the tax surcharge on individuals was $6½ billion in the second half of 1968 and rose to a maximum of $11 billion in the second quarter of 1969.[24] The saving ratio did not return to the high levels of early 1968 until the second quarter of 1970. Other influences also helped determine saving during this period, of course, and the effect of the surcharge is hard to isolate. It nevertheless appears that a good part of the initial effect on individuals' spending was offset by a change in their saving rates.

A third explanation is that fiscal policy as conventionally measured in the national income accounts excludes direct loans of federal agencies and indirect lending via subsidies and guarantees. The figures quoted above follow this practice. Yet it is dubious that direct federal expenditures have an effect on GNP that is sharply different from the effect of federal lending. Federal lending also supports private expenditures which to some extent would not otherwise be made. Of course, some private expenditures financed with federal loans would be made anyway with loans from nongovernmental sources. But, similarly, some direct federal expenditures may also substitute for private expenditures which are then not made. This is apt to be true of certain grants-in-aid to states and localities.

Federal loans are financed by taxes or Treasury borrowing, and their exclusion from the NIA budget makes the reported deficit appear to be smaller. The amounts are substantial. In the second half of 1968, the net acquisition of credit market instruments by federal agencies in the flow of funds accounts—consolidating the federally sponsored agencies that are excluded from the unified budget—was $6.1 billion at an annual rate. That raises the budget deficit in the national income accounts for the second half of 1968 from $1.5 billion at an annual rate to $7.6 billion. The annual rate of deficit in the first half on the same basis was $19.6 billion.

The annual rate of federal lending alone, which declined by $4.5 billion from the first to the second half of 1968, also contributed to

---

[24] See Okun, op. cit., Table 1. Okun argues that the effect of the surcharge was delayed, not because the tax was viewed as temporary, but because all such effects on consumption have a lag.

fiscal restraint—along with the tax surcharge. It is possible that changes in lending affect the economy with a longer lag than expenditures do, however, because of a lag in the private economy between borrowing and spending. If so, the second half of 1968 was influenced by federal lending activities in previous quarters. Thus the sizable increase in lending in the first half of 1968 over 1967 may have worked to offset the tax surcharge in the second half.

In assessing the effect of fiscal policy, these issues have yet to be settled. Although all of these complications were known in 1968, they were largely ignored until the surcharge proved wholly inadequate for curbing the runaway inflation. Thus was it possible for fears of "overkill" to freeze monetary policy into disastrous inaction throughout 1968.

Behavior of Interest Rates. Perhaps no other development has confused the conduct of monetary policy more in recent years than the astounding increase in interest rates. From 1965 until mid-1970 Treasury bond yields rose almost three percentage points, municipal bond yields four percentage points, and high-grade corporate bond yields more than five percentage points. These increases represented about a doubling of 1965 levels. Short-term rates also rose spectacularly, though they peaked at the beginning of 1970. Over half of the increase came after mid-1968. Apart from panics, U.S. interest rates had never climbed so high in so short a period of time. This gave an appearance of intense tightness to financial markets which, in 1965 and again in 1967-68, helped justify faster monetary growth than the inflationary economy warranted.

The increase in interest rates can be attributed in part to monetary restraint in 1966 and 1969, but the restraint, though important while it lasted, had only a temporary effect. Part of the overall increase since 1965 reflected an expanded demand for capital goods. In the second half of the 1960s, the post-World War II "baby boom" began to augment the labor force and, for the first time since the mid-1950s, many industrial plants operated at high levels of capacity.

But these effects seem incapable of fully explaining the behavior of interest rates. Anticipations of inflation also played an important role. Financial assets such as bonds whose principal is fixed in dollars depreciate in real value during inflation. If prices rise 4 percent per year over the life of a bond, a nominal yield of 8 percent returns 4 percent in real terms. Lenders can compensate for this depreciation by obtaining higher nominal rates of return, and they will look for inflation hedges until bonds offer nominal yields which reflect the anticipated rate of inflation. Businesses will try to borrow more funds until higher interest charges take away all the anticipated gains from inflation.

Years ago economist Irving Fisher of Yale University pointed to this effect of inflation on nominal interest rates. He used it to explain the behavior of bond yields before World War I. Now it helps to account for their rising trend since the mid-1950s. From 1952 to 1955 long-term U.S. bonds fluctuated narrowly around $2^3/_4$ percent. Then from mid-1956 to mid-1959, following the 1955-56 inflation, they climbed to 4 percent and stayed close to that level until 1965. Following the reemergence of inflation in that year, they rose much further, as did all other interest rates (see Figure 2).

There is no reason to believe that anticipations are based solely on past or current rates of inflation. They will be influenced also by current events which portend future developments. This is particularly true for bonds with a maturity many years ahead. The bond yields of recent years suggest that the anticipated rate of inflation has been below the actual rate but that the gap has been closing.

The extent to which high interest rates reflect anticipations of inflation is not easily determined. It must be inferred. Rising wage increases in the new three-year union contracts negotiated since 1965 are one indication of higher anticipations. The decline in interest rates following the imposition of the wage-price freeze of August 1971 appeared to reflect a reduction in the anticipated rate of inflation. But sometimes what might seem to reflect anticipations of inflation in fact do not. During 1969, for example, "equity kickers" became widespread on loans made by life insurance companies. Borrowers agreed to pay a percentage of the gross revenue on mortgaged properties in addition to interest, and this was widely interpreted at the time as an inflation hedge extracted by lenders. Yet the kickers completely disappeared in 1970 when financial markets eased. They had simply been an unusual way of obtaining a higher return in the tight markets of 1967, and were no longer needed in 1970. If they had been primarily an inflation hedge, they would still be popular.

Another problem in determining the effect of inflationary anticipations on interest rates is that short-run monetary conditions produce wide fluctuations in interest rates, whereas anticipations of inflation seem unlikely to be so volatile. Thus in 1969-70 the implicit price deflator for the GNP rose 5 percent per year, whereas high-grade corporate bond yields in that two-year period started out at $7^1/_2$ percent, rose well beyond 9 percent during the first half of 1970, and then fell rapidly almost to $7^1/_2$ percent again by the early months of 1971 before turning up once again. In terms of the GNP price deflator, the real return on bonds ranged from $2^{1}/_{2}$ to over 4 percent and back again in a period of two years.

The anticipated rate of inflation, though not easily determined, is not simply a theoretical curiosity. The failure to distinguish nominal and anticipated real rates of interest has bedeviled the conduct of monetary policy. The reports of the Federal Reserve Open Market Committee frequently took note of the tightness in financial markets as reflected by the high and rising interest rates, but made no mention of the fact that the anticipated real rate of interest was probably much lower, and often falling rather than rising. The increased difficulty of interpreting interest-rate movements in an inflationary period finally led the committee in 1970 to demote (though, unfortunately, not abolish) the role of interest rates as a major indicator of monetary policy.

The greater stress now placed on achieving predetermined rates of growth of monetary aggregates in the Open Market Committee's directives can result in larger fluctuations in interest rates, since the new policy implies that less attention will be paid to moderating those fluctuations. The precipitous decline in short-term interest rates during the second half of 1970 was a first example. Yet interest rates need not fluctuate more on the average under this policy, because the fluctuations in the past were just as much a result of variations in monetary growth as of other influences, and any reduction in monetary variations would help to stabilize interest rates.

Behavior of Prices. Critics of the administration's economic policy during 1969 claimed that monetary restraint was not working. One reason for that claim was that the restraint came, as noted, a half year later than the announced shift in policy. But there was no reason to question the ultimate effect on aggregate demand, which slowed in the fourth quarter; the lag was actually short by historical experience. Yet the critics were right about prices if not about output. Inflation showed little tendency to yield to policy intentions. The unexpected persistence of rising prices made it politically harder to persevere with an orthodox anti-inflation policy (see Figure 4).

The rate of increase of most prices had declined in the second half of 1966, following the application of monetary restraint. The wholesale price index for industrial commodities, a bellwether indicator of subsequent movements in retail prices, rose at an annual rate of 3.4 percent from January to July 1966 and, over the next six months, at a rate of only 1.2 percent. In the next six months this index was virtually constant. For the consumer price index, the annual rate was 4.2 percent in the first period and 2.5 percent in the second. Excluding

138

foods, the deceleration was only slightly less. By contrast, from the second half of 1969 through the first half of 1970 these indexes showed little deceleration. The index for wholesale industrial commodities rose 4.1 percent per year in the first period and 3.8 percent in the second. The consumer price index rose 5.9 percent per year in the first period and 6.0 percent in the second, and excluding foods accelerated to 6.5 percent in the second period.

It was not that there were no signs of improvement in the year following the 1969 slowdown in activity. Consistent with the usual sequence, wholesale prices of crude industrial materials responded first. They reached a plateau in the second quarter of 1970 and remained roughly at that level for the remainder of the year. Intermediate industrial materials rose at an annual rate of 4.3 percent in the first half of 1970, 2.2 percent in the third quarter, and only 1.1 percent in the fourth. But wholesale prices of all industrial commodities had an annual rate of increase of 3.8 percent in the first half of 1970, and this rate fell only slightly to 3.5 percent in the second half. By and large, the pattern of price response was following the usual sequence, but at a snail's pace.

In the first half of 1971, wholesale price increases speeded up, as was to be expected in the first stage of a business recovery. The industrial component rose at an annual rate of 4.0 percent in the first half of 1971 compared with 3.5 percent in the preceding half year. The consumer price index slowed down, to be sure. For the first half of 1971 it rose at an annual rate of 4.1 percent and, excluding foods, at only 2.8 percent. But much of this improvement reflected the sizable decline in mortgage interest rates which are counted in household services. The private GNP price deflator (chain index), which does not cover mortgage rates, continued rising at 5.6 percent per year in the first half of 1971.

Why were prices responding so slowly to slack demand? There are really two questions here. First, why did consumer prices rise more than 5 percent during 1970 at a time when unemployment was rising from 3½ to above 6 percent? Second, why was inflation cooling so much more slowly than in 1966-67?

The common answer to the first question was framed in terms of "cost push." All the old theories of excessive union wage demands and administered pricing discarded in the late 1950s were dusted off and paraded out. No doubt most price increases in 1970 reflected a passing along of higher costs, since demand was too weak to pull prices up. But where did the cost increases originate? "Excessive" increases in administered prices were hard to find. Corporate profit

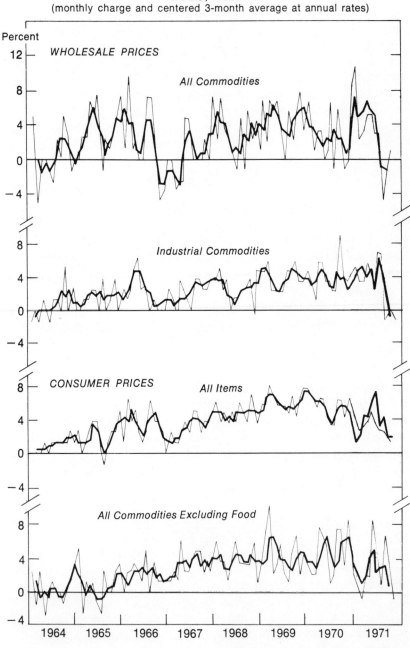

Figure 4
PRICES, 1964-71
(monthly charge and centered 3-month average at annual rates)

Percent

WHOLESALE PRICES

All Commodities

Industrial Commodities

CONSUMER PRICES   *All Items*

All Commodities Excluding Food

Last month plotted, November 1971. Consumer prices seasonally adjusted.

margins were generally declining during 1969 and 1970, which does not indicate a use of administered pricing to maintain profits. In its two "Inflation Alerts" issued during 1970, the Council of Economic Advisers singled out some of the important price increases. Only three were questioned as perhaps not entirely justified by cost or demand pressures—those in petroleum, copper, and cigarettes. Studies of inflation which looked for an influence of concentrated industries generally failed to find that it was disproportionate.

Wages became the scapegoat. One certainly saw plenty of outlandish displays of union power: the construction trades, the teamsters, and the new militancy on the part of state and municipal unions received considerable publicity. Union wage settlements tended to accelerate in 1970 while nonunion wages slowed down slightly. The median increase for 1970 in manufacturing was 7.4 percent per year for union establishments and 5.8 percent for nonunion establishments, compared with 6.9 and 6.0, respectively, for 1969. High union settlements were widely publicized in 1970, giving administration officials cause for hand-wringing despair.

A pattern of union militancy is common to inflation. Unanticipated past increases in the cost of living make workers angry. They feel justified in insisting that their money incomes catch up and provide for future increases over the life of contracts. It is not always clear that even the large gains of over 10 percent put union wages ahead *in real terms.* Such settlements can represent a catching up with past real losses due to cost-of-living increases. The catching up can require 6 to 8 percent for a three-year contract just ended, and the average increase in productivity adds another 3 percent per year. While the data do not indicate that wages in general lagged behind prices in the period since 1965, wages under three-year contracts probably did lag until each contract was renewed. Then, as unions become conscious of inflation, they also bargain to cover anticipated increases in prices over the life of new contracts, which in recent years could add another 4 to 5 percent per year. These sizable increases due to anticipations were built into the second and third year of the contracts, as well as the first. The resulting large increases made militant unions heady, and bringing them back to reality was turning out to be difficult.

The increasing power of unions poses a problem here, not in starting inflation, but in keeping it going. Anticipations of inflation are probably no greater for union workers than for the rest of the economy. But their power enables them partly to disregard slack demand and to translate those anticipations into wage increases which are inconsistent with a policy of curbing inflation. The whipsaw process of each handsome settlement giving rise to militant demands by other unions for equal or better treatment has created the alarming prospect of a very slow cooling of the rampant inflationary psychology.

While union pressures on wages can greatly delay the response of prices to monetary restraint, the persistence of inflation in 1970-71 cannot be explained solely by unions. Wages and salaries continued to rise on a broad front. Median wage adjustments in nonunion manufacturing establishments were still rising 5.0 percent in 1970 compared with 5.1 percent in 1969, and average hourly earnings of production workers in manufacturing (excluding overtime and inter-industry shifts) rose 6.9 percent in 1970 compared with 6.0 percent in 1969. In the first half of 1971 the annual rate of increase was still as high as 6.3 percent. Total compensation per manhour for the private economy even accelerated to an annual rate of 8.6 percent in the first half of 1971, compared with 7.0 percent for all of 1970. These increases could not all be attributed to monopoly unions. The wage inflation had much broader origins.[25]

The main reason for the persistence of inflations, even apart from unions, was simply that inflations do not stop immediately unless activity contracts severely. Prices and wages are set periodically, each time adjusting to an accumulation of cost influences since the previous setting. A price increase in one sector pushes up costs in others, and each increase then works its way through the price structure. At the stage of final goods and services, price increases add to the cost of living, feeding back on wages and costs in the earlier stages of production, then to work forward again. The process of sequential increases in costs and prices, once set in motion by an excessive aggregate demand, unwinds slowly.

The perplexing question was why the process was unwinding more slowly than usual in 1970-71. Unions have grown stronger since inflation was curbed in the second half of the 1950s. That seemed to be one reason. Another reason was the greater magnitude and duration of price increases in the preceding years than in any of the previous inflationary periods since World War II. The new outbreak in 1965 added to the upward trend of prices since World War II, making anticipations of future inflation stronger than ever. General anticipations are not, of course, observed directly. Surveys of consumer and business price anticipations are neither comprehensive nor quantitative and do not help much. Indirect indications

---

[25] See also discussion of wages by Estey, this volume, chapter 3.

of anticipated inflation, however, have been increasingly evident. As has been noted, part of the increase in interest rates appears to have reflected anticipations of higher rates of inflation. (The 1970 decline in stock prices, however, did not indicate a reduction of inflationary anticipations, because the market recovered most of the loss by early 1971. The decline largely reflected the more attractive yields from debt securities in real terms and the deterioration of corporate profits.) Despite the 1970 contraction in activity, fears of business recessions have lessened since World War II. Such fears used to contract investment expenditures at the first signs of an economic downturn, but business investment continued at a high level throughout 1970, notwithstanding a slackening in aggregate demand and declining profit margins. (The administration had unintentionally encouraged business optimism during 1969 by predicting a mild slowdown in early 1970 and a resumption of economic expansion thereafter.) Newspapers reported the course of inflation fully, along with a consensus view of economic commentators that no President seeking reelection could any longer safely allow the economy to depart from full employment for very long. The implication was that prices are seldom going to decline, will frequently rise, and, once inflation gathers speed, the counteractions of policy will be gentle and not very effective.

The significance of strong anticipations of inflation is that they can reduce the influence of demand on prices, even without strong unions. Cost increases are more readily and fully passed along, despite weakness in demand, if that weakness is viewed as temporary and prices are expected to follow an upward trend. Then the process of costs pushing up prices and vice versa moves along with less friction and is harder to interrupt by curtailing demand. The process only gradually slows down when cost increases are not fully passed along and anticipations eventually respond to a slackening in the actual rate of inflation.

Given little or no moderation in wage increases, a crucial contribution to curbing inflation could be made by an increase in productivity. The productivity of the U.S. economy—as usually measured by the ratio of output to hours of labor—has grown on the average of 3 to 3½ percent per year. But it fluctuates over the business cycle, typically slowing as the economy approaches full employment as it did during 1969, causing an acceleration in the rise of labor costs per unit of output. While a decline in output tends to reduce productivity at first, the decline induces firms to improve efficiency, and output per manhour usually begins to rise midway through a con-

143

traction. As a result, the rise in unit labor costs starts to slow down despite large wage advances. Unit labor costs in the private economy rose 5.5 percent per year in the first half of 1970, 5.0 percent in the second half, and 2.8 percent in the first half of 1971. In the third quarter of 1971 the annual rate was 2.0 percent. If the rate of increase continues to slow down, wage costs will push prices up less rapidly. This will allow anticipations of inflation to slacken, which will eventually have a moderating effect on wage increases.

The recovery from the 1970 recession has therefore been a critical phase in the unwinding of inflation. The recession set business to the task of improving efficiency by trimming the working force, but most of the benefits from such a process do not show up in unit labor costs until output recovers. Then the rate of increase in unit labor costs declines if wages do not accelerate. It is important that the recovery not tighten markets to the point of creating new demand pressures on prices. If demand remains slack, the diminishing increases in unit labor costs are translated into a deceleration of prices. Such a process is not new. Inflation of the mid-1950s finally disappeared in the aftermath of the 1958 recession. While a recession sets up the pre-conditions for reducing inflation, therefore, the expansion of output following it can be the vehicle by which prices begin to decelerate. The mild recovery during the first half of 1971 meant that increases in productivity were low; nevertheless, unit labor costs as noted above did decelerate from 5.0 to 2.8 percent per year.

The wage-price freeze of August 1971 came in the midst of this process. No one can be sure of the effects. The freeze and subsequent controls might speed up the deceleration of unit labor costs by holding wage increases down. It might also reduce anticipations of inflation and thus remove part of the increases in wages and prices that were being added on to compensate for future inflation. These effects would help to decelerate the inflation. But the controls might postpone wage and price increases which will be posted in full after it expires. It would then have little lasting effect and, because of postponements and a relaxation of monetary and fiscal restraint, actually prolong inflation.

The effect of the President's program initiated in August will be long debated. A full assessment must await the subsequent course of inflation. Unfortunately, wage and price controls distort the measures by which the outcome is assessed. If controls are imposed for a long time, it will be difficult to tell what is happening and, more important, what would have happened had they been removed in a short time or not been imposed at all.

Direct Controls.[26] Although the wage-price freeze was imposed in August for only 90 days, either a simple lifting or extension of the freeze was not seriously contemplated. A freeze creates too many distortions to last for long, and 90 days is not long enough to attain its objectives. It had to be replaced by some kind of review procedure to enforce wage-price guideposts. But none of the various options were attractive, because they all posed serious problems of enforcement and effectiveness. This had been learned from the history of steps either taken or contemplated in the year and a half preceding the August freeze.

During 1970, as it became clear that prices were responding more slowly to economic slack than they had been expected to, policymakers examined the distasteful choices. To subdue inflation fairly rapidly, unemployment would have to be raised to unacceptably high rates. But if unemployment were reduced to 5 percent or so and held there, which seemed temporarily acceptable even though not permanently desirable, inflation could not be reduced very rapidly— according to some estimates, only one percentage point a year or even less. Even then the reduction of inflation might not go very far, since some economists argued that a permanent unemployment rate of 5 percent or more might be necessary just to keep inflation down to 2 or 3 percent a year. No one could be sure of the final outcome, except that neither permanently high unemployment nor permanently high inflation was generally acceptable. The frustrating lack of a quick solution created a willingness to reconsider direct controls which had previously been stoutly resisted.

The business community was attracted to a wage-price freeze in the belief that this was the only means of stopping runaway wage increases. But a freeze can serve only as the initiating step to other direct controls. Since individual wages and prices cannot be kept absolutely constant for long, increases must very soon be allowed, which requires a sizable agency to decide every allowed increase and to try to enforce the decrees. Experience with this apparatus during World War II and the Korean War convinced many of its unattractiveness, especially the government officials who would be responsible for its administration. Also, there was no telling how long such controls might have to be maintained, and few could be sanguine

---

[26] See also discussion of incomes policy by Estey and Moore, this volume, chapters 3 and 4.

about wrapping the economy up in such a straitjacket for a long time.

Middle-of-the-road opinion outside the government therefore gravitated during 1970 to an "incomes" policy of one kind or another. Proposals covered a wide range: the publication of general "guideposts" for wages and prices, as the Council of Economic Advisers had done in the early 1960s; establishment of a high-level board to review the appropriateness of wage and price increases with authority to publish findings but not enforce them, as Federal Reserve Board Chairman Burns had proposed; or more elaborate commissions authorized both to review increases and delay them, as Britain had had for several years until it abandoned the effort completely in January 1970. Earlier the Nixon administration had rejected such schemes as ineffective and philosophically obnoxious. But by the end of 1970 it was prepared to apply selective "jawboning," which relies on publicity to focus public disapproval and other kinds of government pressure on errant unions and firms.

Although the Council of Economic Advisers began in August 1970 to issue periodic reports on inflation which highlighted specific price increases, the administration applied pressure only in a few instances: During 1970, in an effort to counter rising petroleum prices, restrictions were relaxed on the importation of oil from Canada and on the production allowed from federal offshore leases. In January 1971, an announced increase in steel prices was reduced substantially under the threat of a possible relaxation of steel import quotas. In March 1971, the construction unions agreed to help set up a voluntary wage review board for the industry, in exchange for continuing enforcement of "prevailing wages" on federal construction projects under the Davis-Bacon Act. In July 1971, the President called upon management and workers in the steel industry to reach a "constructive settlement" in their new wage contract.

A case could be made for each of these steps on its own. After all, the federal government supports or enforces import quotas in oil and steel, and much of the power of construction unions to raise wages derives from federal legislation. To curb price and wage increases that could not occur without federal support, a reduction of this support was appropriate. Board sentiment existed for curbing runaway wages in the construction industry, where 1970 contracts awarded a median first-year increase of 18.3 percent while unemployment among construction workers was unusually high.

But such steps, even aside from their limited enforcement, were too selective to have much effect on the general rate of inflation. A general effect required the imposition of wage and price guideposts for all or most of the economy. This step the administration had originally rejected. Aside from objections based on political philosophy, there was little practical evidence of their effectiveness. The Kennedy administration had initiated guideposts in the early 1960s. They were enforced selectively to head off or roll back announced wage increases which deviated, after allowing for certain adjustments, from an average increase in labor productivity of $3^1/_4$ percent per year. Prices, except for special circumstances, were to remain constant. While the pressure appeared to work in some cases, the overall accomplishment was limited.[27]

Experience abroad had been no more favorable.[28] Several European countries had struggled with "incomes" policies having various powers of enforcement. Generally, the policies could not overcome trade union intransigence and gradually crumbled. In the case of every country that tried them, serious difficulties arose when inflation accelerated. Governments were in the absurd position of asking workers to refrain from raising wages to match past price increases fully or in anticipation of future increases; in effect, workers' money incomes were not to keep up with inflation. Such a policy has only a slim chance of working when aggregate demand is weak; it had no chance in the runaway inflation of 1965-69.

To fasten hopes on guideposts as a means of curbing inflation in 1970 or 1971, after the demand pull on prices had subsided, implied a particular view of why inflation persisted. In this view, the persistence reflected excessive wage settlements due to union power and to anticipation of continuing inflation at the same rate as in recent years. These guideposts might counteract union power and reduce anticipations. But, if the rise in wages and prices in 1971 reflected a catching up commensurate with past inflation, guideposts would distort relative wages and prices and would be hard to enforce. For guideposts to be successful, therefore, it was implicitly assumed that the catching up had largely been done before 1971 or that it was possible to enunciate guideposts which allowed for catching up.

Even then, however, advocates of this view faced a practical dilemma in opposing anticipatory increases in wages. To pretend that prices would not increase at all was ridiculous. Yet to select any particular rate of increase put policy in a box: too low a rate invited

---

[27] A favorable assessment of the guideposts by George Perry is that they reduced manufacturing wage increases by about 2 percentage points per year for the period 1962-66. Difficulties with this estimate suggest that it is too high. See the discussion in the *American Economic Review*, June 1969, pp. 251-69.
[28] See Eric Schiff, *Incomes Policies Abroad* (Washington: American Enterprise Institute), April 1971.

derision and union opposition, while too high a rate predicted the failure of anti-inflation policy. Unfortunately, these unattractive high and low zones overlapped in 1970-71, providing no middle ground.

One way around this problem would be to supplement guide-posts for wages with mandatory cost-of-living escalator clauses. Such clauses had been widely used in the 1950s, but had fallen into disfavor because employers often found cost-of-living payments to be larger than expected and unions disliked the limit on such payments which contracts at that time usually specified. Escalators were thought to accelerate inflation by speeding up the transmission of wage and price increases through the economy. Yet, it is unfair and futile to rely on a lag in wages to hold back inflation. If the clause has no upper limit, as in the General Motors agreement of 1970, wages remain roughly stable in real terms over the life of the contract. Then, if policy manages to reduce inflation, the increase in nominal wages will be correspondingly low; while if policy fails to slow the inflation, the wage increase will prevent a reduction in workers' real incomes.

Even with escalator clauses, however, guideposts pose serious problems for controlling wages. The expediency of holding increases in all wages equal to the growth in average productivity offers no solution, because there must be allowance for deviations in particular industries and crafts, from the average. This need makes enforcement of guideposts in specific cases arbitrary and difficult. The problems are vastly more intractable for prices. Yet controls on wages but not prices seem politically unacceptable; they had to cover both, as well as dividends and perhaps interest.

The administration's decision was to ply a middle course. The lid it put on the inflationary steampot had plenty of holes to let off the pressure. The strategy was to avoid setting up strong political opposition by bending the guidelines upward where necessary, but to achieve a sufficient reduction of increases elsewhere to produce a sense of waning inflation. Then anticipations would weaken and remove their pressure for increases in wages and prices. The initial effect on anticipations appeared to be favorable (judging by financial markets). Confusion over how the new controls would work inci-dentally served the additional purpose of creating uncertainty, which delayed the business recovery and kept markets slack. But permanent success against inflation depended upon the advance in aggregate demand. If markets remained slack, a slow unwinding of the inflation could continue. If policy stimulated the economy too rapidly, even a lid with holes could not contain the resulting build up of inflationary pressures.

Lessons of Recent Monetary Experience

The inflation that began in 1965 has created an almost made-to-order experiment for testing monetary effects on the economy. Monetary restraint was imposed in 1966 and again in 1969 to curb the inflation under circumstances which left no doubt that the reductions in monetary growth were policy decisions and not an automatic response of the monetary system to changes in the demand for money or credit. The resulting developments provide new evidence on the effects of monetary policy and on the nature and problems of inflation.

Effects of Monetary Policy. Monetary policy has long been downgraded, even by the monetary authorities themselves, as having limited power to influence the course of economic activity. Since changes in the money stock are typically produced via Federal Reserve sales or purchases of financial assets, no immediate effect on business sales or national income need occur. An effect on interest rates and then on investment demand occurs as the public subsequently adjusts to the change in money balances. A common view has been that the ultimate effect on aggregate expenditures is highly uncertain and probably fairly weak.

The recent experience has made clear, however, that monetary effects are not weak. Inflation began in 1965 when excessive monetary growth pushed the economy into the zone of increasing prices. Economic activity faltered in 1967 and contracted in 1970 after monetary policy became restrictive. There was nothing new here; such effects have been seen in the past. But the causal role of money was widely doubted on the grounds that monetary growth passively reflects changes in economic activity, not vice versa, or that other influences are responsible for the appearance of a common variation in activity and monetary growth. For the recent episodes these alternative explanations can be readily dismissed. Monetary policy has finally come center stage.

The recent experience not only verifies that money affects aggregate expenditures but also that it does so with a lag. It is the lag which explains why the effects have often been overlooked. In 1966 and 1969 the length of the lag was about two quarters from the step peak in monetary growth to the peak in the level of economic activity—a lag on the short side compared with past cycles but not far out of line. The effects on the *rate of change* of activity occur somewhat earlier. Thus, the monetary model of the Federal Reserve Bank of St. Louis, which has had a fairly good record in forecasting, uses a distributed lag in which changes in GNP are affected by monetary growth concurrently and in the previous four quarters. The average length of this distributed lag is about $1^{1}/_{2}$ quarters. Different forms of this relationship give different estimates of the lag pattern, however. The lag time is not easy to pin down, largely because it varies from one episode to the next. Predictions of monetary effects are therefore subject to considerable error, and this has often led to confusion in the conduct of monetary policy.

In view of the variable lag in the effects of monetary policy, fiscal policy used to be viewed as the key to stabilizing the economy. The acclaimed success of the 1964 tax cut helped to certify fiscal measures as a practical tool of government policy. But the disappointing failure of the 1968 tax surcharge—first the delay in getting it enacted and then its inability to curb the business boom—raised serious questions about the reliability and practicality of fiscal measures. Neither fiscal nor monetary policy has proven to be an effective stabilizer of the economy in the very short run. It is more accurate to say that both have been major sources of instability.

At the center of these policy shortcomings stands the sorry record of forecasting. After more than a decade of research on complicated econometric models, crucial changes in the economy are still missed, causing serious policy mistakes. The beginning of inflation in 1965 was generally not recognized until it had gathered momentum. The strength of the business recovery following the slowdown in the first quarter of 1967 was underestimated. The downturn of 1969 was first predicted for early in that year and, when it finally came at the end of the year, its depth and duration were generally underestimated. As a result, the application of monetary restraint in 1966 was late, and its reversal in 1967 was far too strong. The restraint in 1969 also came too late and was overdone.

The financial crunches of 1966 and 1970 resulted from the delay and then overapplication of monetary restraint. The severe restraint unsettled financial markets, raised interest rates sharply, and channeled the limited supply of credit in favor of particular sectors. Housing especially suffered—in large part because savings institutions, which are the main suppliers of residential mortgage credit, could not compete effectively for deposits and were forced to curtail their mortgage lending. The housing problem was partially alleviated by the expansion of federal support of the mortgage market. But to avoid severe contractions of home building in the future, savings institutions need greater flexibility so that they can offer competitive rates on their deposits and attract funds even in tight markets. Basic reforms are needed to free these institutions from deposit-rate ceilings and other regulations.

The conduct of monetary policy in the 1965-70 period made additional errors by relying too much on movements in bank credit and interest rates as indicators of monetary effects. Both were particularly misleading in those years. Because of deposit-rate ceilings, time deposits experienced wide fluctuations as market rates rose above and then fell below the ceilings. Bank credit reflected these variations in time deposit growth and in nondeposit sources of funds which banks contrived to borrow on the open market until discouraged by the imposition of new regulations in 1969. The variations in growth of bank credit did not indicate parallel changes in the total supply of credit. Interest rates were also a poor indicator, because they reflected more than just monetary policy. In addition to shifts in the demand for credit, anticipations of inflation contributed to the rise in interest rates from 1965 to 1969. On the whole, growth in currency and demand deposits was a better indicator of the effects of monetary policy on aggregate expenditures.

Given the lags in monetary policy and the difficulties of forecasting, a policy of stable growth in the money stock has much appeal. But deposit-rate ceilings and other banking regulations cause problems here too. The large fluctuations in time deposits just described reflect portfolio transfers in and out of other assets, mostly securities but to some extent demand deposits also. Hence, a given growth rate of demand deposits could have varying effects on the economy because of substitutions between demand and time deposits. The money stock defined to include demand deposits plus currency is still the best single indicator for monetary policy, given the large fluctuations in time deposits. But, under such circumstances, even this indicator is less than ideal. A dismantling of deposit-rate ceilings and improved control over monetary growth is badly needed.

The Nature and Problem of Inflation. The current inflation has proved unexpectedly tenacious despite less than full employment since early 1970. Looking to past experience, the inflationary upsurge of 1955-56 did not finally subside until 1958, but many prices had begun to decelerate before or soon after business activity turned down in 1957. This time deceleration came more slowly. Inflation began to slacken in early 1969, but as of mid-1971 gave little indication of a steady decline.

This does not mean that monetary restraint has been ineffective. The restraint has curtailed aggregate expenditures and activity, as noted above. Inflation continues to be a problem because the slowdown in the economy has been reflected primarily in output and hardly at all in prices. Price increases have developed a built-in momentum which seems to be generated and maintained by the widespread public anticipations of continuing inflation. The anticipations in turn affect prices, indirectly by raising wage settlements and directly by weakening the depressing influence on prices of the slack in aggregate demand.

As people come to anticipate inflation, they adjust to it. Then in theory it has less tendency to redistribute wealth and income and is less of a burden, though there continue to be individual cases of hardship. And, indeed, recent studies have found redistributive effects to be small, at least between major economic sectors.[29] The loudest complaints in recent years have come instead from sectors hurt by the financial stringencies of 1966 and 1969, which resulted from monetary efforts to curb the inflation.

Although anticipations of inflation seem to have made inflation easier to live with, at the same time they have reduced one of its alleged benefits by making a given trade-off between inflation and unemployment harder to sustain. Where inflation of 5 percent per year could have offset the wage increases of an earlier date and produced a demand for labor sufficient to keep unemployment at 4 percent of the labor force, now nominal wage demands anticipate the 5 percent inflation, and the same employment level requires a higher rate of inflation. This upward shift in the trade-off relation would be repeated as each higher rate of inflation came to be anticipated.

Until August 1971, policy acted to maintain moderate slack in the economy until inflation came gradually under control. The consequences of inflationary anticipations were that inflation would take longer to curb and, if not curbed, would get worse. Although unit labor costs decelerated during 1971 and promised to reduce the pressure under rising prices, the administration responded to widespread impatience with the slow signs of progress by abruptly changing course. In August the President announced a 90-day wage-price

[29] Andrew F. Brimmer, "Inflation and Income Distribution in the United States," *The Review of Economics and Statistics*, February 1971, pp. 37-48, and Edward C. Budd and David F. Seiders, "The Impact of Inflation on the Distribution of Income and Wealth," *American Economic Review Papers and Proceedings*, May 1971, pp. 128-38.

freeze and other measures to stimulate the economy and to deal with a worsening balance of payments. The freeze was followed in November by guidelines for wages and prices. Since the administration had long expressed opposition to direct controls on the economy in peacetime, the change of mind holds momentous implications for the range of economic policies now likely to be considered acceptable in the future.

The belief that inflation has become inevitable due to full-employment policies arose in the early post-World War II years, subsided during the early 1960s, and has now revived. The belief is strongly entrenched and partly validates itself by hardening anticipations of inflation. It accounts for the impatience with traditional monetary restraint and for the resort to controls. Yet, there is no necessary incompatibility between price stability and reasonable full employment. Inflations are started when policy overshoots full employment. Once entrenched and anticipated, inflation is very difficult to eradicate. But the slow inroads against inflation by monetary restraint do not mean that it is having no effect. The problem is that the speed of the effect does not meet current standards of political acceptability. Whether wage-price controls will henceforth become an acceptable part of policies to curb inflation is the issue now being tested.

3
WAGES AND WAGE POLICY
1962-71

Marten Estey

Introduction

The decade 1962-1971 was in many ways an extraordinary one so far as the labor market is concerned. It began with a unique experiment in wage restraint, the wage-price guideposts of 1962, which were the first American attempt in peacetime to establish a national wage stabilization policy; compliance, it was hoped, would be voluntary. It ended with another unique experiment in wage restraint, the 90-day wage-price freeze of August 15, 1971 and its sequel, Phase II, complete with Pay Board, Price Commission, and Cost of Living Council, the first American use in "peacetime" of formal controls over wages and prices generally.

In some respects, the circumstances surrounding these two experiments were remarkably similar—so much so that we almost seem to have come full circle:

> Both the guideposts and the freeze were introduced at a time of considerable slack in the economy. In January 1962, when the guideposts were issued, the seasonally adjusted unemployment rate was 5.8 percent; in August 1971, when the freeze was announced, it was 6.1 percent.
>
> In both 1962 and 1971, the administration was confronted with a serious balance of payments problem, which reinforced concern about the domestic consequences of inflation.
>
> Both the guideposts and the freeze were preceded by months of public discussion of the need for wage and price restraint—although the pressure for intervention was both more intense and more widespread in 1971 than in 1962.

But there was one major—indeed, crucial—difference between the economic situation in 1962 and that in 1971, and thus in the task that wage policy was designed to perform.

At the beginning of 1962, wages were not only increasing at the slowest pace in six years, but, more important, they were rising at nearly the same rate as productivity. In short, wage behavior at that time was *not* significantly inflationary. The primary objective of the guideposts, therefore, was *preventive:* to keep wages from starting to rise faster than productivity and thereby becoming inflationary.

In 1971, on the other hand, wages were increasing at near-record rates and far outstripping the growth of productivity. Wage behavior was inflationary, and the goal of the freeze was *corrective.* It was designed to stop an inflationary process that was already well advanced, and to give the administration time to prepare a policy and a program which would move toward noninflationary wage behavior.

This study traces the development of wage policy and the behavior of wages and productivity during the decade from the introduction of the guideposts in 1962 to the announcement of the wage-price freeze in 1971, and it examines the impact of these factors on and their relation to the problem of inflation.

Labor Cost Stability, 1961-65

The Wage Guideposts. An appropriate point to begin an appraisal of the role of wages and the labor market is January 1962 when the Council of Economic Advisers (CEA) published what it described as "Guideposts for Noninflationary Wage and Price Behavior." In its view, the "central guidepost" for wage settlements was productivity. More specifically, the general guidepost for noninflationary wage behavior was that "the rate of increase in wage rates (including fringe benefits) in each industry [should] be equal to the trend rate of over-all productivity increase." [1] General acceptance of this standard would lead to stability of unit labor costs for the economy as a whole, and so long as the price guideposts were observed, to price stability as well.

There were a number of important exceptions to the guideposts, but the crucial relationship, so far as the wage guideposts were concerned, was the tie between wages and productivity.

---

[1] *Economic Report of the President* (Washington: Government Printing Office), 1962, p. 189; hereinafter referred to as *Economic Report*, with year of publication. For the text of both the general wage and price guideposts and their most important exceptions see Thomas Moore, chapter 4, this volume.

The concept of tying wages—or, more accurately, compensation—to productivity did not originate with the publication of the guidepost policy in 1962. As Douty notes, "The elements of a productivity-based wage and price policy may be found in the Economic Reports of the President throughout the postwar period." Thus, as early as 1947, he adds, the President's mid-year economic report stated that, aside from special circumstances, "wage increases should be related to general trends in productivity. . . ." And the 1953 *Economic Report of the President* suggested that "the preferable general formula . . . is for money wages to increase with productivity trends in the whole economy." [2]

Nor was a wage-productivity formula exclusively a product of national economic policy. In 1948, the General Motors-United Automobile Workers' agreement had included an "annual improvement factor," which provided automatic wage increases based upon *national* trend productivity. The same settlement introduced a cost-of-living escalator clause. Taken together, these two clauses insured production workers at General Motors that real wages would at least keep pace with trend productivity. Although the objective in that case was to use productivity as a guide to *minimum* rather than to *maximum* wage increases, it is significant that the wage-productivity concept had roots in collective bargaining as well as in national economic policy.

The introduction of the guideposts in January 1962 was well timed. The economy was just recovering from its third recession in a decade, and conditions for making a *preventive* move were favorable. First, and most important perhaps, was the fact that overall wage behavior was essentially noninflationary. In 1961, the 3.8 percent increase in compensation per man-hour had been the smallest in six years, while output per man-hour had risen a strong 3.5 percent. The result was the smallest increase in unit labor costs in six years, a rise of only 0.3 percent. The impact of collective bargaining also appeared generally noninflationary. In 1961, the median first-year wage adjustment for all major settlements was only 2.8 percent and for those in manufacturing alone only 2.4 percent, each less than the current increase in productivity. Moreover, the 2.4 percent gain in average hourly earnings in the total private economy was the smallest since 1947.

---

[2] Harry Douty, "Some Problems of Wage Policy," *Monthly Labor Review*, July 1962, p. 733. This contradicts Moore's suggestion that the antecedents of the guideposts go back only to the Eisenhower administration. Moore, *U.S. Incomes Policy*, pp. 9-10.

Second, unemployment appeared to have peaked, having dropped from a high of 7.0 percent (seasonally adjusted) in May 1961 to 6.0 percent in December 1961. The prospects for economic expansion were encouraging.

Finally, the steel negotiations, perhaps the most critical of all union-management negotiations in terms of their impact on prices generally, were coming up in early 1962. In letters to both the major steel companies and to the union, the President had already indicated his interest in a noninflationary settlement.

With the economy expanding and wages rising unusually slowly, it seemed an opportune time to emphasize the kind of wage and price behavior that would prevent the anticipated expansion from becoming inflationary, and to suggest restraint before wages and prices started to accelerate, rather than try to slow them down after they picked up speed. Furthermore, concern over our unfavorable balance of payments position provided an added incentive to try to preserve domestic price stability.

In summary, the introduction of the guideposts in 1962 can be described as an essentially *preventive* measure designed to preserve the status quo, in contrast to the situation in 1971, when the objective of Phase II was essentially *corrective*, designed to reduce the current rates of increase of both wages and prices.

The 1962 guideposts were designed to apply not to the economy as a whole, or even to the whole private sector, but only to *discretionary* wage and price decisions. As the Council of Economic Advisers put it:

> There are important segments of the economy where firms are large or employees well-organized, or both. In these sectors, private parties may exercise considerable discretion over the terms of wage bargains and price decisions. Thus, at least in the short run, there is considerable room for the exercise of private power and a parallel need for the assumption of private responsibility.[3]

It was further indicated that the guideposts were intended for individual wage and price decisions that assumed "national importance," either because they directly involved "large numbers of workers and large amounts of output," or because they were "regarded by large segments of the economy as setting a pattern."[4]

Rejecting mandatory controls over wage negotiations and indi-

---

[3] *Economic Report*, 1962, p. 185.
[4] *Ibid.*

vidual price decisions as neither desirable nor practical, the CEA offered the guideposts as a means by which the public could judge whether or not particular wage-price decisions were inflationary, and thus presumably help create an atmosphere in which the private decision makers would exercise their discretionary power "responsibly." The guideposts, therefore, were initially offered as a contribution to public discussion rather than as operational policies.

In keeping with this view, the council issued no guidepost figure in 1962, although it did discuss alternative measures of productivity. In 1963, concern with the slow pace of expansion overshadowed the fear of future inflation, and the *Economic Report of the President* gave no further clue as to what the administration considered the most appropriate measure of productivity. Not until 1964, when the President's economic report included a trend productivity figure of 3.2 percent for the five years ending in 1963, was there a single recognized wage guidepost figure.

Nevertheless, the guideposts were turned into operational policy within weeks after they were issued. This occurred in April 1962 when the steel industry, following the acceptance of a "noninflationary" wage settlement by the Steelworkers Union, announced its intention of increasing the price of steel. The ensuing uproar—the famous confrontation between President Kennedy and the leaders of the steel industry, and the vigorous efforts of the administration to force the industry to back down—needs no recounting here. Its outcome, according to the Council of Economic Advisers' classic understatement, was that "the price increase was rescinded after the President expressed the country's concern over the serious threat to price stability and our balance of payments." [5]

The furor over the confrontation between President Kennedy and the top management of the steel industry has diverted attention from the collective bargaining agreement which preceded it and from the fact that, in addition to satisfying the then unquantified wage guideposts criteria, that agreement had called for *no* general wage increase in 1962 and had eliminated the cost-of-living wage escalator. [6] The 1962 settlement in steel, in fact, consisted entirely of improvements in fringe benefits, estimated at about $0.10 an hour, or 2.5 percent. [7]

---

[5] *Economic Report*, 1963, p. 87. For a detailed account of the steel confrontation see Moore, chapter 4, below.

[6] U.S. Department of Labor *Monthly Labor Review* (Washington: Government Printing Office), April 1962, p. III.

[7] The percentage increase is from John Sheahan, *The Wage-Price Guideposts* (Washington: The Brookings Institution, 1967), p. 34.

But the most significant aspect of the no-wage-increase settlement in steel was in the extent to which it set a pattern for no-wage-increase agreements. In 1962 that pattern was followed in the aluminum and can industry settlements, both of which involved the Steelworkers Union. In 1963 the no-wage-increase pattern was extended for another *two* years in steel, aluminum and cans, and in 1964 it was adopted for the first year of a new agreement in the auto industry.

The 1962 Wage Record. To what extent the guideposts contributed to the wage record for 1962 is still a matter of controversy. But regardless of the causes, the final measures of wage and labor cost change for 1962 were encouraging in terms of avoiding inflation.

Although the rate of increase in compensation per man-hour in the total private economy rose from 3.8 percent in 1961 to 4.4 percent in 1962, considerably more than the guidepost would have allowed, the increase was more than offset by the 4.7 percent gain in output per man-hour, the largest gain in productivity since 1950. Accordingly, unit labor costs actually decreased for the first time since 1955, declining by 0.3 percent.

On the collective bargaining front, the picture remained predominantly noninflationary. The median first-year wage adjustment for all major collective bargaining agreements (those covering 1,000 workers or more) was 2.9 percent, little higher than the 2.8 percent of 1961. In manufacturing, it remained unchanged at 2.4 percent, largely because of the absence of a general wage increase in steel. In the building trades, the rate of increase in union scales (rates) eased slightly, from 3.9 percent in 1961 to 3.7 percent in 1962. On the other hand, the median first-year wage adjustment in nonmanufacturing (excluding construction) rose from 3.6 percent to 4.0 percent.

Among the most substantial increases in compensation in 1962 were those made by the administration itself. That year, pay increases to federal employees averaged 8.6 percent for postal employees and 5.5 percent for those in the classified Civil Service. These increases were designed as the first step in making the compensation of federal employees comparable to that of persons in private industry. Thus they appear to fit one of the exceptions to the general guideposts: namely, that "Wage rate increases would exceed the general guide rate in an industry . . . in which wage rates are exceptionally low compared with the range of wages earned elsewhere by similar labor. . . ." [8]

[8] *Economic Report*, 1962, p. 189.

1963. Wage and compensation increases in 1963 were generally *smaller* than in 1962, because of both an unusually light collective bargaining schedule and a worrisome reversal of the downward trend in unemployment. Unemployment rose from 5.5 percent (seasonally adjusted) in the fourth quarter of 1962 to 5.8 percent (seasonally adjusted) in the first and second quarters of 1963. The rate of increase in compensation per man-hour slowed from 4.4 percent to 4.1 percent, and that of output per man-hour from 4.7 percent to 3.5 percent. Unit labor costs rose, but only a minimal 0.3 percent.

Wage changes under collective bargaining also remained moderate in 1963. The collective bargaining schedule had reached the low point in the three-year cycle of such activity; only 2.5 million workers were subject to contract renewals, while 3.0 million received deferred increases. Some 2.3 million workers, or 29.0 percent of those under major collective agreements, received no wage increase during the year.

The fact that so many union members received no wage increase was in large part due to the continued emphasis in the steel and aluminum industry negotiations on improvements in job and income security rather than on general wage increases. In both industries, agreements were made at scheduled wage-reopening dates in 1963 to forego general increases for an additional two years, until 1965.

Reflecting this pattern, wage gains under collective bargaining showed little change from 1962. The median first-year wage adjustment for all industries was 3.0 percent (versus 2.9 percent in 1962), and for manufacturing, 2.5 percent (versus 2.4 percent in 1962). In nonmanufacturing excluding construction, the median adjustment declined from 4.0 to 3.4 percent. In the building trades, the 3.6 percent rise in the index of union scales was the smallest since 1955, the boom in residential construction, which is largely nonunion, having had little impact on union wages.

As in 1962, among the most substantial wage increases in 1963 were those resulting from government actions rather than from business decisions: the 14.4 percent pay increase for the Armed Forces and an increase in the federal minimum wage from $1.15 to $1.25 for some 2.6 million workers.

The slow pace of wage increases in 1962 and 1963, together with the slow pace of reduction in the unemployment rate, was not lost on the AFL-CIO, which at its convention in November 1963 criticized the CEA and called for a *faster* rate of increase in real wages.[9]

---

[9] *AFL-CIO Executive Council Report*, 1963, p. 86.

Furthermore, although 1963 was by most measures a less expansionary year in the labor market than 1962, profits before taxes had reached a record $59.4 billion. The Council of Economic Advisers felt compelled to warn in its 1964 report that "many workers are restive, especially in industries that have been making above-average gains in productivity and profits," and that such profits constituted "a lure for strongly intensified wage demands," particularly in cases where they reflected failure to *reduce* prices in accordance with the price guideposts.[10]

1964. In January 1964, recognizing that the expected tax cut would "increase the opportunity and the temptation to raise prices and wages contrary to the public interest," [11] the Council of Economic Advisers published data on trend productivity in the private economy, including the figure of 3.2 percent for the five years ending with 1963. With this, it provided for the first time a specific figure for the general wage guidepost.

As anticipated, the personal income and corporate profits tax cut was enacted in February 1964, and the pace of expansion picked .up again.[12] Unemployment resumed the downward trend begun in 1961, dropping from 5.5 percent (seasonally adjusted) in January to 5.0 percent in December, while nonfarm employment rose by 1.7 million. As the labor market began to tighten, most measures of wage change accelerated. Average hourly earnings rose 3.5 percent, versus 2.7 percent in 1963. Compensation per man-hour rose 5.1 percent, the largest increase in seven years. Output per man-hour rose strongly, 3.9 percent, but not enough to match the rise in compensation, so that unit labor costs rose 1.1 percent.

Compensation rose less rapidly under collective bargaining than in the economy as a whole. A study of 20 key contracts covering 2.25 million workers in 11 major industries showed a median increase in compensation (as distinct from wages only) of 3.5 percent over the life of the contract—well below the 5.1 percent rise in compensation in private economy.[13]

The measures of *wage* change under collective bargaining were strongly influenced by settlements in a single industry, the auto industry. The automobile settlement provided *no general wage increase* in the first year (thus extending for a third year the pattern

---

[10] *Economic Report*, 1964, pp. 115 and 120.

[11] *Ibid.*

[12] For an extensive discussion of the economic analysis underlying the 1964 tax cut, see Charles E. McLure, Jr., chapter 1, above.

[13] *Economic Report*, 1965, p. 55; and *Economic Report*, 1968, p. 108.

first set in steel in 1962) and postponed the customary "annual improvement factor," or productivity increase, until the second year. Instead, it called for substantially liberalized pension benefits and a large wage increase in the third contract year, 1966.

Despite this, the automobile package exceeded the guidepost figure of 3.2 percent, being generally estimated at 4.5 percent.[14] But the fact that it provided no wage increase contributed both to the small increase in the median first-year wage adjustment for all industries (3.2 percent versus 3.0 percent in 1963) and, more significantly, to the *decline* in the median first-year wage adjustment in manufacturing, from 2.5 percent to 2.0 percent.

In nonmanufacturing industry, on the other hand, first-year wage adjustments rose by 3.6 percent, as compared to 3.4 percent in 1963. And in construction, although the index of union scales increased only slightly faster than in 1963 (3.7 percent compared to 3.6 percent), average hourly hearings increased by 4.1 percent, compared to 3.0 percent in 1963.

The federal government's behavior as an employer stood out in 1964, when federal employees received *two* general salary increases. In January they received the second step of an increase initiated in 1962, amounting to 2.6 percent for postal employees and 4.1 percent for classified employees. In July postal employees received a 5.6 percent raise and classified employees 4.2 percent. A 2.5 percent raise for the armed services became effective in September.

1965. The year 1965 was the last year of essentially inflation-free expansion. The turning point between economic stability and inflation was President Johnson's announcement on July 28, 1965 of the shift to large-scale military involvement in Vietnam.[15] But the full extent of its economic impact was not felt until the fourth quarter, so that the economic performance for the year 1965 as a whole remained fairly stable.

Employment conditions continued to improve throughout 1965. For the first time since 1957 the *annual* unemployment rate fell below 5.0 percent to 4.6 percent. And the decline in unemployment accelerated in the third and fourth quarters so that, by December 1965 the rate was down to 4.1 percent (seasonally adjusted), just short of the interim unemployment target of 4.0 percent. Nonfarm

---

[14] *New York Times*, September 13, 1964, p. 51.

[15] The monetary growth rate, however, doubled as early as June 1965. See Cagan, chapter 2, this volume.

employment rose by 2.0 million between 1964 and 1965 and by 2.5 million from December 1964 to December 1965.

Although the expansion continued apace throughout the first three quarters of 1965 and accelerated in the fourth quarter, the overall labor cost picture in 1965 was actually somewhat better than it had been in 1964. Compensation per man-hour in the total private economy rose less rapidly than it had in 1964 (4.1 percent in 1965 as against 5.1 percent in 1964). Output per man-hour also eased, but proportionately less than compensation (rising 3.4 percent in 1965, compared to 3.9 percent in 1964), so that unit labor costs in the total private economy rose less than in 1964 (0.8 percent versus 1.1 percent). In manufacturing, unit labor costs actually declined by 1.4 percent in 1965.

The most important single collective bargaining negotiation in 1965, from the point of view of economic policy, was the steel negotiation, the first overall contract renewal in that industry since the historic confrontation over prices in 1962. The administration went to some lengths both to minimize the possible adverse effects of a strike—by timing the distribution of an increase in social security benefits for September 1—and to encourage a settlement within the guideposts. To that end, the Council of Economic Advisers, on May 1, 1965, released a report on steel prices in which it noted that "stable steel prices since 1959 have been made possible by the stability of labor costs per unit of steel output"; it also emphasized that "the stability of steel prices is second only in importance to the stability of average labor costs in explaining the absence of inflation during the past four years of record-breaking expansion." [16]

When the contract expired at the end of August 1965, having been extended because of a key union election, the President intervened to avoid a strike by appointing a special mediation board consisting of the secretary of labor, the secretary of commerce, and the chairman of the Council of Economic Advisers, with the latter as "statistical umpire." The CEA subsequently reported that "a settlement was achieved within the wage guideposts. According to the best estimates of its cost available to the government, the settlement averaged 3.2 percent a year, computed over the full 39-month period." [17] However, Sheahan notes that if the cost of the settlement had been computed from the effective date of September 1, 1965, rather than from figures retroactive to the original expiration date

[16] *Monthly Labor Review*, June 1965, p. 673.
[17] *Economic Report*, 1966, p. 89.

of May 1, 1965, the average would have been *above* 3.2 percent.[18]

In any case, the 1965 steel agreement represented a significant turning point in the collective bargaining pattern: The wage increase effective September 1, 1965 was the first general wage increase in the steel industry in nearly four years (since October 1961). Whether it was within the guideposts or not, the settlement unmistakably signaled the end of the "unemployment psychology" and the preoccupation with job security and fringe benefits which had accompanied it. Instead, interest had shifted to current wage increases and to front-loading (concentrating a disproportionate part of the total increase in the first year of a long-term agreement) in order to catch up with rising prices.

The steel settlement had a significant impact on collective bargaining data, primarily because it affected such a large proportion of the workers involved in negotiations in 1965. Thus, largely because of the steel settlement, the median first-year *wage* adjustment in manufacturing was 4.0 percent in 1965, double the 1964 figure of 2.0 percent, while the median first-year adjustment for all industries rose from 3.2 percent in 1964 to 3.8 percent in 1965. In nonmanufacturing, the median adjustment was 3.7 percent, up from 3.6 percent in 1964.

Steel also contributed to the fact that an unusually high proportion of workers subject to collective bargaining received wage increases in 1965. Only 10.0 percent of the workers under collective bargaining received *no* increase, as against 23.0 percent in 1964 and 29.0 percent in 1963.

Because the automobile settlement in 1964 resulted in a relatively small first-year wage adjustment in manufacturing in 1964, and the 1965 steel settlement in a relatively large one in 1965, these two settlements tended to distort the 1964-1965 data on wage changes under collective bargaining, probably *understating* the gains in 1964 and *overstating* them in 1965. This led to the analysis of collective bargaining settlements in terms of changes over the life of the contract, a measure which shows a moderate but steady increase in wages under collective bargaining from 2.3 percent in 1963 to 3.0 percent in 1964 and 3.3 percent in 1965.[19]

Although the steel settlement met the guidepost criteria, this was not the case with all major settlements. In aerospace and construction, negotiated increases exceeded the guideposts; but in rub-

---

[18] Sheahan, *op. cit.*, p. 50.

[19] *Current Wage Developments* (Washington: Department of Labor, Bureau of Labor Statistics), No. 216, Supplement, December 1, 1965, p. 3.

ber, maritime, New York newspapers and aluminum, as well as steel, the settlements were within or close to guidepost standards.

The federal government may have contributed more to the acceleration of wages and prices in 1965 than did any single private industry. In addition to a $900 million increase in social security benefits effective on September 1, 1965 and to an increase in minimum wages under the Fair Labor Standards Act, the government gave a pay increase averaging 3.6 percent to some 1.7 million federal civilian employees [20] and a military pay increase of approximately $1 billion. The latter was credited by the Council of Economic Advisers with being one of the three "most prominent" elements in the 1.8 percent rise of the GNP deflator.[21]

1961-65 Summary. As suggested above, 1965 marked the end of an era of unusually stable prices, in which the annual increase in the consumer price index (CPI) for the five-year period, 1961-1965, was only 1.3 percent.

A brief review of the period highlights its economic patterns and emphasizes its exceptional character.

Productivity. A distinguishing and vitally important feature of the economic picture for the years, 1961-1965, was the rapid growth of productivity, or output per man-hour. For the five-year period as a whole, productivity in the total private economy increased at an average annual rate of 3.8 percent, the highest rate for any five-year period since 1950-1954 and substantially better than the average of 2.3 percent per year in the preceding five years, 1956-1960. The 4.7 percent increase in productivity in 1962 was the largest since 1950 and the second largest one-year gain in the 23-year period, 1947-1970.

At the same time, the five-year average benefited substantially from the fact that the smallest annual increase in productivity was 3.4 percent. The period 1961 through 1965 was, in fact, the first five-year period since World War II in which annual productivity gains consistently exceeded even as low a figure as 2.0 percent.

The productivity record from 1960 to 1965, therefore, was clearly exceptional, both in terms of its high average and its consistency.

Compensation Per Man-hour. At the same time that unusually

---

[20] According to the 1966 *Economic Report* (p. 89), this increase was kept "within the guideposts" only after the President threatened to veto a larger increase proposed by Congress.

[21] *Ibid.*, p. 65.

166

large productivity gains were being registered, compensation per man-hour was increasing at substantially less than its previous pace.

Compensation per man-hour in the total private economy increased at an average annual rate of 4.3 percent during the five years, 1961-1965, significantly less than either the 5.1 percent annual average of the preceding five years, or the 5.4 percent average of the period, 1947-1960. Like the productivity data, compensation per man-hour was unusually stable during the years, 1961-1965. In only one year, 1964, did the rate of increase in compensation exceed 5.0 percent.

Unit Labor Costs. The combination of above-average increases in productivity and below-average increases in compensation produced almost unprecedented results in terms of unit labor costs. In the years 1961 through 1965, the average annual increase in unit labor costs in the total private economy was 0.4 percent. This increase in unit labor costs of less than one-half of one percent per year was the smallest annual average for any five-year period since 1947, and, in fact, subsequently proved to be the smallest increase for any consecutive five-year period between 1947 and 1970.

It is evident that whatever the guideposts contributed to the restraint of increases in compensation, the price stability of 1961-1965 was as much a function of exceptional productivity gains as it was of moderate increases in compensation. These exceptional productivity gains, in turn, were possible in part because of the excessive slack in the economy associated with high levels of unemployment.

For those who may look back in envy to the "golden years" of 1960-1965, it should be obvious from this summary that the conjuncture of such *prolonged* high productivity and low compensation gains may be hard to duplicate, even with enforced wage restraints. It must be emphasized, too, that although the performance of productivity, compensation, and unit labor costs was unusually favorable from the point of view of inflation, one price that was paid for this performance was five years of high unemployment averaging 5.6 percent.

Wages Under Collective Bargaining. Like other measures of compensation, collective bargaining settlements were unusually moderate during the 1961-1965 period. The median first-year wage adjustment for all major settlements of 2.8 percent in 1961 was the smallest since 1954, when data on the costs of collective bargaining settlements were first published. For the five-year period as a

167

whole, the annual average of the median first-year adjustments was 3.1 percent, compared to 4.3 percent for the period 1954-1960.

In manufacturing, the first-year wage adjustment averaged 2.7 percent for 1961-1965, while in nonmanufacturing (excluding construction) the average was 3.7 percent. And even in construction, although the index of union scales increased an average of 3.8 percent per year in 1961-1965, this was substantially less than the average increase of 5.9 percent in 1947-1960.

These figures do not include fringe benefits, which generally rose more rapidly than wages during this period. Nevertheless, they suggest that rather than creating inflationary pressures, compensation under collective bargaining lagged behind compensation gains in the total private economy, as is customary during the early stages of expansion.

Real Compensation. During the period, 1961-1965, real compensation per man-hour (compensation adjusted for changes in the CPI) rose at an average annual rate of 2.9 percent, or less than the average increase in output per man-hour of 3.8 percent. Largely as a result of this lag of real compensation behind productivity, employee compensation declined from 70.8 percent of the national income in 1961 to 69.8 percent in 1965.

But while labor's share of national income was declining, corporate profits before taxes rose from 11.8 percent to 13.8 percent of national income. This situation increased the pressure for an acceleration in wage increases beginning in 1966. In fact, organized labor's recent demand for profits control in Phase II stemmed in part from its desire to avoid a shift in income distribution similar to that of 1961-1965.

The Rise in Labor Costs, 1966-70

1966. At the beginning of 1966, the Johnson administration found itself in a dilemma with respect to the measurement of trend productivity, the basis of the general wage guidepost. Having indicated in the 1964 *Report of the Council of Economic Advisers* that the current five-year average was the appropriate measure of trend productivity, it was now confronted with two shortcomings with that particular measure:

First, revisions of GNP data for the five years, 1959-1963, had raised the original trend productivity figure for that period from 3.2 to 3.4 percent. Although such data revision is routine procedure, in

Figure 1

RATES OF CHANGE IN OUTPUT PER MAN-HOUR,
COMPENSATION, AND UNIT LABOR COSTS,
TOTAL PRIVATE ECONOMY, 1960-1970

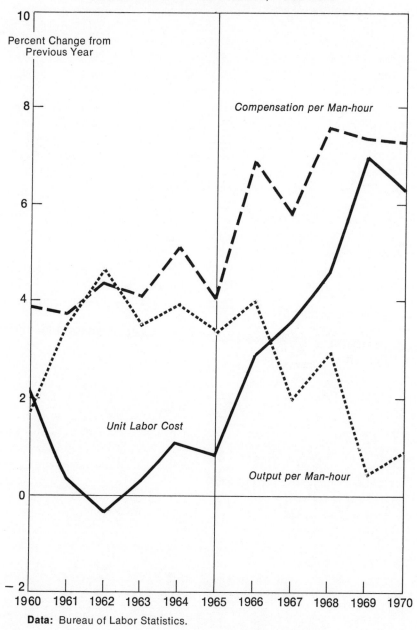

Data: Bureau of Labor Statistics.

this case it left the administration vulnerable to the criticism, especially from organized labor, that the original guidepost figure had been too low, and hence unnecessarily restrictive so far as wages were concerned. On the other hand, the new data meant that wages were, if anything, less inflationary than they had appeared from 1960 to 1965.

Second, by 1966 the use of the current five-year average meant dropping the 1959 and 1960 figures and adding those for 1964 and 1965, thus replacing low productivity years with high productivity ones and further raising the five-year trend.

The net result of these changes was a trend productivity figure of 3.6 percent for the five years 1961-1965. But the council rejected this figure as inappropriate, on the grounds that it was abnormally high, could not be sustained (a view which was subsequently substantiated by experience) and was, therefore, not an accurate measure of the true trend of productivity. Instead, the council, in its first specific recommendation of a guidepost figure, urged continued adherence to the original guidepost figure of 3.2 percent.[22]

While the administration's decision to stick with the 3.2 percent guidepost figure may have been required by the fight against inflation, it served to intensify organized labor's opposition to the guideposts. The AFL-CIO Executive Council, meeting in February, remained "firmly opposed" to guidelines on the grounds that they only served to hold down wages.

This inauspicious beginning ushered in what proved to be a disastrous year for the guideposts. But the fundamental problem was not so much the opposition of unions, important as that may have been, as the inexorable pressures of the rising demand for labor.

In late 1965 and 1966 the demand for labor rose dramatically, in the largest and most rapid expansion since 1951. In 1966, nonfarm payroll employment increased by more than three million, up 5.1 percent from 1965; and in durable goods manufacturing, the private sector most stimulated by the escalation of the war in Vietnam, payroll employment rose by one million, or 7.7 percent. In addition, the armed forces were expanded by 400,000 in 1966, or nearly 15.0 percent.

Unemployment reached the long-sought interim target of 4.0 percent (seasonally adjusted) in January 1966. During the first quarter of 1966, unemployment eased further, to 3.8 percent, at which point it leveled off and remained virtually steady (with minor fluctu-

---

[22] *Economic Report*, 1966, p. 92.

ations) throughout the remainder of 1966 and 1967. The factory work week rose to 41.4 hours in 1966—the highest since World War II—of which an average 3.9 hours was at overtime rates.

Under the pressure of this great rise in the demand for labor in an economy already operating at close to efficient capacity, five years of wage and labor cost stability came to an abrupt end. Compensation per man-hour rose 6.9 percent, the largest increase since 1951, reflecting a combination of increased wages and benefits, more overtime, the shift to higher paying jobs, and increased employer contributions to social security. Although the 4.0 percent increase in output per man-hour (up from 3.4 percent in 1965) was the second highest in 11 years, it fell far short of matching the rise in compensation.

The resulting 2.9 percent increase in unit labor costs was the largest in nine years, and the first since 1960 to exceed 1.1 percent. Not surprisingly, the accompanying rise of 2.9 percent in the CPI was also the greatest in nine years. Inflation, once a potential problem, had become an actual one.

Fortunately from the point of view of restraining inflation, the collective bargaining schedule for 1966 was a light one. Only 3.4 million workers were subject to current wage increases, while 4.9 million were eligible for deferred increases, and 1.7 million (including the steel-workers) were scheduled to receive no general wage increase. The schedule was especially light in manufacturing where only 1.4 million workers were subject to wage negotiations, compared to an average 2.4 million in the years, 1960-1965.[23] Although a light collective bargaining schedule obviously does not affect the size of wage increases under collective bargaining, it does reduce the number of workers who get them. Thus it makes the impact of collective bargaining on average compensation gains less than it would have been if the schedule had been heavier.

In addition, surprising as it may seem, there was no acceleration in the size of negotiated wage gains as a whole in the first half of 1966. Although negotiated wage increases in excess of the guideposts began in January in the New York transit case, the median first-year wage adjustment in major collective bargaining settlements in the first six months of 1966 was actually *less* than it was for first-half 1965 (3.9 percent as against 4.0 percent). As the Council of Economic Advisers conceded, this figure was "only moderately in excess" of the general wage guidepost.[24]

---

[23] Bureau of Labor Statistics, *Current Wage Developments*, April 1, 1967, p. 4.
[24] *Economic Report*, 1967, p. 127.

The acceleration of wage increases in collective bargaining settlements came in the second half of the year. The airline mechanics settled for a 5.0 percent increase that seriously damaged the guideposts, and workers in electrical equipment manufacturing and in telephones won increases which were "about $1^1/_2$ percentage points in excess" of the general wage guideposts, or close to 4.7 percent.[25] It is significant that one official source, a Labor Department publication, acknowledged that the big gains of third and fourth quarters of 1966 occurred "in part because of the rapid increase in the CPI," [26] which had risen at an annual rate of 3.4 percent in the first and second quarters of 1966.

As a result of the substantial gains in the second half, the median first-year wage adjustment for all of 1966 was 4.8 percent, up 0.9 percentage point from 1965, representing the most rapid acceleration since 1959, the first year for which these data are available. But the primary source of this acceleration was not in manufacturing, where the median first-year adjustment rose only moderately, from 4.0 percent in 1965 to 4.2 percent in 1966; rather, it was in nonmanufacturing, where the sharp rise from 3.7 percent in 1965 to 5.0 percent in 1966 was also the greatest since 1959.

Rapid as it was, the acceleration of wages under collective bargaining appears to have been less rapid than that of other wages. The medium wage and benefit (compensation) increase in settlements covering 5,000 workers or more was 4.1 percent (equal timing) or 4.5 percent on a time-weighted basis; either way, it was considerably less than the 6.9 percent gain in compensation in the private economy. Furthermore, in manufacturing, the only sector in which we have both union and nonunion wage data, the median wage increase in nonunion establishments was 4.4 percent, compared to 4.1 percent in union establishments.

Nevertheless, despite the fact that wage increases under collective bargaining were somewhat moderated by the light calendar, 1966 can only be described as disastrous so far as the guideposts are concerned.

Although efforts to maintain adherence to the guideposts were redoubled and although the number of cases in which the administration made overt attempts to keep settlements within the guideposts reached a peak, most of the government's publicized confrontations were failures. Increasing numbers of settlements were

---

[25] *Ibid.*
[26] *Current Wage Developments*, April 1, 1967, p. 3.

reached which openly ignored both the guideposts and the administration's pleas for their observance.

The impact of these jawboning efforts is succinctly summarized by Arthur Okun, later chairman of the CEA. Noting that in a number of cases *price* decisions appeared to have been affected by the council's activities, Okun wryly adds, "Similarly favorable responses by labor leaders could not be reported." [27] More to the point, however, was Okun's conclusion that "the tides of excess demand could not be talked down." [28]

The first major collective bargaining settlement of the year, that of the New York transit employees, exceeded the guideposts by providing a 4.0 percent increase in the first year and 11.0 percent the second. Hard on the heels of the transit case, the Operating Engineers Local 825 and the Associated General Contractors of New Jersey announced the terms of a three-year agreement providing, according to Labor Department estimates, package increases averaging from 7.6 percent to 9.0 percent per year. Since the agreement had not yet been signed, the CEA invited the parties to discuss it in the hope of modifying the size of the wage and benefit packages. Although the parties voluntarily submitted their dispute to a special mediation panel consisting of the secretary of labor and the New Jersey commissioner of labor and industry, the final agreement, reached in September, gave the union "substantially what it had tried for in the first place." [29]

However, the Operating Engineers' case was not the total loss that it appeared to be at the time, for among the measures proposed for coping with the problems of wage and price stability in construction was a national wage review board. Union leaders "categorically" rejected the proposal at that time. However, it is an encouraging sign of progress in dealing with wage restraints in this industry that five years later, in 1971, the administration was able to win the cooperation of the building trades in just such a program.

But the case that is generally considered as having damaged the guideposts beyond repair and having considerably reduced the efficacy of presidential involvement in collective bargaining was that of the airline mechanics. One of the factors in the Machinists Union's insistence on an above-average wage increase was the exceptionally favorable profit position of the major airlines. Although

---

[27] Arthur Okun, *Political Economy of Prosperity* (Washington: The Brookings Institution, 1970), p. 76.

[28] *Ibid.*, p. 77.

[29] Sheahan, *op. cit.*, p. 53.

a tentative settlement estimated at 4.3 percent was negotiated under White House auspices and announced to the nation by President Johnson himself, it was rejected by the membership. The final agreement provided a package estimated by the CEA at 4.9 percent, and the head of the Machinists Union boasted that it had destroyed the guideposts: "It completely shatters them for all unions." [30]

A similar conclusion, in fact, had already been reached independently by the President's Advisory Committee on Labor-Management Policy. Although it continued to support the guidepost principle of relating wages to national productivity trends, the committee warned, in a memorandum to the President on August 18, that "it is impractical if not impossible to translate the goals reflected in the guideposts into formulae for application to every particular wage or price decision." It concluded that "any policy to achieve price stability will be acceptable and effective only if it bears equitably on all forms of incomes." [31]

Perhaps the administration's chief success in 1966, so far as guideposts were concerned, was to enforce them with respect to its own employees for the second year in a row. Having warned that "Government pay increases should be consistent with the guideposts," [32] in July the administration succeeded in getting congressional approval to hold increases for the armed forces and federal civilian employees to an estimated 3.2 percent. As Sheahan points out, this was not only a recognition that the federal government serves as an example to private industry, particularly with respect to the policies it seeks to enforce, but also that the federal payroll has a significant effect on aggregate demand. [33]

1967. The Council of Economic Advisers took to heart the criticisms of the President's advisory committee and the unions—and the results of collective bargaining in 1966. In its 1967 report, it acknowledged that the rise in consumer prices made settlements at the guidepost level unrealistic, that "corporate profits have increased considerably more than aggregate labor income . . . since 1961," and that both had contributed to union resistance to the guideposts. [34] While refusing to sanction full cost-of-living escalation on the ground that it would be inflationary, the council reluctantly concluded that "If restraint cannot mean an average wage advance

[30] *New York Times*, August 21, 1966.
[31] *Monthly Labor Review*, October 1966, p. 1122.
[32] *Economic Report*, 1966, p. 13.
[33] Sheahan, *op. cit.*, p. 55.
[34] *Economic Report*, 1967, p. 127.

only equal to the rise in productivity, it surely must mean wage advances which are substantially less than the productivity trend plus the recent rise in consumer prices." [35] Although the administration abandoned the use of a specific guidepost figure in 1967, its qualitative standard could be translated into quantitative terms; the administration clearly hoped that wage gains in 1967 would be "substantially less" than 6.5 percent (3.2 percent, plus the current estimate of a 3.3 percent rise in the CPI for 1966).

In short, the original guidepost standard, which tied wages to trend productivity, was abandoned. It was a victim of the airline mechanics settlement, the failure of the price guideposts, rising profits, and, ultimately, the pressures of the labor market.

It is somewhat ironic, then, that the surging expansion of 1966 did not carry over into 1967, which proved to be a year of consolidation and relatively slow growth, sometimes described as a mini-recession. Employment rose slowly, with total nonfarm payroll employment up only 3.3 percent and payroll employment in manufacturing up only 0.8 percent. And although the annual unemployment rate remained at 3.8 percent, the same as in 1966, the seasonally adjusted unemployment rates edged up throughout the year, from 3.7 percent in the first quarter of 1967 to 3.9 percent in the fourth. Unemployment rose to 4.3 percent in October because of strikes in the auto industry.

Reflecting the slowdown in economic expansion, compensation per man-hour rose considerably less rapidly than it had in 1966, increasing 5.8 percent compared to the previous 6.9 percent. But the key element in the 1967 labor cost picture was the abrupt deceleration in the growth in output per man-hour, from 4.0 percent in 1966 to 2.0 percent in 1967, the lowest level since 1960. The combined effect of these changes in compensation and output per man-hour was the continued acceleration of unit labor costs, from 2.9 percent in 1966 to 3.6 percent in 1967, and in turn the continued rise in the CPI at the rate of 2.9 percent.

In contrast to 1966, the collective bargaining calendar for 1967 was a heavy one, with 4.4 million workers, the largest number since 1960, covered by scheduled contract negotiations.

Wages under collective bargaining continued to accelerate in 1967, but somewhat less rapidly than they had in 1966. The median first-year wage adjustment for all industries was 5.7 percent, up from 4.8 percent in 1966. This rise, furthermore, was due entirely to the sharp increase in the size of the median adjustment in manufac-

---

[35] *Ibid.*, p. 129. See also Okun, *op. cit.*, p. 77.

turing, which rose from 4.2 percent in 1966 to 6.4 percent in 1967. There was no acceleration in wage adjustments in nonmanufacturing, which remained unchanged at 5.0 percent. The substantial rise in wage gains in manufacturing, in turn, was due largely to the settlement in the auto industry, which featured an unusually large first-year wage increase, estimated at between 5.5 and 7.0 percent. In addition, "several prominent settlements substantially exceeded 6.0 percent a year." [36]

As the Council of Economic Advisers noted, "Unions negotiating in 1967 had the background of two years of rising living costs, low unemployment—especially for adult men—and relatively high profits to support their negotiating positions." [37]

The performance of wages under collective bargaining in 1967 provided a foretaste of what was to come in 1970: The mini-recession failed to slow the pace of collective bargaining gains at least in manufacturing. On the other hand, as we have noted, there was no acceleration in the rate of wage gain in nonmanufacturing. And in 1967, for the first time in the 1960s, the median wage increase in unionized manufacturing plants was greater than in nonunion plants—5.5 percent as against 5.0 percent.

Moreover, at least in the view of the council, 1967 marked a switch, perhaps temporary, to cost-push rather than demand-pull inflation. "Because the basic inflationary force in 1967 was rising costs, the pattern of wage and price changes was rather different from that of 1966, when excessive demands were the chief inflationary force." [38]

On the wage front, the administration continued to follow its own policy prescriptions with respect to its employees. Federal pay increases, effective in October 1967 for both civil servants and the armed forces, ranged from 4.5 percent for classified civilian employees to 6.0 percent for postal employees. In line with the policy set forth in the 1967 economic report, these increases were equal to the increase in trend productivity plus an increase *less* than the full rise in the CPI. In other words, they were less than the sum of productivity (3.2 percent) and the full increase in the CPI (2.9 percent).

1968. In the 1968 report, the Council of Economic Advisers warned that even without further acceleration, the continuation of the 1967

---

[36] *Economic Report*, 1968, p. 125.

[37] *Ibid.*, p. 108.

[38] *Ibid.*, p. 106.

pattern of wage and benefit increases (averaging 5.5 percent over the life of the contract) would lead to an "appreciably larger" rise in compensation for the economy as a whole, since deferred increases due in 1968 would be generally greater than in 1967.

Whatever faint hopes the administration may have had for avoiding further acceleration of wages were swept away by the unexpected vigor of the recovery. GNP rose by $71 billion from 1967 to 1968—some $10 billion more than anticipated—while real GNP rose nearly $40 billion, or nearly 5.0 percent, clearly exceeding the estimated increase in the economy's potential of roughly 4.0 percent. Nonfarm employment rose by 2.0 million, or 3.0 percent, and the decline in unemployment to 3.3 percent (seasonally adjusted) in December resulted in an annual unemployment rate of 3.6 percent, the lowest in fifteen years.

This combination of excess aggregate demand and an extremely tight labor market was reflected in the renewed acceleration of compensation per man-hour, which rose from 5.8 percent in 1967 to 7.6 percent in 1968. This was the largest gain since 1951, and, as we now know, the largest gain of the period 1966-1970. Though output also rose in response to the recovery, the substantial gains in productivity witnessed in the period, 1960-1965, were no longer possible. Thus, although output per man-hour rose 2.9 percent (compared to 2.0 percent in 1967), unit labor costs continued to accelerate, from 3.6 percent in 1967 to 4.6 percent in 1968, the greatest increase in unit labor costs since 1956.

Unlike the expansion of 1966, when a light bargaining schedule blunted the ability of organized labor as a whole to take advantage of the expansion, the 1968 bargaining schedule was unusually heavy, with 4.9 million workers subject to current negotiations. This included nearly one million in basic steel, whose impact on prices is particularly heavy. Accordingly, wage increases under collective bargaining were not only the largest in ten years but, more significantly, they accelerated more rapidly than in any other year of the five-year period, 1966-1970. Thus, the median first-year wage adjustment for all major collective bargaining settlements rose to 7.2 percent, over 25.0 percent more than the 5.6 percent increase of 1967.

The principal source of this rapid acceleration in the size of wage gains, however, was not in manufacturing, where settlements tended to follow the pattern set in the auto industry in late 1967 (the $0.20 first-year wage increase in the 1968 steel settlement, for example, was identical to that in autos) and accelerated rather moderately, from 6.4 percent in 1967 to 6.9 percent in 1968. Instead, the impetus came mainly from nonmanufacturing, where the median settlement was 7.5 percent, half again as large as the 5.0 percent rise in 1967.

Acceleration in the rate of wage increase was not confined to union settlements, however. Average hourly earnings in the private economy increased by 6.3 percent, compared to a 4.7 percent gain in 1967; this acceleration was even more rapid than that of first-year wage adjustments under collective bargaining.

1969. When the Nixon administration took office in January 1969, its primary domestic goal was to bring inflation under control. Its plan for achieving that goal was to rely primarily on monetary and fiscal policy to reduce aggregate demand, assuming that the slowdown in economic activity would in turn lead to a reduction in the rate of wage and price increases. The plan for 1969 pointedly "did not include an attempt to revive wage-price guideposts." [39] Instead, the administration's strategy was to supplement monetary and fiscal policy by exercising its influence in markets where it was a direct participant, either as buyer or seller, by avoiding inflationary behavior on its own part, and by correcting market malfunctions which might contribute to inflation. [40]

It was this approach, rather than that of direct restraint, that was first used by the Nixon administration to attack the problem of accelerating wage increases in the construction industry. In September 1969 the government announced that it would cut new contracts for direct federal construction by 75.0 percent until conditions eased in the economy or in the construction industry. In addition, the President established the Construction Industry Collective Bargaining Commission, which was to explore ways for improving the functioning of both the construction labor market and of bargaining processes in the industry. [41]

On the supply side, the administration initiated the so-called Philadelphia Plan, which was designed to increase the number of blacks employed on federal construction projects (thereby simultaneously working to reduce discrimination *and* inflation) by requiring contractors bidding on these projects to try to meet minority hiring goals, generally described as quotas. [42]

---

[39] *Economic Report*, 1970, p. 23.

[40] *Ibid.*, p. 25.

[41] *Ibid.*, pp. 42-43.

[42] *Ibid.*, p. 116.

But the new monetary and fiscal policies had little impact on the labor market in 1969; the record-breaking pace of expansion continued almost unabated, although it eased slightly as the year progressed. Nonfarm payroll employment increased by 3.4 percent to 70,139,000, as against a 3.0 percent gain in 1968. The unemployment rate declined still further, from 3.6 percent in 1968 to 3.5 percent for the full year 1969, the lowest level in 17 years. On a quarterly basis, however, the seasonally adjusted unemployment rate showed the first signs of the changed economic policies. It edged up from a low of 3.4 percent in the first quarter of 1969 to 3.6 percent in the third and fourth quarters.

Under these circumstances, compensation continued to rise, though at a slightly decelerated rate of 7.4 percent compared to the 7.6 percent of 1968. More important, in terms of its impact on inflation, was the dismal performance of productivity. In the first half of 1969, output per man-hour actually declined, while on an annual basis it rose a scant 0.5 percent, the smallest gain since 1956. This in turn led to a record-breaking rise of 7.0 percent in unit labor costs, the highest such increase since World War II, and to a consequent acceleration of inflation. The annual rate of increase in the CPI rose from 4.2 percent in 1962 to 5.4 percent, the largest increase since 1951.

Collective bargaining was at the low point of its customary three-year cycle, with only 2.5 million workers scheduled for contract negotiations and 7.3 million eligible for deferred increases set in previous years. Because of the high proportion of deferred increases, the median *effective* wage adjustment (the combination of current and deferred adjustments) was smaller in 1969 (5.1 percent for all industries) than in 1968 (5.5 percent). Thus the *net* impact of collective bargaining on compensation per man-hour in the private economy appears to have been less in 1969 than in 1968—not as a result of administration policy or union restraint, but as a fortuitous result of the collective bargaining calendar.

The median first-year wage adjustment, however, continued to accelerate, though not as rapidly as it had in 1968, rising from 7.2 percent in 1968 to 8.0 percent in 1969. As in 1966 and 1968, most of this rise was attributable to settlements in nonmanufacturing industries, which rose from 7.5 percent in 1968 to 10.0 percent in 1969. In manufacturing, on the other hand, first-year gains were only slightly higher than in 1968—7.0 percent compared to 6.9 percent.

Wage increases averaged over the life of the contract, on the other hand, accelerated considerably more rapidly than first-year increases. They rose by 6.8 percent for all industries, compared to 5.2 percent the previous year, suggesting that new contracts were less "front-loaded" than before—i.e., that emphasis was shifting from catching up with past inflation toward hedging against future inflation.

Other significant factors in the rise in compensation per man-hour included a 6.7 percent increase in average hourly earnings, the largest in eighteen years; another round of pay increases for federal employees, 9.1 percent for the armed forces and classified civil servants and 4.1 percent for postal employees; and an increase in the federal minimum wage.

1970. In 1970 the effects of the restrictive monetary and fiscal policies set in motion in early 1969 showed clearly in the labor market, most noticeably in the unemployment rate. The seasonally adjusted unemployment rate rose steadily throughout the year, from 3.5 percent in December 1969 to 5.0 in July 1970, and by December 1970 to 6.0 percent, the highest monthly rate since December 1961. The annual unemployment rate rose by 40.0 percent, from 3.5 percent in 1969 to 4.9 percent in 1970. Nonfarm payroll employment (seasonally adjusted) dropped steadily from March to November, ending with an *annual* gain of only 0.6 percent, the smallest annual increase since 1960.

Despite talk to the contrary, the slackening of the labor market *was* reflected promptly, if not substantially, in wages and compensation generally. For the second year in a row, there was a slowdown in the rate of increase in compensation per man-hour, from 7.4 percent in 1969 to 7.3 percent in 1970 (the figures then available indicated a shift from 7.2 percent to 7.1 percent). This was the first *two-year* deceleration in the growth of compensation since the recession of 1960-1961.

Output per man-hour rose a scant 0.9 percent, but nonetheless was up from an even poorer 0.5 percent gain in 1969. For the first time since 1958, however, the gain was due to cutbacks in man-hours rather than to increased output.[43] The slowdown in the growth of compensation and the rise in productivity produced a slowdown in the growth of unit labor costs from 7.0 percent to 6.3 percent, the first such slowdown since 1965. But because of the acceleration in unit *non-labor* costs—interest, depreciation, and

---

[43] *Monthly Labor Review*, May 1971, p. 3.

taxes—prices rose slightly faster than in 1969, up 5.9 percent as against 5.4 percent in 1969.[44]

The growth in average hourly earnings also slowed, down to 6.3 percent from 6.7 percent in 1969, largely because the reduction in the average workweek meant a cutback in overtime pay. On the other hand, wage gains under collective bargaining continued to accelerate, apparently unaffected by rising unemployment. The median first-year wage adjustments were 10.0 percent for all industries (as against 8.0 percent in 1969), 7.5 percent in manufacturing (versus 7.0 percent in 1969), and 14.2 percent in nonmanufacturing (up from 10.0 percent in 1969).

While few analysts expected union rates to be as sensitive to the slowdown in economic activity as other wages, the administration was particularly concerned by the performance in construction, where the median first-year adjustment for 1970 as a whole was 16.3 percent, or more than twice the 7.5 percent in manufacturing, and where the *average* (as distinct from the median) first-year wage adjustment had accelerated from 15.5 percent in the first quarter of 1970 to 22.1 percent in the third quarter, the period of peak construction activity.

1966-70 Summary. The distinguishing economic feature of the period 1966-1970 was accelerating inflation, associated with slow productivity growth and rapid gains in compensation.

Productivity. Although in 1966, in response to the surge of demand produced by the escalation of the war in Vietnam, the rate of gain in productivity accelerated from the 3.4 percent of 1965 to 4.0 percent, from 1966 to 1969 productivity grew more and more slowly and finally came to a complete halt. In the first half of 1969, in fact, productivity actually declined, while for the year as a whole it rose a scant 0.5 percent. In 1970, although the rate of productivity gain rose slightly, this reflected not a quickening of economic activity but the fact that man-hours declined even more than output. Taking 1969 and 1970 together, the productivity gain was the lowest for any two consecutive years since 1947, and the only two-year period when the average annual increase was less than 1.0 percent.

For the five years, 1966-1970, the average annual increase in productivity was only 2.0 percent, little more than half the 3.8 percent average of 1960-1965 and, more important, the smallest

---

[44] *Ibid.*

average increase for any five-year period since World War II. It was also well below the 1947-1965 average of 3.4 percent.

Compensation Per Man-hour. So far as compensation per man-hour is concerned, the period 1966-1970 offers a sharp contrast to the preceding five years. From 1960 to 1965, as we have seen, the rate of increase in compensation fluctuated around an average of 4.3 percent per year, and compensation was not increasing substantially faster in 1965 (at 4.1 percent) than in 1961 (at 3.8 percent).

In 1966, however, compensation per man-hour accelerated sharply, from 4.1 percent to 6.9 percent, the sharpest acceleration since 1956. After a slowdown in 1967, another acceleration brought the rate of increase in compensation in 1968 to 7.6 percent, the largest gain since 1951.

The average annual gain in compensation for the period 1966-1970 as a whole was 7.0 percent, the highest such increase for any five-year period since World War II, and substantially above the average annual increase of 5.0 percent from 1947 to 1965. But it is significant that, since 1968, the rate of increase in compensation slowed for two consecutive years, declining from 7.6 percent in 1968 to 7.3 percent in 1970.

Unit Labor Costs. Under the combined impact of record declines in productivity growth and record gains in compensation, unit labor costs accelerated to new records during this period. From a low of 0.8 percent in 1965, unit labor costs in the total private economy accelerated for four consecutive years to a high of 7.0 percent in 1969, a figure which exceeded the previous postwar record gain of 6.4 percent set in 1951.

A turning point may have been reached in 1970, however, when a deceleration in compensation coincided with a slight gain in productivity, to produce the first reduction in the rate of growth of unit labor costs (from 7.0 percent in 1969 to 6.3 percent in 1970) since 1965. Despite the easing of unit labor costs in 1970, their average annual increase for the five years 1966-1970 was 4.9 percent, more than ten times the average annual increase in the preceding five years, and more than triple the 1947-1965 average of 1.6 percent. It seems clear, however, that the rapid increase in unit labor costs during the years, 1966 through 1969, is as much due to the decline of productivity gains as to the rise in compensation. *Both* are responsible.

Wages Under Collective Bargaining. Wage increases in collective bargaining settlements accelerated continuously throughout the period 1966-1970. The median first-year wage adjustment for major settlements in all industries rose from 4.8 percent in 1966 to 10.0 percent in 1970 and, for the five-year period as a whole, the annual average of the median first-year wage adjustments was 7.1 percent, more than double the 3.1 percent for the period 1961-1965. In manufacturing, the median first-year wage adjustment rose from 4.2 percent in 1966 to 7.5 percent in 1970, while in nonmanufacturing, it rose from 5.0 percent in 1966 to 14.2 percent in 1970.

Of particular interest is the fact that the acceleration in the size of collective bargaining settlements continued unabated in 1969 and 1970, although the rate of increase in compensation in the total private economy slowed slightly in both years. Thus the experience of 1966-1970 was the counterpart of 1961-1965. In both cases, wages under collective bargaining were slower in responding to changes in economic conditions than was compensation in the total private economy.

Real compensation. During the period 1966-1970, real compensation per man-hour rose, but at a decreasing rate—from 3.3 percent in 1966 to 1.2 percent in 1970. Nevertheless, its average annual rate of increase of 2.5 percent was slightly higher than the average annual increase in output per man-hour of 2.1 percent. As a consequence, employee compensation rose from 70.2 percent of national income in 1966 to 74.9 percent in 1970.[45] The 1966-1970 record thus contrasted sharply with that of 1961-1965, when real compensation lagged behind productivity and the share of national income going to employee compensation declined.

The Evolution of Incomes Policy, 1970-71

In the first few months of 1970, as we have seen, the effectiveness of restrictive monetary and fiscal policy in slowing down the economy became evident. Unemployment increased by 800,000 (seasonally adjusted), or nearly 30.0 percent, in just three months (from December 1969 to March 1970). But the pace of inflation continued to accelerate. Concern thus shifted from reducing excess demand to trying simultaneously to induce expansion and cope with cost-push inflation.

With this shift began a prolonged and widespread public dis-

---

[45] *First Inflation Alert*, II, p. 26.

cussion of the desirability of some form of incomes policy [46] to further supplement monetary and fiscal policy. Indeed, few other labor market policies have been so thoroughly debated as was the issue of incomes policy in the 18 months between February 1970 and August 1971, when President Nixon announced the 90-day wage-price freeze.

In March 1970 the majority of the Joint Economic Committee criticized the administration's "hands-off" wage policy as a failure and called for a "consciously enunciated price and incomes policy" as a "standard part of the policy mix." [47] Chairman Wright Patman and Representatives Henry Reuss and William Moorehead went still further, calling for a temporary moratorium on price and wage increases in order to allow time to develop an appropriate price and incomes policy. [48]

Public discussion of incomes policy by top government officials began in 'May, in what were described as breaks with administration policy, when Arthur Burns, the recently appointed chairman of the Federal Reserve Board, suggested that "There may be a useful albeit very modest, role for an incomes policy to play in shortening the period between the suppression of excess demand and restoration of price stability" [49] and Secretary of Housing and Urban Development Romney simultaneously urged the use of inflation alerts.

In mid-June, after it became known that unemployment had reached 5.0 percent in May, the President took a short step in the direction of incomes policy by announcing a plan (the one suggested by Secretary Romney) for inflation alerts to spotlight significant wage and price increases and by creating both a National Commission on Productivity and a Regulations and Purchasing Review Board. The latter was charged with reviewing the impact on inflation of federal procurement practices.

---

[46] "Incomes policy" is a broad term. It has been applied to measures ranging from the inflation alerts issued by the Nixon administration to statutory wage and price controls. In general, incomes policies involve restraints on *both* incomes and prices. In many European countries, they are viewed as more than just anti-inflationary devices and are utilized to implement basic social policy, such as income distribution, as well.

Gottfried Haberler has classified as a second type of incomes policies antitrust and labor policies designed to make the economy more competitive. See his *Incomes Policies and Inflation: An Analysis of Basic Principles* (Washington: American Enterprise Institute, 1971).

[47] U.S. Congress, Joint Economic Committee, *1970 Joint Economic Report* (Washington: Government Printing Office, 1970), p. 21.

[48] *Ibid.*, p. 58.

[49] *New York Times*, May 19, 1970.

Two inflation alerts were published in 1970 and one in 1971. The first, issued August 7, 1970, emphasized the importance of increased productivity in improving cost-price performance and noted that the response to inflation seems to depend "not only on the rate of the inflation but also on its longevity." On the collective bargaining side, it displayed some concern over the rate of wage increase in construction.

The second alert, published December 1, 1970, was essentially a review of third-quarter developments. Its chief concern was the failure of wages to "slow down in response to the slack in the economy. . . ." [50] In particular it noted that in spite of an unemployment rate in the construction industry of 11.9 percent (seasonally adjusted) in October, the average first-year wage adjustment in that industry was 22.1 percent in the third quarter.

Following the November elections, whose results were disappointing for the administration and generally attributed to dissatisfaction with domestic economic performance, the administration promptly began to move toward more direct intervention on the wage front. In a wide-ranging speech to the National Association of Manufacturers on December 4, the President warned that the structure of collective bargaining in the construction industry might need to be "consolidated" [51] and that unless labor and management in the industry reformed themselves, the government might intervene in wage negotiations on federal projects. This warning, of course, was in line with the administration's initial policy of utilizing procurement as an anti-inflation device; it was not a move towards a general incomes policy.

These developments also led Arthur Burns to renew his public fight for an incomes policy, as well as to offer an 11-point list of measures to aid in the fight against inflation. The list included among others the suspension of the Davis-Bacon Act and the establishment of a national wage-price review board. [52]

The presidential warning to the construction industry, however, produced no plan, and late in February 1971 the President suspended the Davis-Bacon Act, under which the federal government requires that contractors on federally financed construction projects pay "prevailing" wages, a term generally synonymous with union wages. The suspension was short-lived, however. In late

---

[50] *Ibid.*

[51] Antitrust enthusiasts note: this was a call for further centralization, *not* decentralization.

[52] *New York Times*, December 7, 1970.

March it was terminated and the Davis-Bacon Act restored. In turn came a wage review board for the construction industry—the Construction Industry Stabilization Committee—with authority to approve wage settlements in construction. The suspension of the Davis-Bacon Act appears to have been only a tactical maneuver to force the building trades unions to accept the wage review board.

Since the experience of the Construction Industry Stabilization Committee may be indicative of what to expect from stabilization policy during Phase II, its criteria for acceptable wage increases are of particular significance. According to these criteria, which are set forth in Executive Order 11588 establishing the committee, wage and benefit increases may reflect *both* productivity and cost-of-living trends (possibly a reflection of the Council of Economic Advisers' limited endorsement of escalator clauses in its 1971 report). However such increases are not to exceed the "average of the median increase in wages and benefits over the life of the contract in major construction settlements in the period 1961 to 1968"—a figure generally estimated at approximately 6.0 percent. In addition, equity adjustments are permitted. (These standards closely resemble those subsequently adopted by the National Pay Board.)

It soon became apparent, however, that the 6.0 percent target was intended as a long-run goal, not one which was expected to be reached in 1971. In fact the average wage increase in major settlements (those covering 1,000 workers or more) approved by the Construction Industry Stabilization Committee in the six-month period, April-September 1971, was 11.3 percent over the life of the contract,[53] or roughly three-fourths the average 15.5 percent increase in the comparable period in 1970. While the experience in construction suggests that the Pay Board may move rather slowly toward its 5.5 percent productivity plus cost-of-living wage target, it also furnishes one clue as to the degree of improvement that is feasible.

The establishment of the Construction Industry Stabilization Committee marked another step in the administration's shift toward active wage restraints, but it did little to quell the continued clamor for a general incomes policy. And the economic pressures which fueled this clamor continued unabated. After easing from a high of 6.2 percent (seasonally adjusted) in December 1970 to 5.8 percent in February 1971, the unemployment rate rose for three consecutive

---

[53] "Major Collective Bargaining Settlements, First Nine Months 1971," Bureau of Labor Statistics Release, October 29, 1971, p. 2.

months, reaching 6.2 percent again in May 1971. And in May, the CPI increased at an annual rate of 6.0 percent.

The administration was being pushed toward a decision. In mid-June Paul McCracken, chairman of the Council of Economic Advisers, announced that the President would decide "in July or August whether to stay with the plan or propose new stimulants." Arthur Burns continued to lead the fight for a general incomes policy.

Initially the administration appeared determined to stay with the plan: A high-level review of the economic situation at the end of June brought an announcement of "no change" from Secretary of the Treasury Connally, as well as the report of specific decisions against establishing either wage-price review boards or mandatory wage and price controls. But even this apparently unequivocal decision failed to silence its critics. Arthur Burns, whose position as chairman of the Federal Reserve Board gave him a degree of independence, promptly announced his continued concern over the spread of inflationary psychology.

Perhaps the first clue to the final change in the administration position came in the President's news conference of August 4, 1971, when he asserted that although he was not convinced about wage-price review boards, "we have an open mind" about proposals for dealing with wages and prices. Eleven days later he announced the 90-day wage-price freeze.

Important as it no doubt was, Burns's persistent fight for a general incomes policy could hardly have succeeded had it not been that the data on economic activity for the first half of 1971 made painfully clear how little progress was being made in reducing either unemployment or inflation. The overall unemployment rate of 5.8 percent in July was no lower than it had been six months earlier, in February; indeed, unemployment was expected to rise in August due to widespread layoffs in steel. In some significant aspects the unemployment picture had worsened: the unemployment rate for blacks had risen to 10.1 percent, compared to 9.5 percent in January, and the number of long-term unemployed (those unemployed 15 weeks or more) had reached 1,300,000 (seasonally adjusted), the highest figure since 1963, both in absolute and in percentage terms.

The wage picture was hardly more encouraging. Omitting construction settlements, only nine of which were included in the reports on major collective bargaining settlements in the first six months, the annual rates of wage increase over the life of the contract were higher in the first half of 1971 than in the full year of 1970. Thus, in manufacturing, the life of the contract increase in the first-half of 1971 was 6.4 percent, against 6.0 percent for the full year of 1970, and in nonmanufacturing 10.5 percent compared to 10.2 percent for the full year of 1970. Moreover, first-year wage increases in manufacturing were 8.7 percent versus 8.1 percent for the full year of 1970, although in nonmanufacturing there was an easing of first-year wage increases to 11.9 percent, down from 14.2 percent for the full year of 1970.

On the price side, after easing in the first quarter of 1971, the CPI had turned up again in the second quarter. Thus after rising at an average rate of 0.2 percent per month, or 2.4 percent on an annual basis, during the first quarter of 1971, the CPI accelerated so that by June it was rising at an annual rate of 6.0 percent. Perhaps equally disconcerting was the 0.7 percent (8.4 percent on an annual basis) rise in wholesale industrial prices in July, the steepest increase since August 1956.

Compelling as the domestic economic problem was, however, the conclusion is inescapable that the decisive factor in the administration's about-face on incomes policy was the growing threat of a run on the dollar in the international money markets in the second week in August. Indeed, in a television appearance on July 25, Secretary Connally had indicated that persistent international monetary and balance-of-payments problems could trigger a change in the administration's wage policy. Thus, as in 1962, the decision to restrain wages and prices was directly affected by the demands of foreign economic policy.

The sequel to the 90-day wage-price freeze was announced by President Nixon on October 7, 1971. As widely anticipated, wage and price control could not be terminated after 90 days, for such a brief pay pause, however effective, could not be sufficient to end inflation. The freeze was to be replaced by Phase II, with wages to be regulated by a tripartite Pay Board and prices by a Price Commission. The overall objective was to reduce the rate of price increase to an annual rate of 2.0 to 3.0 percent by the end of 1972.

The Pay Board, in announcing its general pay standard, or basic wage formula, on November 8, stated that permissible general increases would be "those normally considered supportable by productivity improvement and cost of living trends" (a principle identical to that set forth in the executive order establishing the Construction Industry Stabilization Committee). It specified that "Initially, the general pay standard is established as 5.5 percent." [54]

Given the Pay Board's assumption of a long-term productivity trend of 3 percent, it is clear that the 5.5 percent pay standard is consistent with the administration's goal of 2.0 to 3.0 percent price increases. But both the experience of the Construction Industry Stabilization Committee and the administration's announcement of its price target for the "end of 1972" suggest that it would be realistic to regard late 1972 as the target date for the general pay standard as well.

Analysis

The Guideposts. In appraising the effectiveness of the guideposts, the pertinent data generally indicate that wages increased less rapidly *during* the guidepost period than either before or afterward. Thus, during the period from 1961 through 1965, the first four years of the guideposts and the period generally treated as the one in which they were effective, key wage developments were as follows:

> Straight-time average hourly earnings of production workers in manufacturing increased at an annual rate of 2.7 percent, compared to 3.1 percent annually in the preceding four years, 1958-1961.
>
> Median first-year wage adjustments in major collective bargaining agreements averaged 3.2 percent per year, conforming almost exactly to the general wage guideposts. This compares to an annual rate of 3.4 percent in the preceding four years.
>
> Even in construction, generally considered the bellwether of rapid wage increases, the index of union wage rates increased at a rate of only 3.8 percent per year, as against 4.3 percent in the four years, 1958-1961.

In contrast, in the period 1966 through 1970, as the labor market grew tighter and the guideposts were first seriously damaged (1966) and then completely abandoned (1969), the results were these:

> Straight-time average hourly earnings in manufacturing increased at an annual rate of 5.2 percent. In 1970 alone they increased by 5.9 percent.
>
> Median first-year adjustments in major collective bargain-

---

[54] *New York Times*, November 9, 1971.

ing settlements rose from 4.8 percent in 1966 to 10.0 percent in 1970, and averaged 7.1 percent over the five years.

The index of union wage rates in construction rose by an average 7.4 percent per year—and by 12.3 percent in 1970 alone.

Using these measures of wage change, it is evident that wages rose less during the four-year guidepost period, 1962-1965, than in the years preceding or following that period. Furthermore, both straight-time hourly earnings in manufacturing and first-year collective bargaining settlements stayed within the limits of the guideposts for the years, 1962-1965.

It should be noted however, that fringe benefits rose more rapidly than wages during this period, particularly under collective bargaining. Indeed, for all but the last four months of the period, 1962-1965, there was *no* general wage increase in the steel industry; general increases consisted entirely of fringe benefits. Thus the increases in wages alone, without including increases in fringe benefits, *understate* the actual increase in compensation and *overstate* the apparent impact of the guideposts.

A glance at other measures of wage changes since 1962 shows what happened to wages *not* subject to the guideposts. In manufacturing, the only industry for which we have direct comparisons between union and nonunion wages, we find that during the period, 1962-1965, nonunion wages consistently rose more rapidly than those in unionized plants. The median annual increase in nonunion wages was 3.7 percent, compared to 3.2 percent in unionized plants. Moreover, the most rapid increase in average hourly earnings from 1961 to 1965 was the 3.9 percent annual increase in the retail trades, an industry in which not more than 15.0 percent of the employees are unionized. Part of this rapid increase, undoubtedly, is attributable to the impact of the rise in the federal minimum wage and its impact on retail trade.

The fact that wages rose most rapidly in the sectors not covered by the guideposts—the nonunion and the service sectors of the economy—lends additional support to the contention that the guideposts were effective where they were intended to be. But it also reveals their basic limitation, the fact that they were not designed to cope with the problems of wage increases in nonunion situations or in competitive industries, regardless of how rapidly those wages might be rising. Yet even after the guideposts were abandoned, wage pressures were generally greater in the nonmanufacturing and service industries than in manufacturing. Clearly the problem of wage restraint in these industries is one that must be taken into consideration in any future stabilization plan.

Nevertheless the evidence is clear that *when* and *where* the guideposts were applied, wages increased less rapidly than otherwise. But the question still remains: To what extent, if any, was this pattern the *result* of the guideposts? Or to be more precise, were wage increases any less than they would have been without the guideposts?

The main problem in evaluating the impact of the guideposts is that they coincided with a period of relatively high unemployment, which permitted substantial expansion before the labor market got tight, and of unusually large productivity gains, which were in themselves a powerful anti-inflationary factor. In short, even without the guideposts, wages and unit labor costs would have risen less rapidly than usual.

Perhaps the leading defender of the effectiveness of the guideposts is George L. Perry, who concluded that, during the first 17 quarters of the operation of the guideposts, wages in manufacturing rose *less* rapidly than would have been expected on the basis of wage trends from either 1947-1960 or 1953-1960, and that by 1968, 18 months after the guideposts had been breached, wages rose *more* than predicted by the same equation. His conclusion was that "on the present evidence, I feel one must now try to *disprove* the impact of the guideposts, rather than the other way round." [55]

On the other hand, Otto Eckstein is perhaps representative of the critics when he concludes that "the impact of the guideposts could not begin to match the size of the unexplained residuals." [56] In addition, John Sheahan, in *The Wage-Price Guideposts*, the most comprehensive study of this subject, asserts that "it is impossible to prove or disprove the hypothesis that the guideposts were an important factor in this achievement . . . because no one can be completely sure of what would have happened if they had not existed." [57]

On balance, we conclude that the impact of the guideposts in restraining wages during the period 1962 through 1965 is *uncertain*. Whatever their effectiveness, of course, it was felt in only a limited part of the economy, the area in which discretionary pricing power

---

[55] George L. Perry, "Wages and the Guideposts," *American Economic Review*, September 1967, pp. 897-904; and "Wages and the Guideposts: Reply," *ibid.*, June 1969, p. 369.

[56] Otto Eckstein, "Money Wage Determination Revisited," *Review of Economic Studies*, April 1968, p. 139.

[57] Sheahan, *op. cit.*, p. 79.

existed, which is the only area in which *voluntary* wage restraints are feasible.[58]

The case for guideposts, or perhaps for a more comprehensive method of restraining wages, rests less on the evidence of their effectiveness than on the economic and social costs of the alternative of imposing restraint by unemployment. The basic problem is that unemployment is not only a costly way of restraining wages, but a clumsy and inefficient way of doing so as well. As we have been pointedly reminded in 1970 and 1971, unemployment may rise to politically and socially unacceptable levels *before* it brings about a significant reduction in the rate of wage increase. In the absence of stronger evidence that wage restraints are of *no* value, there is great pressure to impose them in the hope that they may help reduce inflation to an acceptable level more rapidly or with lower unemployment levels than would otherwise be the case. In August 1971, the pressure proved irresistible.

Voluntary versus Mandatory Restraints. One problem of *voluntary* guideposts of the kind we had from 1962 through 1966 is that their application is necessarily limited to firms and unions possessing discretionary power with respect to wages and prices. Where discretionary power is lacking, there *is* no choice, and neither firms nor unions can *voluntarily* modify their behavior.

This limitation poses no problem *if* the primary source of cost-push pressures is, in fact, the firms and unions with discretionary power, although the problem of obtaining their cooperation would remain. But as we have seen, the most rapid wage increases generally have come from the service-producing industries, where relatively few firms possess discretionary power over prices, and where, except in transportation, unions are generally rather weak. Indeed, the evidence strongly suggests that inflationary pressures may be stronger in the service-producing industries than in the goods-producing industries. Not only do wages tend to rise faster in the service-producing industries, but productivity growth tends to be slower than in the goods-producing sector. Finally, the service-producing sector is not only larger but growing more rapidly than the goods-producing sector. In the twenty years, 1950 to 1970, employment in the service-producing industries rose from 59.1 percent to 66.9 percent of nonagricultural payroll employment; the trend is likely to continue.

Thus the mandatory restraints of Phase II have the potential of

---

[58] For a somewhat different assessment of the guideposts, see Moore, chapter 4, this volume.

being more effective than the 1962-1966 wage guideposts, not only because they are enforceable, but also because they have wider applicability than voluntary restraints.

Cost of Living. One of the fundamental weaknesses of a straight productivity standard for wage increases, such as was followed in the 1962 wage guideposts, is that whatever acceptability it may have with labor is contingent upon price stability. But when prices are rising substantially, as they have been since 1966, adherence to a productivity guidepost for wages would lead to declining real wages, an obviously unacceptable situation for labor.

One solution to this problem would be some form of cost-of-living clause that would provide for wage adjustments related or tied to the rise in the Consumer Price Index and thus protect the worker against the erosion of his real wage. This could be done through escalator clauses in union contracts, an approach which received at least cautious encouragement from the Council of Economic Advisers in the 1971 report, or more directly, by including the cost of living as a factor in the basic wage policy, as has been done in both the construction industry stabilization program, and in the general pay standards announced by the Pay Board for Phase II. The cost-of-living factor, in fact, is probably the most important substantive difference between the current wage policy and the 1962 wage guidepost.

Equally important from the policy standpoint is that cost-of-living adjustments make it possible to avoid (in the case of unlimited escalators with no ceiling), or to minimize, the tendency of unions with long-term contracts to try to compensate for *past* inflation by the use of "catch-up" wage increases when contracts are renewed. So long as wage decisions reflect *past* problems, they are less responsive to *current* economic conditions than they might be—a circumstance which helps explain the failure of collective bargaining settlements in 1970 and the first half of 1971 to fully reflect the high unemployment rates then prevailing.

But with some form of cost-of-living clause, workers would be compensated (more or less fully) for price rises on a current basis and therefore would have less need to "catch up" at contract renewal time. Perhaps most significant of all, when inflation does begin to recede, wages determined by collective bargaining might respond more quickly, there being less need either to correct for previous errors or to try to anticipate future price changes.

Obviously, the decision as to how much cost-of-living adjustment should be permitted is a vital one. While unions are likely to prefer full or unlimited escalation, the need for more rapid progress in the fight against inflation may dictate imposing limits on cost-of-living adjustments. This appears to be the policy adopted by the Pay Board.

Productivity. A review of the inflationary performance of the economy from 1965 through 1970 makes it clear that the rise in unit labor costs during that time cannot be explained by wage pressures alone. Responsibility for the rise must be shared roughly equally by the pronounced and prolonged slowdown in productivity. For the four years, 1967-1970, for example, output per man-hour rose at an average of only 1.5 percent, less than half of either the 1947-1970 average of 3.2 percent or the 1947-1965 average of 3.4 percent. And for the five years, 1966-1970, the average annual increase in productivity was 2.0 percent, the slowest growth of any five-year period in the quarter century 1946-1971.

Given this subnormal rate of increase in productivity, it is clear that even *if* compensation increases had been successfully restrained to the guidepost figure of 3.2 percent throughout the period 1966-1970, compensation per man-hour would have exceeded output per man-hour each year from 1967 through 1970, and unit labor costs would have risen and prices along with them. In short, even without the acceleration in compensation, the slowdown in productivity would have led to increasing unit labor costs and to cost-push pressures on prices.

Now, of course, this is only part of the story. Compensation *did* rise, and rapidly, and it substantially *reinforced* the cost-push provided by declining productivity growth.

Conversely, *if* the rate of productivity growth had remained constant on the 3.4 percent trend of 1947-1965, the rise in compensation would have brought about rising unit costs and cost-push inflation.

The point is, then, that the four-year spurt in unit labor costs from 1965 through 1969 was the product of *two* forces, accelerating compensation growth and decelerating productivity growth, either of which by itself was strong enough to raise unit labor costs and create inflationary pressures. Taken together they were sufficient to push unit costs, and subsequently retail prices, to their greatest increases in a quarter-century. This suggests that the prompt restoration of trend rates of productivity growth is as crucial to the fight on inflation as effective wage restraint. Both are essential to the success of the stabilization program.

Having made this point, a word about the nature of productivity is in order. Although output per man-hour is commonly referred to as "labor productivity," it must be emphasized that it is not a measure of the productivity of labor alone, but simply a measure of the output *associated with* a particular unit of *input*—namely, one hour of production labor. A variety of factors affect this output, one of its most important determinants being the amount of capital equipment involved in the process. Labor effort *may* also affect output per man-hour, but it is not the sole or even necessarily the most important variable.

It is also important to realize that higher productivity does not necessarily mean *more output*. Higher productivity also results when the same output is achieved with fewer man-hours of input. In 1970, as we have seen, productivity rose even though output dropped, because man-hours dropped even more than output. And when higher productivity is the result of the same output with less input, it usually means less employment. This possibility, by no means unrealistic as recent experience indicates, is the basis for workers' fears about productivity and for their not infrequent opposition to technical advances which promise higher productivity.

To put it another way, increased productivity may be the basis for increased real income and higher living standards, or it *may* also mean producing the same income with fewer people, in which case it becomes a road to increased unemployment. In that event, higher productivity could become simply a mechanism for substituting unemployment for inflation, a dubious gain indeed.

It is clear, therefore, that the task of public policy is to insure that productivity growth be utilized to provide more output, not more unemployment.

Table 1
OUTPUT PER MAN-HOUR, TOTAL PRIVATE ECONOMY
(Index 1967=100)

Year	Index of Output Per Man-Hour	Percent Change
1947	51.3	
1948	53.6	4.5
1949	55.3	3.2
1950	59.7	8.0
1951	61.5	3.0
1952	62.7	2.0
1953	65.3	4.1
1954	66.9	2.5
1955	69.9	4.5
1956	70.0	0.1
1957	72.0	2.9
1958	74.3	3.2
1959	76.9	3.5
1960	78.2	1.7
1961	80.9	3.5
1962	84.7	4.7
1963	87.7	3.5
1964	91.1	3.9
1965	94.2	3.4
1966	98.0	4.0
1967	100.0	2.0
1968	102.9	2.9
1969	103.4	0.5
1970	104.3	0.9

Source: Bureau of Labor Statistics.

Table 2
COMPENSATION PER MAN-HOUR, TOTAL PRIVATE ECONOMY
(Index 1967=100)

Year	Index of Compensation Per Man-Hour	Percent Change
1947	36.2	
1948	39.5	9.1
1949	40.1	1.5
1950	42.8	6.7
1951	46.9	9.6
1952	49.8	6.2
1953	52.9	6.2
1954	54.5	3.0
1955	55.9	2.6

Table 2 (continued)

1956	59.5	6.4
1957	63.3	6.4
1958	66.0	4.3
1959	69.0	4.5
1960	71.7	3.9
1961	74.4	3.8
1962	77.7	4.4
1963	80.8	4.1
1964	84.9	5.1
1965	88.4	4.1
1966	94.5	6.9
1967	100.0	5.8
1968	107.6	7.6
1969	115.6	7.4
1970	124.0	7.3

Source: Bureau of Labor Statistics.

Table 3

UNIT LABOR COSTS, TOTAL PRIVATE ECONOMY
(Index 1967=100)

Year	Index of Unit Labor Costs	Percent Change
1947	70.6	
1948	73.7	4.4
1949	72.5	−1.6
1950	71.7	−1.1
1951	76.3	6.4
1952	79.4	4.1
1953	81.0	2.0
1954	81.5	0.6
1955	80.1	−1.7
1956	85.0	6.1
1957	87.9	3.4
1958	88.9	1.1
1959	89.8	1.0
1960	91.8	2.2
1961	92.1	0.3
1962	91.8	−0.3
1963	92.1	0.3
1964	93.1	1.1
1965	93.8	0.8
1966	96.5	2.9
1967	100.0	3.6
1968	104.6	4.6
1969	111.9	7.0
1970	118.9	6.3

Source: Bureau of Labor Statistics.

Table 4

MEDIAN FIRST-YEAR WAGE ADJUSTMENTS [a]
IN MAJOR COLLECTIVE BARGAINING SETTLEMENTS [b]
1954-1970

Year	All industries	Percentage Increase Manufac- turing	Nonmanu- facturing
1954	3.1 c		
1955	5.4 c		
1956	5.4 c		
1957	4.9 c		
1958	3.9 c		
1959	3.9	3.5	4.0
1960	3.2	3.2	3.3
1961	2.8	2.4	3.6
1962	2.9	2.4	4.0
1963	3.0	2.5	3.4
1964	3.2	2.0	3.6
1965	3.8	4.0	3.7
1966	4.8	4.2	5.0
1967	5.6	6.4	5.0
1968	7.2	6.9	7.5
1969	8.0	7.0	10.0
1970	10.0	7.5	14.2

Source: Bureau of Labor Statistics.

a Major settlements are those covering 1,000 workers or more.

b Wage adjustments include settlements in which wages were unchanged or decreased, as well as those involving wage increases.

c Estimated.

4

INCOMES POLICY, ITS RATIONALE AND DEVELOPMENT

Thomas Gale Moore

In 1962, the Kennedy administration started the American government on an experiment to stem inflation through rules, guidelines, and moral suasion. The effort at first appeared to be successful, later broke down, was abandoned with the Republicans, then was partially resurrected, and finally culminated in the wage-price freeze of August 15, 1971. This paper is a history and analysis of this American experiment with incomes policies, as such efforts have been termed.*

Cost-Push Inflation During the 1950s

The specter of rising prices and rapidly mounting wages at a time of substantial unused capacity and unemployment—1955 to 1958—continued to haunt public policy throughout the 1960s. Only in light of this experience are guideposts, jawboning, and the fiscal

---

*The effectiveness of incomes policies has recently been discussed by Gottfried Haberler, *Incomes Policies and Inflation: An Analysis of Basic Principles* (Washington: American Enterprise Institute, 1971). Professor Haberler divides incomes policies into two types, those in which the government attempts to induce particular price and wage behavior through guidelines and/or controls and those in which the government attempts to make the economy more competitive through antitrust and labor policies. To keep this study manageable, it has been confined to Haberler's first type of incomes policy. However, it is recognized that measures promoting a more competitive economy would probably make the problems of stabilization easier. For other recent discussions of incomes policies, see Eric Schiff, *Incomes Policies Abroad* (U.K., Netherlands, Sweden and Canada) and Colin D. Campbell, ed., *Wage-Price Controls in World War II, United States and Germany*, both published by the American Enterprise Institute in 1971.

policies of the Kennedy and Johnson administrations understandable.

The combination of inflation and unemployment in the late 1950s revived discussion of cost-push and administered price inflation. During the Great Depression, Gardner Means had alleged that some industries "administered" prices so that their charges were maintained by reducing output in the face of depressed demand. Thus he argued these industries contributed to high unemployment and the lack of aggregate demand and thereby prolonged the depression. The alleged ubiquity of rigid "administered" prices and their lack of flexibility, especially downward, generated considerable controversy and academic study. It is probably fair to say that there were many economists on both sides of the issue and that, as far as the application of the theory to the 1930s is concerned, the profession would have had to render the Scotch verdict of "unproved."

More germane to our study has been the revival of interest in "administered" prices as an explanation for rising prices between 1955 and 1958. In 1957, Means presented to a Senate committee a now famous chart in which he classified product groups as to whether they were administered, mixed, or market-established and indicated for each class the percent price change between 1953 and 1957.[1] Substantial price increases predominated for the product groups he had classified as administered while decreases or no changes were shown for those classified as market-determined. This chart has been the subject of much controversy and analysis. The classification of products has been called "whimsical" by Stigler[2] and shown to lead to no correlation if products are classified by concentration.[3] The lack of correlation has been disputed by Weiss;[4] in another study, he found a significant relationship after changes in labor costs and in raw material and semi-fabricated prices were taken into account.

Others attributed the 1955-58 inflation to rises in costs, specifically due to union activity. For example, Eckstein and Fromm at-

[1] Hearings before the Subcommittee on Antitrust and Monopoly of the Committee on the Judiciary, U.S. Senate, 1957 (Washington: Government Printing Office, 1957), Part 1, p. 90.

[2] George Stigler, "Administered Prices and Oligopolistic Inflation," *Journal of Business* (January 1962).

[3] Horace J. Depodwin and Richard T. Selden, "Business Pricing Policies and Inflation," *Journal of Political Economy* (April 1963).

[4] Leonard W. Weiss, "Business Pricing Policies and Inflation Reconsidered," *Journal of Political Economy* (April 1966), pp. 177-87.

tributed most of the increase in steel prices to "an extraordinary rise in wages which is the result of bargaining between a strong union and a management with strong market power in the product market. Government intervention has probably accelerated this process." [5]

The theoretical underpinnings of both cost-push inflation and administered price inflation are weak. Conceptually cost-push inflation stems from an arbitrary rise in the cost of some factor (usually labor) that is then passed on in the form of higher prices, with the result that the gain in real income to the factor is eroded. This in turn leads labor—if that is the factor—to demand further wage increases which continue the spiral. Without government action, however, cost-push inflation cannot go on indefinitely. The complete theory, therefore, argues that strong unions push up wages which in turn leads to higher prices. The higher prices reduce sales which leads to reduced demand for labor and to unemployment. Since the government is committed to full employment, steps are taken to increase aggregate demand, with the result that the original wage increase and price increase are validated. But the wage increase has now been eroded in real terms and therefore new wage demands are made and granted and the inflation continues.

The practical problem facing the policymaker is whether the presence of unions with substantial market power changes the level of unemployment that is consistent with stable prices. Only about 25 percent of the labor force is unionized, and of this portion only a small part has significant market power. Lewis,[6] concludes that for "considerably less than 6 percent [of the labor force] . . . the relative wage effect is 20 percent or more."

Presumably the effect of strong unions is to raise the relative wage in their industries while depressing it elsewhere. Even if the proportion of the labor force which had significant market power were 50 percent rather than less than 6, there is no theoretical reason to believe that unions could distort the unemployment-inflation "trade-off." Higher monopoly wages would simply be offset by lower wages in competitive sectors as labor that is displaced from highly unionized sectors moves into other employment. Only if the government attempts to forestall the labor shift by

[5] Otto Eckstein and Gary Fromm, "Steel and the Post-war Inflation," Study Paper No. 2 prepared in connection with the *Study of Employment and Growth, and Price Levels* for consideration by the Joint Economic Committee (Washington: Government Printing Office, 1959), p. 34.

[6] H. Gregg Lewis, *Unionism and Relative Wages in the United States* (Chicago: University of Chicago Press, 1963), p. 7.

increasing aggregate demand sufficiently to maintain *union* employment would inflation be the "result" of union activity.

But could not strong unions push up wages continuously? They could, but at the cost of reduced employment and union membership. While the objective of unions is unclear, it is obvious that at some point the membership and the union leaders become unwilling to trade higher wages for decreased employment in that sector. At that point, union wages stop pushing up costs and prices and displaced labor stops depressing real wages in competitive sectors (dollar wages in a growing society never need fall).

Consequently "cost-push" inflation, if it exists at all, must only be a temporary matter as strong unions push up wages. Continuing inflation would exist only if the government viewed the temporarily unemployed labor from the strong union sector with sufficient alarm to cause it to increase aggregate demand.

The administered price inflation hypothesis is even harder to justify theoretically. Unlike unions in demanding wage increases, companies and industries face market situations in which there is some price (or prices) which maximizes profits. Since a price higher than that level can only reduce profits, and no one claims that higher prices are wanted in themselves, how continuing inflation can or would occur remains unexplained. Apparently, firms with market power arbitrarily raise prices leading to inflation. To the extent this happens, firms with market power must have been setting their prices below profit maximizing levels before they raised them. They must have had, in Galbraith's words, "unliquidated monopoly gains." [7]

The only sound theoretical explanation for "administered price" inflation would seem to lie in the hypothesis that oligopolistic industries or monopolistic industries lag in raising prices in an inflation. In this subset of industry, lags in adjusting prices to changes in demand and lags in changes in costs are greater than elsewhere. Instead of "administered price inflation," the theory might better be called "lagged inflation."

To make sense of this hypothesis, some explanation must be offered as to why oligopolistic industries are slower in adjusting prices than other industries. To the extent that prices are set by collusion either implicit or explicit in oligopolistic industries, prices may be more rigid than in more competitive circumstances. Change

---

[7] John Kenneth Galbraith, "Market Structure and Stabilization Policy," in Hearings before the Subcommittee on Antitrust and Monopoly, U.S. Senate, "Administered Prices," Part I, 85th Cong., 1st Sess., 1957, p. 65.

is costly. Securing agreement on a new appropriate price level is costly; opinions may differ as to the extent of the inflation, the appropriate price level, the elasticity of demand, the reaction of governments and unions, et cetera. Many firms apparently believe that buyers prefer stable prices to rapidly changing ones and thus are reluctant to make rapid changes.

Moreover, there is some evidence that union wages lag in a rapid inflation, at least initially.[8] To this extent costs and particularly marginal costs are held down in unionized industries; most concentrated industries are largely unionized. If marginal costs remain constant, there is no reason for the industry or a monopolist to raise prices even if demand shifts to the right, unless the shift decreases the elasticity of demand. Thus increasing demand in an inflation would be consistent with constant prices if marginal costs do not rise, or only slowly rising prices as marginal costs edge upwards.

"Lagged inflation" might even occur in a world without significant market power. In some markets which are workably competitive, prices may be changed only infrequently. For example, college tuitions are usually adjustable only once a year, natural gas, oil, and coal are often sold on long term contracts with prices adjustable at intervals, and rents are normally specified for at least one year and sometimes for more. In the labor market, many unions have no appreciable market power with the result that union wages average over time no higher than the competitive level; but since contracts may be negotiated for as long as three years, wages may not change rapidly with shifts in demand. Consequently, during an inflation some prices will respond more quickly to increases in demand than others. Commodities sold on exchanges will respond almost instantaneously, but the prices of other products will move up more slowly, and some may not adjust completely for several years, especially if the inflation follows a period of substantial price stability.

The inflation process might work as follows. Suppose there is a period of substantial price stability and relative prices are in equilibrium. If this is followed by an inflation stemming from a rapid once-and-for-all increase in the money stock, some prices will rapidly move up to a new equilibrium, while others will remain at pre-inflation levels. The more responsive prices, however, will be held down by the substitution possibilities with products whose prices are more sticky. Eventually the more sluggish prices will

---

[8] Lewis, *op. cit.*, pp. 4-6.

adjust to higher levels but this in turn will result in a change in relative prices, with the result that other prices will have to adjust further. Thus a once-and-for-all large jump in the stock of money might produce an inflation spread over several years; prices would still be rising long after all inflationary pressure was apparently over, even though all markets were reasonably competitive.

What policy prescriptions can be derived from our "lagged inflation" hypothesis? None, really. It is not obvious that delaying the impact of inflation worsens either the distribution of resources or income, and, in fact, it could be argued that it improves both. To the extent that oligopolistic industries price below the profit-maximizing level, their charges are closer to the competitive level and, at least during the upswing, resources are more appropriately allocated. When an industry finally catches up and returns to profit maximizing, resources are no more poorly allocated than they were prior to the inflationary outburst. Moreover by delaying and spreading the inflation over a longer period, individuals and firms are given more time to adjust to the inflation and so misallocations stemming from the general increases in prices are reduced.

Some observers and believers in "administered price inflation" have related the concept to "target return pricing." [9] Professors Adams and Lanzillotti have claimed that in the 1950s U.S. Steel arbitrarily raised its target rate of return and thus pushed prices and costs up in the steel industry. Why U.S. Steel allegedly did so is not made clear, but the facts in the case are also not clear. A careful study of the impact of costs on steel prices during the 1950s [10] indicates that, of the increase in revenue per ton between 1947 and 1958, only 6.4 percent could be attributable to an increase in profits per ton. It is a little weak to hang a theory on a factor that is responsible at most for only 6.4 percent of a total phenomenon. What about all the other factors?

The "target return pricing" hypothesis of administered pricing seems even weaker than the "lagged inflation hypothesis" and is apparently strictly ad hoc. Inflation occurs (or is continued) because for some mysterious reason some large firm or firms have decided to increase their target rate of return.

In any case, the most careful study of the period, that done by

---

[9] Walter Adams and Robert F. Lanzillotti, "The Reality of Administered Prices," in *Administered Prices: A Compendium on Public Policy*, Subcommittee on Antitrust and Monopoly of the Committee on the Judiciary, U.S. Senate, 88th Cong., 1st Sess. (Washington: Government Printing Office, 1963), p. 19.

[10] Eckstein and Fromm, *op. cit.*

Leonard Weiss,[11] presents strong evidence that there is a correlation between price increases from 1953 to 1959 and concentration, once other factors such as labor costs, raw material costs, and changes in demand are taken into account. Such evidence is consistent with some version of the "administered price inflation" hypothesis, although other factors could explain it. In fact, Selden [12] argues that the inflation during this period was strictly a matter of demand increases in certain sectors including steel. Nevertheless, the best explanation of price behavior during this period was probably given by Weiss:

> These results do not necessarily imply continuously creeping inflation. . . . (B)ut a half-decade recoupment of potential profits foregone ·by monopolists who had been checked earlier by the direct controls of the World War II and Korean War periods and by public-relations considerations during the intervening period of open inflation seems quite consistent with rational entrepreneurial behavior. A period of rising prices in the mid-1950's would then imply only that some of the earlier inflation has been deferred.[13]

In other words the inflation of the late 1950s could be called "lagged inflation."

Price movements during a "lagged inflationary" period would be expected to increase but at a decreasing rate as the various industries caught up with their profit-maximizing positions. The data appear to confirm this pattern. Leaving aside food prices which in the short run are mainly a function of shifts in supply due to weather and other factors, the inflation of the 1950s was beginning to diminish before the 1957-58 recession started. Seasonally adjusted unemployment reached its lowest level (3.9 percent) in September and October of 1956 and again in March and April of 1957, while the wholesale price index of intermediate materials started to move up less rapidly by the fourth quarter of 1956.

The end of the inflation is well pictured in Figure 1, taken from the Council of Economic Advisers' *Inflation Alert* of August 7, 1970. This chart shows that the rate of inflation diminished first for crude materials, then for intermediate materials, then for wholesale

---

[11] Weiss, *op. cit.*

[12] Richard T. Selden, "Cost-push Versus Demand-pull Inflation, 1955-57," *The Journal of Political Economy* (February 1959).

[13] Weiss, *op. cit.*, p. 183.

Figure 1

PRICE CHANGES AT SELECTED STAGES OF PRODUCTION, 1955-59

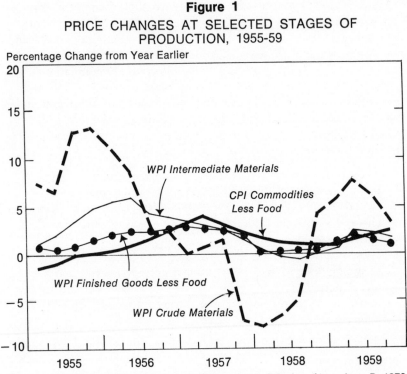

Percentage Change from Year Earlier

WPI Intermediate Materials

CPI Commodities Less Food

WPI Finished Goods Less Food

WPI Crude Materials

Source: The National Commission on Productivity, *Inflation Alert*, Aug. 7, 1970.

prices for finished goods, and finally for consumer commodities. Given lags in the economic system, this would be the expected pattern for price changes as an inflation ended. The consumer price index for all items except food actually reached its peak rate of increase in April 1967, the last month of the lowest rate of unemployment. After that the rate of increase of consumer prices started to decline as unemployment started to increase.

Wage increases also followed traditional patterns during this inflation. Median first year wage increases in union contracts went from 3.1 percent in 1954 to 5.4 percent in 1955 and 1956 and then declined to 4.9 percent in 1957 with the start of the recession and fell further to 3.9 percent in 1958 and 3.2 percent in 1960.[14]

A careful study of this period by Throop [15] indicates a significant increase in the union-nonunion wage differential during the 1950s.

---

[14] Report to the National Commission on Productivity by the Council of Economic Advisers, *Inflation Alert*, August 7, 1970, II-6.

[15] A. U. Throop, "The Union-Nonunion Wage Differential and Cost-Push Inflation," *American Economic Review* (March 1968).

It appears from his data that the differential ceases to widen after 1958. In part confirming Throop's findings, Lester [16] has presented data on labor union wage settlements and average hourly earnings. His results indicate that increases in average hourly earnings exceeded those in wage settlements in 1951, 1952, 1953, and 1957, while settlements were higher in the other years of the 1950s. Thus with the exception of 1957, union wages appeared to be catching up during the inflationary period.

These data are consistent with the cost-push inflation hypothesis. Union wages rose more rapidly than nonunion wages until 1958, thus increasing cost and possibly prices in the affected sectors. On the other hand, the "lagged inflation" hypothesis also fits the data, assuming that union wages respond more slowly to inflationary pressures than nonunion wages.

In summary, then, the inflation of 1955-1958 would appear to fall in the traditional demand-pull mode. There appears to be no strong evidence to support the hypothesis that it was a union cost-push inflation. While concentrated industries did apparently raise prices more than other industries during this period, the practice seems to have stemmed more from the delayed reaction to prior inflationary periods than to any "administered price" hypothesis.

Development of Guideposts

The trauma of rising prices at a time of substantial unemployment was bound to have a major impact on public policy. As the new administration took over in January 1961, the problem of how to "get the country moving again" without reactivating inflation faced policymakers. President Kennedy in his first economic message to Congress set a "4 percent unemployment rate as a temporary target." [17] His goal was to achieve this target in 1963 without "endangering the price stability of the last four years."

The administration's concern was dramatized in the Annual Report of the Council of Economic Advisers, which devoted its final chapter to the subject of price behavior and inflation in a growing

---

[16] R. A. Lester, "Negotiated Wage Settlements, 1951-67," *Review of Economics and Statistics* (May 1968).

[17] *Economic Report of the President*, 1962 (Washington: Government Printing Office), p. 8; hereinafter referred to as *Economic Report*, with year of publication.

economy. The view of the council on the 1955-57 inflation can best be seen by quoting from its report: [18]

> In contrast to the two earlier inflationary bursts, there is still considerable uncertainty as to the causes of rising prices during this period. A simple explanation running in terms of over-all excess demand is not satisfactory. If aggregate excess demand prevailed at all, it existed only briefly toward the end of 1955. After the end of 1955, capacity utilization slackened as investment created capacity more rapidly than final demands were increasing. Employment of production workers in manufacturing began to decline in the latter half of 1956 and was lower in 1957 than in 1955. The average workweek in manufacturing declined over this period—from 40.7 hours in 1955 to 40.4 in 1956 to 39.8 in 1957. Unemployment as a percent of the civilian labor force, seasonally adjusted, dipped below 4.0 percent in only three months during the entire period. . . .
>
> Elements of major importance in the 1955-58 episode were thus the existence of relatively high demand, principally in one sector of the economy; the use of market power by management to maintain profit margins despite rising costs; the exercise of market power by labor unions in an effort to capture a substantial share of rising profits for their membership; and the transmission of these developments to other sectors of the economy.

Apparently the council believed that cost-push and administered prices were at least partially responsible for the inflation of 1955-58. Such an inflation could easily be reactivated as the economy moved towards full employment. Only substantial unemployment, the council believed, was holding wage demands in check. Better business conditions might also stimulate business to demand higher profit margins or at least to maintain them as labor costs rose. Thus success in achieving the President's target of 4 percent unemployment would risk the rekindling of the inflation after four years of relative price stability.

The council's fear of administered price inflation was quite clearly stated in its report: [19]

---

[18] *Annual Report of the Council of Economic Advisers*, 1962 (Washington: Government Printing Office, 1962), p. 171; hereinafter cited as *Annual Report*, with year of publication.

[19] *Ibid.*, p. 185.

There are important segments of the economy where firms are large or employees well organized, or both. In these sectors, private parties may exercise considerable discretion over the terms of wage bargains and price decisions. Thus, at least in the short run, there is considerable room for the exercise of private power and a parallel need for the assumption of private responsibility.

These conditions and the views held of them by policymakers set the stage for the establishment of some type of incomes policy. Many European nations had experimented with incomes policies with various degrees of success. In the United States, the Eisenhower administration had attempted a mild form of incomes policy when it appealed to business and labor for responsible behavior. For example, the 1957 *Economic Report of the President* pleaded for restraint in the following words.[20]

Economic developments in recent years show the basic role that monetary and fiscal restraints must play if the excesses that often accompany prosperity are to be avoided. At the same time, this experience suggests that fiscal and monetary policies must be supported by appropriate private policies to assure both a high level of economic activity and a stable dollar. When production, sales, and employments are high, wage and price increases in important industries create upward pressures on costs and prices generally. To depend exclusively on monetary and fiscal restraints as a means of containing the upward movement of prices would raise serious obstacles to the maintenance of economic growth and stability. In the face of a continuous upward pressure on costs and prices, moderate restraints would not be sufficient; yet stronger restraints would bear with undue severity on sectors of the economy having little if any responsibility for the movement toward a higher cost-price level and would court the risk of being excessively restrictive for the economy generally.

More specific guidelines on appropriate wage increases were set forth in the President's 1958 economic report.[21]

---

[20] *Economic Report*, 1957, p. 44.

[21] *Economic Report*, 1958, p. v.

. . . Business managements must recognize that price increases that are unwarranted by costs, or that attempt to recapture investment outlays too quickly, not only lower the buying power of the dollar, but also may be self-defeating by causing a restriction of markets, lower output, and a narrowing of the return on capital investment. The leadership of *labor must recognize that wage increases that go beyond overall productivity gains are inconsistent with stable prices,* and that the resumption of economic growth can be slowed by wage increases that involve either higher prices or a further narrowing of the margin between prices and costs. . . . [My emphasis.]

The relationship of wages, productivity, and prices was further spelled out in the next year's report: [22]

. . . But improvements in compensation rates must, on the average, remain within the limits of general productivity gains if reasonable stability of prices is to be achieved and maintained. Furthermore, *price reductions warranted by especially rapid productivity gains must be a normal and frequent feature of our economy.* Without such reductions we shall not be able to keep the price level as a whole from advancing.

A well-informed and vigilant public opinion is essential in our free society for helping achieve the conditions necessary for price stability and vigorous economic growth. Such public opinion can be an effective safeguard against attempts arbitrarily to establish prices or wages at levels that are inconsistent with the general welfare. . . .

As can be seen, the President's 1960 report struck a theme which was to recur again and again under the next administration. This was the reliance to be placed on an informed public opinion to keep wages and prices in line with noninflationary behavior. Similar statements could be quoted from the 1961 report.

Thus, the introduction of the wage-price guideposts by the Democrats in the 1962 *Annual Report of the Council of Economic Advisers* was not such a major innovation. Much of the groundwork for the guideposts had been established by the preceding Republican administration, including some of the general guidelines which

---

[22] *Economic Report,* 1960, p. 8, emphasis added.

were to be the backbone of the incomes policy under the Democrats. Even the wording of the guidepost section was reminiscent of the earlier statements. It is worth quoting extensively the 1962 statement of the guideposts since that statement set the standard for the next eight years: [23]

> *Prices and wages in individual industries.* What are the guideposts which may be used in judging whether a particular price or wage decision may be inflationary? The desired objective is a stable price level, within which particular prices rise, fall, or remain stable in response to economic pressures. Hence, price stability within any particular industry is not necessarily a correct guide to price and wage decisions in that industry. It is possible, however, to describe in broad outline a set of guides which, if followed, would preserve over-all price stability while still allowing sufficient flexibility to accommodate objectives of efficiency and equity. These are not arbitrary guides. They describe—briefly and no doubt incompletely—how prices and wage rates would behave in a smoothly functioning competitive economy operating near full employment. Nor do they constitute a mechanical formula for determining whether a particular price or wage decision is inflationary. They will serve their purpose if they suggest to the interested public a useful way of approaching the appraisal of such a decision.
>
> If, as a point of departure, we assume no change in the relative shares of labor and nonlabor incomes in a particular industry, then a general guide may be advanced for noninflationary wage behavior, and another for noninflationary price behavior. Both guides, as will be seen, are only first approximations.
>
> The general guide for noninflationary wage behavior is that the rate of increase in wage rates (including fringe benefits) in each industry be equal to the trend rate of over-all productivity increase. General acceptance of this guide would maintain stability of labor cost per unit of output for the economy as a whole—though not of course for individual industries.
>
> The general guide for noninflationary price behavior calls for price reduction if the industry's rate of productiv-

---

[23] *Annual Report*, 1962, pp. 188-89.

ity increase exceeds the over-all rate—for this would mean declining unit labor costs; it calls for an appropriate increase in price if the opposite relationship prevails; and it calls for stable prices if the two rates of productivity increase are equal.

These are advanced as general guideposts. To reconcile them with objectives of equity and efficiency, specific modifications must be made to adapt them to the circumstances of particular industries. If all of these modifications are made, each in the specific circumstances to which it applies, they are consistent with stability of the general price level. Public judgments about the effects on the price level of particular wage or price decisions should take into account the modifications as well as the general guides. The most important modifications are the following:

(1) Wage rate increases would exceed the general guide rate in an industry which would otherwise be unable to attract sufficient labor; or in which wage rates are exceptionally low compared with the range of wages earned elsewhere by similar labor, because the bargaining position of workers has been weak in particular local labor markets.

(2) Wage rate increases would fall short of the general guide rate in an industry which could not provide jobs for its entire labor force even in times of generally full employment; or in which wage rates are exceptionally high compared with the range of wages earned elsewhere by similar labor, because the bargaining position of workers has been especially strong.

(3) Prices would rise more rapidly, or fall more slowly, than indicated by the general guide rate in an industry in which the level of profits was insufficient to attract the capital required to finance a needed expansion in capacity; or in which costs other than labor costs had risen.

(4) Prices would rise more slowly, or fall more rapidly, than indicated by the general guide in an industry in which the relation of productive capacity to full employment demand shows the desirability of an outflow of capital from the industry; or in which costs other than labor costs have fallen; or in which excessive market power has resulted in rates of profit substantially higher than those earned elsewhere on investments of comparable risk.

The guideposts as so enunciated were general and contained numerous exceptions including a paragraph not quoted above that provided further "outs" by stating that the guideposts "leave out of account several important considerations." The guideposts were specifically introduced "as a contribution to . . . a discussion" of how to judge which particular wage or price decisions are in the public interest. Yet they were definitely framed and referred to as guides to appropriate behavior. Ostensibly they were intended to be self-enforcing with the whip of public opinion meant to keep labor and management in line. However, since they listed so many exceptions and since no particular measure of productivity was indicated even as a guide to public opinion and "responsible" labor and management, they were woefully inadequate. A table in the report indicates a variety of levels of productivity depending on the period and the subgroup considered. Given this table, a union could claim that a wage settlement as high as 3.5 percent was within the guidelines, while management could argue that anything over 2.1 percent would be inflationary.

Given the wide range of productivity and the number of qualifications which could justify almost any wage package, it is difficult to see how the public could bring moral suasion to bear on price-wage decisions. Moreover, prices were to be a function of changes in productivity within a particular industry provided labor wage rates stayed within the guidelines. Prices were to remain constant only if productivity were equal to the national average, whatever that might be. If productivity lagged, prices could be and should be raised; or if profits were inadequate to attract capital, prices could be increased. Thus for the public to evaluate price increases meant that some judgment had to be made on both the rate of productivity in the industry and the level of profits. Inevitably, if the price guidelines were to have any effect, some government agency would have to interpret their application in a given industry. They could not be, as wage guidelines were, self-enforcing.

With no appreciable change in the unemployment rate, calendar year 1962 was disappointing to the administration. But, as a consequence, the continuation of substantial unused capacity kept prices from rising noticeably with the result that the 1963 *Annual Report of the Council of Economic Advisers* gave much less emphasis to wage-price guideposts than had the report the year before. Only one page out of the five devoted to the subject of prices and wages discussed the guideposts, whereas the 1962 report had an entire chapter on prices and wages with six pages on the guideposts. Inflation seemed like a remote problem in January 1963.

Throughout the year 1963, unemployment remained virtually unchanged from the levels of 1962. While the economy grew, its growth was not fast enough to reduce excess capacity or to stimulate a rise in prices. The administration believed that its first goal should be to eliminate this excess capacity and to return the economy to a more fully employed level. President Johnson said in his 1964 economic report: "I regard achievement of the full potential of our resources—physical, human, and otherwise—to be the highest purpose of governmental policies next to the protection of those rights we regard as inalienable." [24]

But the President and the council were naturally apprehensive that the stimulus of the proposed tax cut would not only reduce unemployment but would also reactivate the inflation of the 1950s. As a consequence, the President asked the council to reaffirm the guideposts. The council did more than that; it amplified them. For the first time it spelled out what it regarded to be the appropriate level of productivity. In a table in the chapter on prices and wages the "trend productivity" was indicated to be derived by taking a five-year moving average, which at that time produced a figure of 3.2 percent. Thus labor and management were on notice as to the level of approved wage increases, although exceptions were still valid.

The qualifications for the guideposts were restated, but with the limitation that "it must be emphasized that they [the exceptions] are intended to apply to only a relatively few cases . . . the most constructive private policy in the great majority of situations would be to arrive at price decisions and wage bargains consistent with the general guideposts." [25]

Thus the guideposts were turned into more definite rules of behavior. Industry and labor were to be judged by the exact standards of the guideposts, although it would still be necessary to have some agency such as the council interpret the guideposts on industry behavior. The 1964 report also emphasized the desirability of price reductions in those industries whose trend productivity gains exceeded the national trend. While not specifically mentioned, it is obvious that the council had the automobile industry in mind.

The 1965 report of the council [26] limited the exemptions from the general guideposts even further: "Because the industries in which market power is concentrated are largely high-wage indus-

[24] *Economic Report*, 1964, p. 3.

[25] *Annual Report*, 1964, p. 119.

[26] *Annual Report*, 1965, p. 108.

tries with a relatively low long-term rate of increase of employment, the first two of these exceptions are rarely applicable." While the table on productivity revised the "trend productivity" for 1963 upwards to 3.3 percent, the level for the most recent year was set at 3.2 percent. There was no change, therefore, in the level of approved wage increases.

Calendar year 1965 was a good year for the council and for the economy. For the first time in eight years, unemployment rates fell below 5 percent and stayed there. Wholesale prices, which had not risen substantially since 1957, remained virtually unchanged during the year. Thus, 1966 started with stable prices and with the economy moving slowly but surely towards the goal set by President Kennedy in his first economic message.

The definition of trend productivity specified in the 1964 report—the average of the previous five-years change in output per man-hour—produced the magic 3.2 percent number cited in the 1964 and 1965 reports of the council, but for the five years prior to 1966 the average was 3.6 percent. Rather than blindly following the formula used in past years, the council decided to keep the 3.2 percent figure. Anything higher would probably exceed the true long-run rate of productivity and thus be inflationary. The council recognized that a change in method of calculating trend productivity would lead to much acrimony and resentment, especially on the part of labor leaders, but concluded that adherence to a formula based on five years of steady growth from the recession of 1960 would mislead and misdirect the economy.

The 1966 report also reiterated the limitations on the exceptions to the wage guideposts set out in the previous report. In addition, it further qualified the exceptions for price changes not in line with the general guideposts. It noted that price increases "may occasionally be appropriate . . . to correct an inability to attract needed capital." But then it added: [27]

> The large firms to which guideposts are primarily addressed typically have ready access to sources of capital; moreover, the profits of virtually every industry have risen sharply and are at record levels as a by-product of the general prosperity in the economy. The . . . exception is thus not widely applicable in the present environment.

While the guideposts had ostensibly been set out as a contribution to a discussion of appropriate wage and price behavior and

---

[27] *Annual Report*, 1966, p. 91.

while, in the absence of compelling reasons otherwise, the guide-posts were to be used to judge behavior by the public, there had been no claim that the government would attempt to enforce them. As will be discussed below, the administration did attempt from the beginning to secure what it considered appropriate behavior by both labor and management. However, in the 1966 economic report there was the first public acknowledgment that the council and the administration had in the case of a wide variety of industries attempted to secure compliance with the guideposts. The report claimed: "On numerous occasions, Government officials have specifically reminded unions or management of the guidepost standards—either publicly or privately, either generally or with reference to specific situations." [28]

The economic pace stepped up considerably in 1966 under the stimulus of the Vietnam War and the domestic Great Society programs. Unemployment, which had dropped 0.5 percentage points from 1963 to 1964 and 0.6 percentage points the next year, fell 0.7 percentage points from 1965 to 1966—a 15 percent fall that took it below 4 percent for the first time since 1953. As the council put it:[29]

> By any standard, then, 1966 was a big year for the economy. Gross national product (GNP) expanded by a record $58 billion in current prices and reached $740 billion. As in the 2 preceding years, a major advance in business fixed investment was a key expansionary force. And the rising requirements of Vietnam added $10 billion to defense outlays. State and local spending and inventory investment also rose strongly.

This rise in activity coincided with a noticeable increase in prices. Actually, wholesale prices had started edging up at the beginning of 1965 but, by 1966 the inflation was becoming obvious. Most of the price rises during 1965 applied to farm products and resulted from special supply conditions. The increases in 1966 were more widespread and reflected growing shortages at existing prices as demand pushed against capacity in a wide variety of markets.

With the fall in the unemployment rate to below 4 percent for the first time in nearly 15 years, wages began to rise more rapidly than they had since the 1950s. Compensation per man-hour in-

---

[28] *Ibid.*, p. 89.
[29] *Annual Report*, 1967, p. 37.

216

creased at an annual rate of 6 to 7 percent in 1966, compared to a rate of about 4.3 percent between 1960 and 1965.[30] Nonunion wages began increasing more rapidly than union wages, although first year union increases were larger than nonunion increases.[31] In fact, the rate of increase of union wages lagged behind nonunion increases until mid-1968.

Prior to 1966, although wages had increased faster than the guidelines would have called for, the increases were not sufficient to push costs up noticeably. But with the new spurt in demand and with the economy reaching relatively fully employed levels, inflation began. The wage guidelines clearly died in 1966.

The death blow was dealt by the airline mechanics strike which resulted in a settlement well beyond the guideposts. This agreement, along with a steel-price boost, prompted Gardner Ackley, chairman of the Council of Economic Advisers, to concede that guidepost policy had "recently suffered some stunning defeats." [32]

The airline strike, which began July 8, 1966 and ended 43 days later on August 19, involved over 35,000 ground crew workers represented by the International Association of Machinists (IAM). Early in the game, President Johnson had appointed an emergency board which recommended a package providing for an annual increase of about 3.6 percent, slightly in excess of the guideline but still labeled noninflationary by the administration. The five airlines accepted the recommendations, but the union rejected them.

Following this impasse, Secretary of Labor Wirtz and Assistant Secretary Reynolds stepped in as mediators. The first real blow to the guidelines came when President Johnson sponsored a July 30th bargaining session in the Executive Office Building that resulted in an agreement providing for a 4.4 percent increase. The President claimed the increase was non-inflationary because the airline industry had been experiencing productivity gains of about 6.3 percent. His reasoning implied that the 3.2 percent national productivity figure was not in fact the relevant one. The appropriate consideration now seemed to be each industry's productivity.

This deviation in policy was immediately recognized by other unions. For example, David Lasser, assistant to the president of the International Union of Electrical Workers (which was beginning

---

[30] Report to the National Commission on Productivity by the Council of Economic Advisers, *Inflation Alert*, August 7, 1970, p. II-18.

[31] *Ibid.*

[32] *Wall Street Journal*, August 8, 1966, p. 3.

contract renegotiations with General Electric) stated that an industry-by-industry basis for guidelines made good sense.[33]

Ultimately, the rank and file of IAM rejected the airline agreement, so the strike continued. The pressure for, and against, strike legislation also continued.

The negotiators finally reached another agreement early Monday morning, August 15, and the contract was ratified the following Friday. The terms of the settlement provided for an annual wage increase variously estimated at from 6 to 8 percent and included a cost-of-living escalator. After the contract had been safely approved by the membership, the administration estimated the increase at 4.9 percent in an apparent attempt to convince other unions that the increase was not as large as it appeared to be. The CEA deplored the size of the gain, but maintained that the settlement would not prohibit a continuing downtrend in airline fares since some of the high productivity advances could be passed along to the public.

There is little doubt that the size of this settlement and the implied shift in relevant productivity figures (from national to industry) severely weakened the guideposts. Treasury Secretary Fowler indicated that the administration was reviewing the question of whether 3.2 percent was the proper figure and even "whether there was one magic number for all industries." Commerce Secretary Connor also doubted "whether any specific mathematical formula" could be applied to all industries.[34]

The airlines' agreement also placed other unions under pressure to produce high settlements. The International Union of Electricians claimed the airline pact showed that the guideposts had no applicability in its talks with General Electric. Furthermore, later contracts between the IAM and other airlines followed the terms of this agreement, while American Airlines and the Transport Workers Union ratified a contract calling for a 6.2 percent increase.

The 1967 report of the CEA clearly reflected these changes in the economic environment. Part of the 1966 inflation was attributed to a failure by both labor and business to observe the guideposts. Some businesses, it was alleged, had generated a rapid rise in profit by failing in particular to reduce prices when costs fell,[35] but the report did acknowledge that the primary source of the rise in prices came from sectors of the economy where the guideposts were not applicable. Farm products and services were two of the areas which were chiefly responsible for the rise in the consumer price index.

---

33 *Wall Street Journal*, August 1, 1966, p. 3.

34 *Wall Street Journal*, August 9, 1966, p. 2.

35 *Annual Report*, 1967, p. 127.

As if to shift the blame for the growing inflation from the government, the 1967 CEA report disclosed the government's activities to enforce the guideposts. It was admitted that the guideposts were intended to be rules for business and labor and that those who failed to adhere to them were considered "violators." The council's primary role in interpreting the guideposts was acknowledged, and it was admitted that the CEA had taken an active role with other government agencies in attempting to persuade labor and management to conform to the guidelines.

It was clear that it was unrealistic to expect or attempt to hold wages to a 3.2 percent productivity increase in the face of a 3.3 percent rise in consumer prices, a rapid increase in wages in nonunion sectors, and record profit levels. The council therefore abandoned the specific guidelines for wage increases. While reiterating its faith in tying wages to productivity, its report implied that wages should rise less rapidly than the sum of the price increases and "trend productivity." Thus organized labor was in fact requested to accept a reduction in its relative share of income in 1967 in order to return to price stability. The CEA's report then went on to acknowledge that some of the problems were resulting from public policies: increased taxes were raising costs; and the 11 percent higher minimum wage would push some wages up much faster than the sum of trend productivity and price increases.

While not repudiating the guideposts, the Council of Economic Advisers in effect had eliminated the specific numbers that facilitated enforcement. In the future the public could not know whether a particular wage settlement, and consequently a price increase, was consistent with desirable performance without government interpretation. Moreover, no union could know what was desired without help from the council, aside from the rule that the sum of the rate of inflation and the trend productivity should be greater than its settlement.

The 1968 report reflected a further retreat from the guidepost strategy. Council efforts, if any, to enforce guideposts were not discussed. The reader was referred to the previous year's report for a detailed discussion of the guideposts. Both labor and management were urged to reduce their demands to the point where each would receive a smaller portion of the income generated. It was argued that if each attempted to secure an increase in income equal to the sum of price rises and productivity increases, inflation would be on a continually increasing treadmill. While price stability was not promised in the 1968 report, it was indicated that the rate of increase might be slowed if both management and labor acted responsibly. Labor was to reduce its first-year union settlements appreciably below the 5½ percent average of the previous year and business firms were urged not only to avoid widening gross margins but to absorb some cost increases.

While inflationary forces had tended to slacken slightly in 1967 due to tight monetary policy, they were clearly not exhausted. Consumer prices moved up 2.8 percent compared to the previous year's 2.9 percent. The GNP deflator rose 3.0 percent, an increase compared to the 2.7 percent gain of the previous year. While wholesale prices did not rise noticeably during the year mainly due to a fall in farm and crude material prices, hourly compensation rose an average of 6.0 percent, pushing unit labor cost up 4.5 percent. As a consequence, there was no way to reestablish price stability quickly and the CEA had to retreat further from the wage and price guideposts.

Inflation became stronger during 1968 despite the council's attempts to secure smaller price increases in key industries, despite its admonitions, and despite the imposition of the surtax in the middle of the year. Consumer prices rose 4.6 percent from January 1968 to the next January; wholesale prices increased 2.8 percent in the 12 months ending December 1968, compared to a rise of only 0.8 in the previous year.

Unlike the inflation a decade earlier, the inflation of 1965-1968 was unmistakably due to demand forces. Even the council's reports acknowledged this fact. In spite of the fact that little confidence could be put in incomes policies as a weapon to fight inflation, the council continued to pay at least lip service to the concept. Its 1969 report claimed success for the wage guideposts in the past and, although admitting the inflation was the result of a rapid growth in demand, still urged restraint: [36]

> The extent to which the satisfactory performance between 1961 and 1965 was enhanced by the efforts of the Administration to urge the observance of the guideposts cannot be precisely assessed. But the history of key wage and price decisions during this period indicates that these efforts did exert a distinct and significant influence.
>
> The blemished price-wage record of the past 3 years reflects primarily an excessive growth of demand. Indeed, the initial departures from the path of price and cost stability were concentrated in farm products, raw materi-

---

[36] *Annual Report*, 1969, p. 119.

als, and services where guideposts have little, if any, applicability. The same forces also influenced price and wage decisions in areas of discretionary market power. Once consumer prices started to move up sharply, increases in compensation no larger than the productivity trend would not have led to any improvement in real income. Workers could not be expected to accept such a result, particularly in view of the previous rapid and consistent rise in corporate profits.

The guideposts section of the 1969 annual report of the CEA continued to eschew establishing firm guidelines for either price or wage behavior for 1970 while advocating restraint. However, Chapter 1 of the report endorsed the standards suggested by the Cabinet Committee on Price Stability in its December 1968 report to the President. These standards were as follows: [37]

> New wage agreements would move halfway back to the ultimate productivity standard next year if labor accepted wage settlements that would bring the average increase in money wage rates a little below 5 percent . . . business should agree to absorb increases of up to 1 percent in unit costs and accept as a guide in price decisions a profit target no higher than the average achieved in the years 1967-68. Responsible pricing requires that businessmen focus on margins before tax and not attempt to pass the temporary corporate tax surcharge on to consumers.

The official guideposts died with the Johnson administration. Its successor was no sooner in power than it repudiated the guidepost approach. While not arguing that guideposts had had no effect during the early 1960s, the position of the Nixon administration was that they would be ineffectual in the face of strong aggregate demand. The 1970 report commented: [38]

> The Administration's plan of policy for 1969 did not include an attempt to revive wage-price guidelines, such as those existing in 1962-66. The results of our own experience and numerous trials of such policies in other countries over the preceding 20 years did not justify confidence that such efforts would help solve the inflation problem in 1969. . . .

---

[37] *Ibid.*, p. 59.
[38] *Annual Report*, 1970, pp. 23-24.

Experience with such policies in other countries has been remarkably consistent. In some cases success in holding down wage settlements or price increases has been achieved in particular industries. There is usually a period in which these programs may have some overall deterrent effect, though evidence here is less certain. After an interval, however, there is a point at which accumulating pressures make the programs ineffective. . . .

With the upsurge of inflation and inflationary pressure after mid-1965, the difficulty of reconciling the guideposts with market forces became more intense. Labor and business were being asked to act as if prices were not rising, when in fact they were. As it became evident that steps necessary to keep prices from rising were not being taken, it also became more obviously unrealistic and inequitable to make these requests in specific cases. By the fall of 1966 the policy was widely recognized to be unworkable, and it was allowed to fade away. In subsequent years, there were only episodic actions with specific companies regarding prices.

Whether the policy changed the overall behavior of the price level before it ran into intense inflation is uncertain. These were years of relative price stability. But they were also years of considerable slack in the economy, relatively high unemployment, and stable or declining farm prices. That is, they were years in which market conditions favored price stability. Econometric studies attempting to isolate a further contribution that guideposts might have made to price stability have produced uncertain results. The findings of some studies are consistent with the view that the guideposts may have had some effect in reducing the increase of the price level; other studies do not support this conclusion.

Whatever the uncertainties about this earlier period, the guidepost policy clearly did not work once the economy ran into strong and serious pressures of inflationary demand. By that time the question was not whether guideposts would have a measurable influence on the rate of inflation. It was whether they had any credibility and viability at all. The evidence is that they did not. The conspicuous cases in which guidepost policy could exercise some influence were too few and were overrun by the general tide of inflation in the economy as a whole.

In other words, the new administration, while not judging the question of whether the guideposts ever had an effect, did not believe they would be effective in the environment of 1970. Unfortunately for the administration, the inflation did not respond to tight monetary and restrictive fiscal policy as quickly as expected or desired. The key industrial commodities portion of the wholesale price index had been rising at a seasonally adjusted annual rate of 4.2 percent in the second half of 1969. In the first quarter of 1970 it rose 3.1 percent (on a comparable basis) but then in the second quarter accelerated to 4.5 percent. Consumer prices, which had been rising at a seasonally adjusted rate of 5.9 percent in the last half of 1969, rose at a 6.3 percent rate in the first quarter of 1970 and 5.8 percent in the second.

Concern with inflation and political pressure made action by the administration mandatory by mid-1970. On June 17 the President went on television to discuss the economy and to announce his intention of appointing a National Commission on Productivity. In his words, "This Commission's task will be to point the way toward this growth in 1970 and in the years ahead. I shall direct the Commission to give first priority to the problems we face now; we must achieve a balance between costs and productivity that will lead to more stable prices." The President also reported that he had instructed the Council of Economic Advisers to prepare periodic inflation alerts. "This will spotlight the significant areas of wage and price increases and objectively analyze their impact on the price level. This inflation alert will call attention to outstanding cases of price or wage increases and will be made public by the Productivity Commission." [39]

The purpose of the inflation alerts has never been clear. Obviously they were aimed partly at quieting the agitation for an incomes policy and for more direct action on prices, and partly at educating the public. Examination of the three alerts issued from August 1970 to the wage-price freeze of August 1971 does not reveal their objective. The first was the most comprehensive and covered not only the recent inflation but also the earlier inflation of the late 1950s. It traced the entire period of the 1960s in some detail in order to develop the background for the then existing situation. One entire chapter out of four was devoted to price behavior in the first half of 1970; the final chapter considered specific price and

---

[39] "Economic Policy and Productivity," Presidential Address, June 17, 1970.

wage developments. It set out its purpose as follows: [40]

> . . . it is difficult to identify particular price and wage changes as inflationary or noninflationary, and that is not the purpose of this section. Its purpose, rather, is to discuss a number of areas where inflationary pressures have had the strongest impact during the first part of 1970, and especially in recent months.

This first alert singled out for attention such industries as construction, metals and metal products, energy, tires and tubes, cigarettes, and motor carriers. It made no real attempt, however, to "blame" management or labor for the price or wage increases, although sometimes it indicated government's role in leading to higher prices.

The second alert, which was released December 1, 1970, was much like the first. It described in considerable detail the path prices had taken since the first alert. The GNP deflator, the wholesale price index, and the consumer price index were broken down into their constituent parts and the reasons for their movement analyzed. Four sectors—automotive products, fuel and energy, local transit, and copper—were singled out for particular comment; wages in the automobile and railroad industries were also discussed in detail. Again little blame was assessed.

The year 1971 opened with few signs that the inflation was abating, with rising and substantial unemployment, and with the substitution of periodic inflation alerts for the abandoned wage-price guideposts. The 1971 CEA report continued to oppose a vigorous incomes policy as unworkable, although in fact the administration was slowly being pushed into the more active posture of attempting to influence prices and wages in particular industries. Such efforts had had their genesis in the Kennedy administration.

Jawboning

Attempts to restrain prices and wages preceded the formulation of the guideposts. The first public effort was made in a letter President Kennedy sent to the heads of the 12 largest steel companies on September 6, 1961. The President acted on the basis of press reports that the steel companies were weighing a price increase that would

---

[40] Report to the National Commission on Productivity by the Council of Economic Advisers, *Inflation Alert*, August 7, 1970, p. IV-1.

coincide with the wage increase due the steel workers on October 1. As quoted in the 1962 report of the Council, the President's letter stated:

> Steel is a bellwether as well as a major element in industrial costs. A rise in steel prices would force price increases in many industries and invite price increases in others. . . .
>
> I do not wish to minimize the urgency of preventing inflationary movements in steel wages. I recognize, too, that the steel industry, by absorbing increases in employment costs since 1958, has demonstrated a will to halt the wage price spiral in steel. If the industry were now to forego a price increase, it would enter collective bargaining negotiations next spring with a record of three and a half years of price stability. It would clearly then be the turn of the labor representatives to limit wage demands to a level consistent with continued price stability. The moral position of the steel industry next spring—and its claim to the support of public opinion—will be strengthened by the exercise of price restraint now.[41]

In the next week, the President wrote the head of the United Steelworkers of America. In that letter he urged that wage demands be limited to advances in productivity. This request, as noted above, was generalized to all industries in the guideposts issued four months later.

The exchange of letters in the fall of 1961 helps explain the virulence of the reaction when the steel industry attempted to raise prices in April of 1962. During the steel negotiations, the secretary of labor had taken an active role in securing an agreement that was widely viewed as noninflationary; it was consistent with the wage price guideposts in that the increase in compensation was estimated to be less than 3 percent. The resultant altercation when U.S. Steel announced a price increase of $3^1/2$ percent on all its products is well known, and it set the stage for future "jawboning" attempts. None was to be as bitter, but its memory would remain and color other disputes.

Whatever the merits of the price rise on the basis of costs, the timing of the rise did not appear to be auspicious. At the time, industry had considerable excess capacity and imports had been rising. Consequently it is possible but by no means certain that, had

---

[41] *Annual Report,* 1962, p. 182.

the President not intervened, the price increase would not have stuck. Certainly there was a clear division of opinion within the industry as to the desirability of the price rise. The chairman of Inland Steel, Joseph Block, had claimed that cost reduction rather than price increases would have been the best way to increase industry profits.[42]

In any event, the forcefulness of the President's response, coupled with veiled threats of antitrust action and the use of the FBI, made a deep impression on the business community. In the future, the steel industry would act with more subtlety and other industries would be more likely to listen carefully to the administration. The steel industry did not attempt another across-the-board price rise until August of 1968, although many price changes and especially increases were made over the intervening years. Instead it generally followed the approach of raising some prices and lowering others, an approach that made a frontal attack by the government more difficult.

The sharp reaction of the business community and the precipitous fall in the stock market may have had an impact on the administration as well. During the next two years there were no known conflicts over price changes with any company or industry. Partly this may have been due to the existence of considerable excess capacity and basically stable prices. The administration did indicate concern over the automobile industry not because prices were increased but because they were not reduced. A major tenet of the guideposts called for prices to be reduced in those industries where productivity gains exceeded the economy-wide average. During this period, the automobile industry never reduced prices.

The administration continued to view the steel industry as the key to its stabilization efforts. In January 1965, the President requested the Council of Economic Advisers to prepare an analysis of steel prices in preparation for forthcoming labor negotiations. While seeking to forestall a price increase, the administration also wanted to prevent another major confrontation with the steel industry. Richard F. Janssen claimed that [43]

> underlying the Administration's intent to accentuate the positive side of steel price stability is a growing belief that President Kennedy's angry outburst in 1962 was a mistake. While his reaction was understandable, officials say,

---

[42] John Sheahan, *The Wage-Price Guideposts* (Washington: The Brookings Institution, 1967), p. 36.

[43] *Wall Street Journal*, April 1, 1965.

the lingering mistrust it aroused in the business community is something the consensus-bent Mr. Johnson would be
loath to revive.

Perhaps even more compelling to some strategists, however, is the belief that a Kennedy-type crackdown not only
displays but readily dissipates Presidential power. "We
have no big stick" over steel prices, one official says,
worrying that the worst mistake would be to frequently
brandish a club that proved to be too fragile, leaving the
President's ability to influence prices much weaker than
before.

Thus, the plan was to use the council's report on the steel
industry to help secure a reasonable wage settlement in line with the
wage guideposts. The report, issued in May, indicated that wages
could rise by as much as 3 percent per year without the steel
industry having to raise prices. The wage settlement that occurred
was officially estimated to be within the guideposts—"an average of
3.2 percent a year, computed over the full 39-month period." [44]
Initially the steel industry continued its practice of raising some
items and lowering others and no further governmental action was
taken.

In the fall, the government was presented with an opportunity
to wield "a stick" when the major aluminum companies announced
an increase in the price.of ingot of one-half cent per pound. The
administration had been negotiating with the industry about the
disposal of the government's surplus stockpile of aluminum.
Promptly after the announcement of the price increase, Secretary of
Defense McNamara, Secretary of the Treasury Fowler, and Secretary of Commerce Connor were called to the White House to
consider ways of speeding the disposal of some of the 1,400,000
tons of government aluminum. On November 7 the government
announced plans to sell 200,000 tons to relieve growing pressure on
prices. A few days later the industry capitulated and rolled prices
back.

The aluminum incident indicated a continued interest in steel
prices because steel and aluminum are substitutes for many uses
and therefore higher aluminum prices would permit and encourage
higher steel prices. It also showed a willingness to take forceful
action to prevent price rises, although few industries were in as
vulnerable a position as aluminum. In particular the government had

[44] *Annual Report*, 1966, p. 89.

no such weapon over steel. However, industry generally viewed the aluminum confrontation as a threat to all industry not to raise prices.

Another confrontation with the steel industry arose at the end of 1965 when steel companies attempted to raise prices on structural steel and pilings. The government, which used about 25 percent of all structural steel, threatened to shift its purchases to firms that did not raise prices. Thereafter, a compromise was reached with a smaller price increase.

During 1966, two costly labor settlements led to the abandonment of wage guideposts and inhibited future jawboning. In January the New York transit strike was settled with a wage increase that was personally termed by the President to be in violation of the guideposts and not in the public interest. In August, after considerable government intervention in the negotiations, the airline mechanics settled their long strike with a package which the union claimed amounted to an 8 percent gain—clearly way in excess of the guideposts. These two settlements made it more difficult for the administration to take vigorous action against price increases by industry.

In August, the steel industry moved again and boosted prices of sheet and strip steel 2.1 percent in violation of the guideposts. The government condemned the action in strong words but was unable or unwilling to take any other action to force a rollback. The price increase stuck. But the administration did win one public battle that year, in July, when the Council of Economic Advisers opposed a 5 percent price increase, in molybdenum, an important element in stainless steel production. After some dissension this price increase was rescinded.

According to its 1967 annual report, the CEA also met with leaders of industries representing "perhaps 50 product lines" for which price increases were either announced or planned by one or more firms. While the council did not claim universal success, the annual report said: "In a number of cases, it is clear that price increases which were announced or contemplated have been rescinded, reduced in amount of coverage, or delayed. Some companies have indicated that their subsequent price decisions were affected even where their decision in the immediate case was not changed." [45]

One of these successes appears to have been in the tobacco industry where, according to public statements by some companies,

[45] *Annual Report*, 1967, p. 127.

an announced price increase was partially rolled back as a result of government pressure. In addition, it was widely reported in the press that a rollback of newsprint prices was the result of administration efforts. However, other efforts and successes, if any, were not reported.

During 1967, the only public confrontations between the government and industry were over steel prices. In September the steel industry ignored pleas from the administration not to follow Republic Steel's price increase on cold carbon and alloy bars. In December, U.S. Steel first increased the price of cold-rolled carbon steel sheets by $5 a ton and then followed a few days later with comparable price increases for galvanized and aluminum-coated sheet. Both the President and the chairman of the Council of Economic Advisers protested but without visible effect.

There seems to be no doubt that during the remainder of the Johnson administration, the council made many private representations to industry leaders to refrain from raising prices or not to follow already announced increases by rivals. Although many members of the council and its staff believe these efforts retarded price increases, there is little objective evidence to support their belief.

During its last year in office, the administration sharply criticized two announced price increases, one across-the-board increase in steel and one for automobiles. In each case, the largest firm in its industry, U.S. Steel and General Motors, increased its prices less than the initial announcement by rivals. Hence in both cases the administration claimed that its efforts had reduced the size of the price increase. However, there is no evidence to indicate what these firms would have done had the government remained silent. The government had apparently been ineffectual the previous year in restraining steel prices, and its power to keep increases down in 1968 was obviously no greater. On the other hand, there is some evidence that it may have brought more pressure to bear on the industry in 1968, including threats of diverting business to those who did not follow the increase.

The Nixon Administration

With the advent of the new administration and the jettisoning of the guideposts, "jawboning" was specifically disavowed. The council dropped even its private efforts to keep price increases restrained. Right from the beginning, however, the administration was under pressure to either reinstate guideposts and jawboning or to institute some other form of incomes policy. The financial editor of the *Washington Post* as well as leading Democrats were vocal advocates of an incomes policy and severe critics of "Nixon's laissez faire."

The new administration refrained from any real jawboning during its first two years. Efforts were made to deal with price problems in lumber and in copper, but in both cases, moral suasion was not the primary tool. However, in 1971, prior to the wage-price freeze, the administration did take action more in line with what its predecessors had done. In January, Bethlehem Steel Corporation announced price increases of about 12 percent for carbon steel plates and structural shapes. President Nixon criticized these increases and expressed his concern that they would lead to further inflation in the construction industry, an industry that was causing the government the most anxiety. Other steel producers announced price increases of about 8 percent and the lower prices prevailed.

The construction industry troubled the Democrats under Johnson and then the Republicans under Nixon. This industry has seemed to follow its own dictates and to ignore economic pressures. In recent years, unemployment in the industry has risen markedly but without obviously affecting the rate at which wages climbed. In 1970, for example, construction agreements called for an average first-year increase of 18.3 percent, while the industry's unemployment rate was nearly double that of the rest of the economy.[46]

In January 1971, the President met with labor and management leaders in the construction industry and asked them to work out with the Construction Industry Collective Bargaining Commission a voluntary plan which would help stabilize costs and prices. This effort soon proved futile and the President suspended the Davis-Bacon Act on February 23. After that blow, labor leaders agreed to participate with the government and management in achieving greater price and wage stability. This led to the establishment of a Construction Industry Stabilization Committee and craft dispute boards to review future labor contracts. It also led to the establishment of an Interagency Committee to develop criteria for determining the acceptability of negotiated wages and prices. In return, the President revoked the suspension of the Davis-Bacon Act, but with the reservation that wage increases in excess of approved levels

---

[46] *Third Inflation Alert*, A Report by the Council of Economic Advisers, April 13, 1971, p. 35.

would not be used in implementing the "prevailing wages" provisions of the Davis-Bacon Act.

It is really too early to measure the impact of these actions on construction wages. The annual rate of growth in the Department of Commerce Composite Construction Cost Index slowed from 9.2 percent in the last six months of 1970 to 6.4 percent in the first six months of 1971. This may be misleading, however, since the decline in rate of growth was concentrated in the first three months of 1971. The rate of growth in the index for the three months ending in June was back up to 10.0 percent. No doubt much of the movement of this index is due to changes in construction material prices.

Effectiveness of the U.S. Incomes Policy

There have been a number of studies bearing on the issue of the effectiveness of the U.S. incomes policy. Professor George Perry presented evidence [47] that the guideposts restrained wage increases in manufacturing between the middle of 1962 and 1966 and that the effect was most pronounced on "visible industries." Perry's evidence was based on an earlier study he conducted which related wage changes to unemployment, consumer price index changes, the average profit rate in manufacturing and the change in the average profit rate in manufacturing.[48] Using quarterly data Perry estimated the relationship for the period 1947-60 and then extrapolated through 1966. He found that the model tended to overestimate the expected wage increase for the guidepost period. Perry also examined two sets of industries, those which were considered to be "visible" and thus subject to government pressure and those which were "invisible." For each set of industries, he prepared the ratio of the average hourly earnings between 1954 and 1957 and between 1963 and 1966—two periods that he argued were comparable. He then took the ratio of the two ratios to express whether wages rose faster or slower in the second period compared with the first. This was done for each industry and the averages presented. Perry found that wages in visible industries had moved up faster relative to those in invisible industries during the earlier period than during the guidepost period.

These results and the conclusions have been sharply challenged

---

[47] George L. Perry, "Wages and the Guideposts," *American Economic Review* LVII (September 1967), pp. 897-904.

[48] George L. Perry, *Unemployment, Money Wage Rates, and Inflation* (Cambridge, 1966).

by Paul S. Anderson, Michael L. Wachter, and Adrian W. Throop.[49] They pointed out that Perry's estimating equation is unstable, that dummy variables for other periods also were significant, that considerable serial correlation would account for long series of residuals of the same sign, that using a different period to estimate the equation leads to reducing the series of negative residuals to the 1964 to mid-1967 period. Professor Anderson also presented data on wage changes that indicated that there had been a downward shift in the distribution of wage settlements rather than a compression, which is what the guideposts would have predicted. The invisible, visible dichotomy was also criticized on the grounds that it was arbitrary, that using percent unionized or concentration indexes led to worse result and that, in any case, the "visible" industries were the ones that had experienced the most rapid wage increases in the 1950s and thus the fact that wages moved up less rapidly in the 1960s was due to the regression fallacy—relative price relationships were moving back towards the norm.

Professor Perry [50] replied that he still believed his evidence and that he found some of the figures presented by his critics confirmed the impact of the guideposts. He also showed that, after 1966, his model again explained wage changes reasonably well. He argued that this too confirmed the impact of the guideposts, since they ostensibly were abandoned by mid-1966.

Perry's results have also been questioned by Simler and Tella [51] in a recent article. They found that if account is taken of the increased portion of the population which moves into and out of the labor force depending on labor market conditions, the published rates of unemployment during the 1960s significantly understated the true levels of unemployment. Correcting for this bias and also utilizing data on wages and salaries per man-hour in the private nonfarm economy results in the virtual elimination of the large negative residuals for the 1962-66 period. Thus it appears from their study that the guideposts had no measurable effect on wages. Simler and

---

[49] Paul S. Anderson, "Wages and the Guideposts: Comment," *American Economic Review* LIX (June 1969); Michael L. Wachter, "Wages and the Guideposts: Comment," *American Economic Review* LIX (June 1969); Adrian W. Throop, "Wages and the Guideposts: Comment," *American Economic Review* LIX (June 1969).

[50] George L. Perry, "Wages and the Guideposts: Reply," *American Economic Review* LIX (June 1969).

[51] N. J. Simler and Alfred Tella, "Labor Reserves and the Phillips Curve," *The Review of Economics and Statistics* XLX (February 1968), pp. 32-49.

Tella concluded: "On balance, there is no tendency to overpredict . . . after mid-1962. The average prediction error for the 20 quarters between 6203 and 6702 is only −0.06 for equation (6.3), compared with −0.55 . . . when" wages in manufacturing are the dependent variable.[52]

A more elaborate and sophisticated study than Perry's was carried out by Robert Gordon[53] who examined the macro behavior of the economy between 1954 and 1970. While he, like Perry, worked with reduced form equations without fully specifying the underlying model, his work is a significant improvement over earlier efforts. His articulated model includes estimates for both disguised and measured unemployment, for price expectations, for tax changes, and for the guideposts. Moreover, his wage variable includes a new fixed-weight index of nonfarm hourly earnings adjusted for fringe benefits that avoids the problems stemming from shifts in the composition of the employed labor force. It is of particular interest to our study that the guidepost dummy was not significantly different from zero, thus indicating, as Gordon asserts:[54] the "equation . . . confirms the conclusion in my previous article that the Kennedy-Johnson guideposts were ineffective in reducing the rate of wage increase."

Other evidence indicating the ineffectualness of the guideposts on wages was presented by Richard Lester, who analyzed negotiated wage settlements from 1951 to 1967 and compared the settlements with increases in straight-time average earnings in manufacturing. He concludes that "the wage-price guidepost policy . . . apparently was not successful in keeping negotiated increases below earnings increases, even in manufacturing where the conditions for its success are favorable."[55]

John Sheahan in his book, *The Wage-Price Guideposts*,[56] reviews most of the studies that had been done on the effectiveness of the guideposts. He admitted that "it is impossible to prove or to disprove the hypothesis that the guideposts were an important factor in achieving more nearly stable prices. This is because no one can be completely sure of what would have happened if they had not existed."[57]

---

[52] *Ibid.*, p. 42.
[53] Robert J. Gordon, "Inflation in Recession and Recovery," *Brookings Papers on Economic Activity*, 1 (1971) pp. 105-66.
[54] *Ibid.*, p. 123.
[55] Lester, *op. cit.*, p. 174.
[56] Sheahan, *op. cit.*
[57] *Ibid.*, p. 79.

Sheahan reports on a number of studies on the effectiveness of the guideposts, most of which find some evidence that prices or wages were reduced. In at least the case of Simler and Tella, he overstates their finding since he concludes that their evidence shows that actual wage increases "turned out to be less than predicted," [58] when they actually found no significant impact from the guideposts.

A fundamental problem with all the wage studies is the failure to develop a fully articulated model indicating the basic structural relationships underlying the studies' equations. In particular, failure to do so makes the meaning of any wage-price guidepost dummy variable ambiguous. All the models include some price variables, such as the consumer price index. If the guideposts had been equally effective on wages and prices, then the effectiveness of the guideposts should be fully reflected in the coefficient for the price variable and no negative residuals or significant dummy variable should be apparent. Thus what Perry and the others claim to have found must be a differential impact of the guideposts on wage rates rather than on prices.

Most observers, however, would argue that the government would have more power over large concentrated industries than over labor unions. As mentioned above, in certain instances the government could threaten to release stockpiles, bring antitrust suits, shift purchases, et cetera; but it has no such potential weapons for dealing with recalcitrant unions. Moreover, right from the beginning unions had refused publicly to be bound by the guideposts. Thus to find evidence that the guideposts were more effective in reducing wages than in reducing prices seems contradictory to our a priori expectation. For example, John Dunlop argued:

> It is my considered judgment that the guideposts probably have had no independent restraining influence on wage changes in private industry. . . . I know of no person actually involved in wage setting on the side of industry, labor organizations, or as a government or private mediator or arbitrator who thinks that the guideposts have had on balance a constrictive influence; and I have discussed the issue in detail with scores of such persons in the past six months. There have been no confrontations on wages as on prices. The evidence from statistical studies of the Phillips curve, relating wage changes and unemployment, appears

---

[58] *Ibid.*, p. 84.

to me inclusive [sic] both to what has happened and the reasons for any possible change.[59]

The evidence of the effectiveness of guideposts on prices is even less compelling than that for wages. A study done by the Federal Reserve Bank of Cleveland showed that the relationship between wholesale industrial prices and unemployment rates had shifted downward during the 1961-65 period compared to earlier periods. All the Cleveland bank did was to plot changes in wholesale industrial prices against quarterly averages of the percent of the labor force unemployed.

There seems to be no doubt that the period of the 1960s was different from the earlier ones but whether this was because of the guideposts is not so certain. During the 1950s there had been a history of rapid inflation, suppressed inflation from controls, and a need for major industries to reestablish prior price relationships. During the 1960s, there had been a period of several years of virtual price stability and rapidly rising productivity. Conditions were certainly different and it is improper to conclude that the guideposts were responsible without more elaborate testing.

Robert Solow did attempt a somewhat more elaborate effort to measure the impact of the guideposts on prices. He found that, for the period 1954 to 1965, year-to-year changes in the wholesale price index for manufactures were related to the McGraw-Hill index of capacity utilization and changes in labor costs per unit of output in manufacturing. His data suggest that wholesale prices rose about 0.7 percentage point slower after 1962 than before but that the difference is not statistically significant. Since the guideposts were also intended to affect wage rates and hence labor costs per unit of output, it is not clear whether he should have found any significant relationship even if the guideposts were very effective. To the extent that his data indicate anything, they suggest that the guideposts were more effective on prices than on wages—which of course is just the opposite of Perry's findings.

In conclusion, the evidence shows that the period of the 1960s differed at least superficially from the period of the 1950s. Whether it differed structurally and fundamentally is an unanswered question. Evidence on both sides can be presented. The impact of the guideposts therefore can not be ascertained with any certainty. A priori it would seem doubtful that they had any long-run impact on wages

---

[59] George P. Shultz and Robert Z. Aliber, eds., *Guidelines, Informal Controls, and the Market Place* (Chicago: University of Chicago Press, 1966), p. 84.

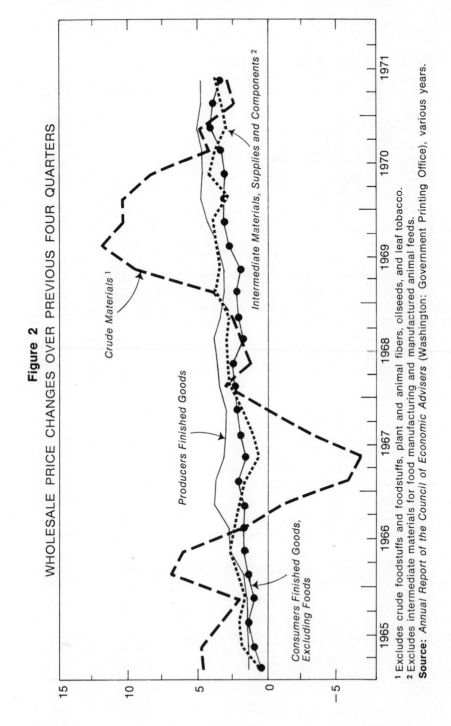

Figure 2

WHOLESALE PRICE CHANGES OVER PREVIOUS FOUR QUARTERS

Crude Materials [1]

Intermediate Materials, Supplies and Components [2]

Producers Finished Goods

Consumers Finished Goods, Excluding Foods

[1] Excludes crude foodstuffs and foodstuffs, plant and animal fibers, oilseeds, and leaf tobacco.
[2] Excludes intermediate materials for food manufacturing and manufactured animal feeds.
Source: *Annual Report of the Council of Economic Advisers* (Washington: Government Printing Office), various years.

since the unions are less subject to pressure than management. In addition, in the long run unions are going to secure whatever premium is possible over nonunion wages. There tends to be a limited ratio of union to nonunion wages that is reasonably constant [60] and it would be unlikely that any incomes policy could change this relationship for long.[61]

On the price side, there is certainly some casual empirical evidence that the guideposts *cum* jawboning had an effect. Some well publicized price increases were rolled back. However, in certain cases, market conditions clearly did not justify the increases and they would not have been likely to stick in any case.

To the extent that prices may have been reduced in certain industries, profits would have been squeezed, with the result that investment would have been retarded. This in turn would have reduced the growth in capacity and the degrees of substitution of modern equipment for older facilities. Both of these effects would result in higher long-run prices, at least until the missing investment could be made up. Thus a successful lid on particular prices might be expected to lead to the same prices rapidly rising in the future, followed by an eventual decline to the long-run equilibrium.

Even if jawboning and the guideposts did hold some specific prices temporarily below what they would have been otherwise, the impact on overall prices is unclear. Presumably if prices were lowered, consumption of the product would have been larger and more resources would have had to be diverted to that industry. Unless the resources specific to that particular industry were underutilized so that no new resources needed to be diverted from other sectors, there would have been cost pressures placed on raw material and perhaps labor markets. Thus it is quite possible that some prices could be held down with the result that other "uncontrolled" prices were increased, leaving consumers no better off and possibly distorting the allocation of resources.

Cost-Push Inflation and the Republican Administration

Whether the guideposts and jawboning were effective or not, they were abandoned with the new administration, as has already been mentioned. The Nixon game plan was to rely on traditional monetary

---

[60] H. G. Lewis, *Unionism and Relative Wages in the United States* (Chicago: University of Chicago Press, 1963), pp. 2-5.

[61] An incomes policy of Haberler's type II that is designed to make labor markets more competitive could change this relationship considerably.

and fiscal policy, especially the former, in order to halt the then raging inflation. In retrospect, it is clear that his administration underestimated the difficulty of reducing the inflation without producing substantial unemployment. It should have been clear from the period of the late 1950s that it takes a long time to squeeze the inflationary pressure out of the economy. The unemployment rate rose above 6 percent in 1958 and remained well above 5 percent until 1965, seven years later; but the rate of increase of gross hourly earnings in the nonagricultural private sector did not decline below 3.5 percent until 1961, four years after the start of a period of substantial excess capacity.

Basically it takes several years to let an inflation run its course. Some prices respond more promptly to inflationary pressures than others, but the inflation will continue until the lagging sectors have brought their prices in line. As will be recalled, the administered price inflation hypothesis argues that concentrated industries will raise their prices and cause inflation even in the absence of excess demand. There is some evidence that suggests that, during the late 1950s, it was the concentrated industries that were raising their prices and contributing to, if not causing, the rise in the price indexes.

On the other hand, Leonard Weiss examined the 1968-69 period and found that concentration had a statistically significant negative effect on prices.[62] In other words, during the 1968-69 period, concentrated industries raised their prices less than unconcentrated industries. It seems unlikely that this disparity will continue. In fact we can be confident that, during 1970 and 1971, concentrated industries raised their prices faster than unconcentrated as they attempted to return their prices to the same relative level as before. Whether this should be called administered-price inflation, cost-push inflation, or lagged inflation is a matter of taste and is of no real importance.

As was pointed out above, increases in union wages lagged behind increases in nonunion wages from 1966 through the middle of 1968. Since organized workers have experienced a relative decline in their wages over a two-and-a-half year period, a catching-up period for union wages as well as for concentrated industries can be expected, with the resultant final adjustment pushed well into the future.

A look at Figure 2 indicates that the pattern of the late 1950s

---

[62] Leonard W. Weiss, Study Reported in an Appendix to the Testimony of Assistant Attorney General Richard W. McLaren before the Joint Economic Committee, July 10, 1970, *1970 Midyear Review of the State of the Economy*, Part I, 91st Cong., 2d Sess., 1970, pp. 108-28.

is again appearing. The rate of increase in the prices of crude materials hit its peak in the first quarter of 1970. As unemployment rose after that, the rate steadily declined. With a one-quarter lag, the rate of increase in prices in intermediate goods also fell, while the rate of increase for producer finished goods continued to rise throughout 1970 and only started to edge down in 1971. It would also appear from the chart that inflation has not been completely squeezed out of the economy since crude material prices are continuing to rise, albeit slower than earlier.

We can conclude this paper then by dismissing the term administered-price inflation and recognizing that, during the late 1950s and in the last few years, the economy has experienced lagged inflation. Conceptually all an incomes policy can do, therefore, is to delay a lagged inflation further. Whether this is desirable or not would depend on the effect on the allocation of resources and on income of the government program. It is quite likely that an incomes policy would discourage investment, retard innovation, and misallocate resources in such a way as to reduce total real income with the result that we all are worse off. On the other hand, it is possible that if it reduced prices only in noncompetitive areas, resource allocation might be improved.

If this analysis is correct, the effect of the wage-price freeze and of the subsequent stage II will be to postpone price rises which would have taken place earlier. Eventually when controls are lifted, prices will rise to their equilibrium level. But this will have to be the subject of a future study.

5
AIMING FOR A SUSTAINABLE SECOND BEST DURING THE RECOVERY FROM THE 1970 RECESSION

William Fellner

The present paper begins with a discussion of appropriate long-run objectives that need to be kept in mind by policymakers now attempting to stage a transition toward a desirable and sustainable state of the economy. Short-run problems relating to the transition itself will be considered subsequently. These short-run problems include, of course, the problem of greatly reducing the inflationary aftereffects of a past period of overfull utilization.

Keeping Our Eyes on the Normal Growth Path While Moving Toward It

Significantly Inflationary Effects of Conventional Full-Employment Policy. As concerns the coming years, even gradual pursuit of a full-employment target by *conventional methods*, and with the usual definition of the American full-employment target in mind, is incompatible with the success of anti-inflationary efforts. It is possible to describe a somewhat unconventional full-employment policy that could be made compatible with reducing our inflation rate to small size and with subsequently keeping it low, and it may well be possible to implement such a program effectively. But overcoming the difficulties would require a good deal of systematic preparation by groups of competent experts who, instead of talking themselves into unwarranted optimism about the possibilities, would undertake to explore the details of a program that is in the nature of a second best.

The conventional method of achieving high employment targets is to keep the effective demand for saleable output at a very high level. This is a level at which there exists a sufficiently high market demand even for those labor categories to which, at given wage rates, the market sector assigns relatively low priority. The target for the national unemployment rate is usually defined as 4 percent or somewhat less. The difficulty here is that, at the corresponding level of effective demand, pronounced shortages develop in a good many of the specific resource-categories that need to be distinguished from one another. Given the characteristics of our wage structure, the demand of the market sector for workers in the more unemployment-prone categories can be increased to the desired extent only by creating undesirable inflationary shortages in the scarce labor categories.

At any high level of effective demand for goods and services at which the unemployment rate of the vulnerable labor categories is

Figure 1

RELATION OF ADULT MALE UNEMPLOYMENT RATE TO NATIONAL UNEMPLOYMENT RATE

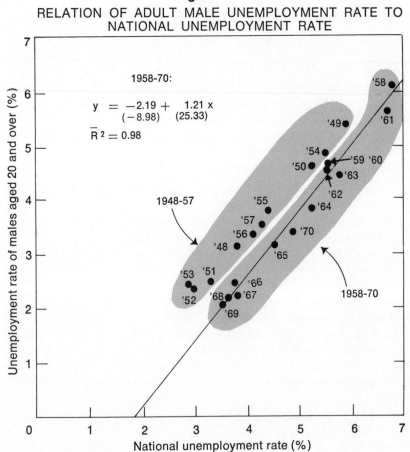

not considered excessive, the excess demand for the scarce types of labor categories (the "shortages") would, of course, become eliminated with no adverse effects on the employment of nonscarce types of labor if the real wages of the scarce types rose sufficiently high *without any rise of the real wages of the others*. But this would require greater flexibility of the wage structure than ours has.

A relationship observed for the post-1957 period and expressed by Figure 1 suggests that when the national unemployment rate is 4 percent the unemployment rate for males aged twenty years and over is 2.6 percent. The corresponding unemployment rate for males twenty-five years and over would be below 2 percent. Since the early postwar years the representation of the adult male category in the unemployment rate has declined appreciably.[1] We even have indications that the regression line drawn in the graph for the post-1957 period hides to some extent a continued gradual trend,[2] so that a rise from the very low national unemployment levels of the late sixties may become associated with a lesser rise of the adult male rate than the line would suggest. The adult male category includes a very large number of subcategories to be defined by educational background, skills, type of interest, work habits, physical health, location, etc., and in some of these subcategories shortages tend to become acute when the unemployment rate of the entire adult male group is about 2 percent for a geographical area of the size of the United States. This is the main reason why conventional full-employment policies are highly suspect of being inflationary in a significant degree. These policies carry the threat of getting us back into the difficulties we now face even if on the present occasion we should succeed in overcoming these difficulties.

Several further circumstances must be taken into account in any attempt to visualize the state of the American economy at a national unemployment rate in the neighborhood of 4 percent. At

---

[1] On changes in the composition of the labor force and of the unemployed and of the unemployment rate by age-sex groups, see George L. Perry, "Changing Labor Markets and Inflation," *Brookings Papers on Economic Activity*, 1970, 3.

[2] The line is drawn as if changes in the ratio of the adult-male rate to the national rate of unemployment had resulted wholly from changes in the national rate. However, by following through in the graph the year-to-year movements of both rates and by looking into the data for various months of the current year (1971) one is led to the judgment that we are faced here not only with a relation between the two variables of the graph but also with a gradual trend toward a lowering of the adult male rate relative to the national rate.

such an unemployment rate a high proportion of the unemployed remains in that condition only for a very short period i.e., is made up of workers who at the time of the survey are between two jobs because they are in the midst of a process of rapid relocation. A small proportion of the 4 percent does experience unemployment of extended duration, but even as concerns this proportion it must be remembered that while the unemployed are by definition persons who at the time of a monthly survey are regarded as job seekers, there exist differences among them with respect to the intensity of their job-seeking effort. On the other hand, even at a 4 percent national rate some labor categories have a higher specific unemployment rate than is needed for avoiding inflationary shortages.

It is understandable that the 4 percent rate is considered socially acceptable at least as an interim target; yet it is understandable also that this rate and rates in its neighborhood have become suspect of involving excess demand for specific resource categories, particularly for specific categories of workers. Indeed, all recent technical-statistical estimates and less formal appraisals with which I am acquainted associate an appreciable rate of inflation with an unemployment rate of 4 percent, though some investigators take the position that it would be possible to keep the resulting rate of inflation steady (nonaccelerating). I will explain later why the accelerationist position seems much more convincing to me than the non-accelerationist, but I will at first take it for granted that a significant rate of inflation is considered highly undesirable in any event. The question will thus be examined whether the shortages developing at an unemployment rate in the neighborhood of 4 percent could not be avoided by relying on methods other than the conventional ones when making the "last mile" of the move toward high employment.

Inflationary methods are the conventional ones for achieving high employment because it is a simple and tempting idea to create significant excess demand for those workers who are in greater demand than others, and thereby to achieve a sufficiently high demand even for the services of those who otherwise would be very much in excess supply. Differently expressed, by the time there is very little excess supply in *any* major labor category, there exists significant excess demand for some major categories, and maintaining the excess demand for these categories by monetary and fiscal policy is a tempting method of helping the workers belonging in the others. But the method is an exceedingly crude one, and I will not shy away from *predicting that circumstances will force us to abandon it.* This is why it is essential to put our minds to working out alternative solutions, and to compare these not with a utopia but with what would happen if we did not find an alternative that at least qualifies as a second best.

If monetary and fiscal policy gradually raised the effective demand for saleable goods and services merely to the point where pronounced shortages in the most needed major labor categories are as yet avoided—let us assume "just barely avoided"—*and if no other measures of employment policy were adopted*, then the excess supply in other labor categories would be greater than is consistent with long-run political and social objectives. I do not believe that the econometric methods occasionally employed for judging the inflationary consequences of maintaining high employment levels, or for judging the unemployment consequences of maintaining noninflationary levels of activity, would be nearly dependable enough for building policy on the precise numerical results so obtained. These levels need to be felt out gradually by policymakers. But for illustration rather than for any more ambitious purpose I will add a few remarks with numerical content about levels of activity carrying the prospect of being noninflationary, or nearly so.

If, using yearly data for the period 1952-70, we explore separately the relation of the rate of unemployment to (a) wage increase, (b) acceleration of wage increase, (c) price increase, (d) acceleration of price increase, then a national unemployment rate of 5 percent is found to be the level of zero acceleration, with a rate of wage increase of 4.7 percent a year and with a "tolerable" price increase of 2.2 percent at this unemployment rate. This is so regardless of whether we represent prices by the consumer price index or the private nonfarm GNP deflator. To be precise, the "wage rate" in question is compensation per man-hour in the private nonfarm sector, and the difference between 4.7 percent and 2.2 percent equals that sector's average productivity increase for the period as a whole. I find this observation worth communicating though results obtained by the oversimplified method of examining a set of two-variable correlations (simple regressions) independently of each other are, of course, not conclusive. In the present case the caveat must be added that wage and price *acceleration* have to do in part with changes in unemployment rather than with the unemployment rate itself (indeed, according to some investigators with whom I disagree, acceleration of inflation results exclusively from *changes* in unemployment). The simple regressions on which I was reporting disregard the fact that, when an explanation is sought for the historical acceleration of wage and price increases, the effect of unemployment and of its changes should be explored jointly. This I had to disregard because the very high positive correlation I found in the time series between the level of unemployment and its changes makes it impossible to distinguish the consequences of low unemployment from those of declining unemployment in any direct or straightforward manner.

Indirect methods for drawing this distinction, or rather methods for obtaining results that *imply* this distinction, *were* used by other investigators. George L. Perry estimates that at a 5 percent unemployment rate inflation would (after an adjustment period) be developing at a rate of about 3 percent, and that at a 4 percent unemployment rate inflation would be developing at $4^1/_2$ percent or somewhat higher. His model yields no acceleration of inflation in the event of constancy of any of the unemployment levels to which the model applies. [3] To the reasons why I consider nonacceleration an unconvincing feature of his model and of some others I shall return. At present I am merely pointing out that there seems to be little controversy about the distinctly inflationary implications of the 4 percent unemployment target and at the same time about the socially undesirable consequences of the high national unemployment rate that would be compatible with a more-or-less noninflationary level of activity. All this is based on samples drawn from past data and hence all this implies the policy practices of the past.

In terms of basic principles, the significantly supernormal vulnerability of specific labor categories to unemployment results largely from rigidities in the structure of real wage rates. These rigidities could be reduced, but in practice they could hardly be reduced to insignificance. Ideally, the real wage rates of workers who are in lesser demand should be at a correspondingly lower level at which employment opportunities would exist for them, and political value judgments concerning minimum living standards should express themselves exclusively in separate measures of subsidization such as do not reduce the incentive to earn income additionally. However, the difficulties standing in the way of putting a general scheme of this kind into effect would probably be insuperable even if the rigidities of the wage structure were much smaller than they are in a world in which the structure is strongly influenced by union activity, by minimum wage legislation, by unemployment compensation, and also by conventions concerning equitable wage differentials. In reality, at a noninflationary employment level, the real wage rates of the vulnerable worker categories are not nearly low enough to

---

[3] To be precise, Perry uses in this context not the official unemployment rate but his measure of labor-market ease (see below).

preclude large unemployment in these categories. In spite of the wage rigidities, the market sector has adjusted *very largely* to the changing relative supply of different types of labor, in that the representation of some of the vulnerable categories in the employed labor force has risen significantly as the relative supply of such workers has risen. But the adjustment has not been complete, and this is what has given rise to the increasingly supernormal representation of these same categories in unemployment. For example, the large relative increase of workers other than white adult males in the supply-mix of the economy has led to a very substantial increase in the proportionate representation of those workers among the employed, but a residual has remained which shows in a significant increase of the weight of the same groups in unemployment.

Outlining a Second-best Solution. Assume now that after (or simultaneously with) greatly reducing the inflationary carry-over from the period 1965-69, monetary and fiscal policy raises effective demand to the point where inflation is at a "tolerable" level, i.e., does not exceed a reasonably selected threshold value, say, remains in the range between 2 percent and 3 percent. Assume also that this involves a national unemployment rate in the neighborhood of 5 percent. If no further measures were taken this result would imply not only the desirable degree of availability of kinds of labor in which there would be shortages at a 4 percent national rate but also an enlarged excess supply in labor categories that would be in lesser excess supply at a 4 percent national rate than at a 5 percent rate. Unemployment compensation and welfare payments would amount to more at a 5 percent than at a 4 percent national rate, and were it not for these welfare-type payments, the vulnerable labor categories would have less unemployment at a noninflationary *national* unemployment rate because the wage structure would be more flexible. In principle, the negative income tax describes a regime under which subsidization of the needy could be made compatible with letting the wage rates of the vulnerable labor categories decline to their equilibrium level. Yet as long as we have not found an administratively manageable general solution of this sort, the rigidifying effect of various institutional arrangements including welfare-type payments remains a fact. It is a fact also that the methods of financing such payments *need not be inflationary* since taxation and even borrowing from the public reduce the expenditures of the rest of the population. At the same time, we should recognize that promoting idleness of persons capable of work is not a reasonable second best.

A more reasonable second best is to offer employment in the public sector—or partly with nonprofit institutions—and to have the government finance the program by noninflationary methods. The scale on which public employment is offered to the non-scarce categories could be such as to reduce *their* specific unemployment rate to that which would otherwise correspond to a national unemployment rate of 4 percent or somewhat less. Essentially this would amount to a small adjustment of the priority ranking of the types of activity undertaken in the economy as a whole to the objective of avoiding strong inflationary pressures. Such a program would be quite different from emergency employment or work relief projects in that here the objective would be that of *reducing the excess supply of those specific labor categories* which, in the absence of the program, would be very much in excess supply in the long run, provided we are aiming for a reasonably noninflationary normal growth path of the economy.

Various difficulties would have to be overcome to put a project of this sort into effect on the scale required for going a long way toward solving the problem with which we are here concerned. While I feel convinced that in the absence of such a program we are heading *either* for stop-and-go policies involving major inflationary disturbances as well as recessions *or* for a chronically low level of employment with substantially rising unemployment compensation and other welfare-type payments, I cannot say that I am equally thoroughly convinced that the program here suggested will prove manageable. But I think there is a very good chance that the program could become manageable, provided a group of experts—including manpower experts—undertook to explore the details in a systematic fashion, and I repeat that the available alternatives to such a program are much more unattractive than the program itself.

As for the orders of magnitude, these would partly depend on how far above a target rate—say, how far above a 4 percent or a 3.8 percent national rate—the reasonably noninflationary unemployment rate is located. Only experience can show this but let us assume for illustration that we are concerned here with the undesirable consequences of a 5 percent unemployment rate. The orders of magnitude with which the program would have to cope depend also on which specific labor categories *need to have* the unemployment rate corresponding to a national rate of 5 percent *to avoid shortages in these specific categories* and to promote the required turnover in them. For example, disregarding at first the continued trend which the line drawn in Figure 1 may hide, we see that for a national unemployment rate of 5 percent that line would indicate a specific unemployment rate close to 3.9 percent for males aged 20 and over. The corresponding rate for white males in those age classes would be close to 3.5 percent (and for white males aged 25 and over, in the neighborhood of $2^1/_2$ percent). Allowing for the trend which our regression line disregards further reduces these figures. [4] We now make the assumption that the resulting average unemployment rate for white males aged twenty and over—involving largely very short-term unemployment—is necessary for avoiding acute shortages; and we add the assumption that it is deemed undesirable to raise the average unemployment rate of the other categories beyond what *their* unemployment rate would be if the national rate were *somewhat below 4 percent*, because these other categories are in ample supply even at such a national rate. We then obtain a rough idea of the orders of magnitude involved in such a program. On these crude illustrative assumptions we would be concerned with arranging additional employment opportunities for roughly 400,000 persons; the need for these arrangements, might in due time be reduced but they would *not* be in the nature of mere emergency measures for the duration of a recession. The gradual trend on which we commented might conceivably raise the number of persons in question into the neighborhood of 500,000 when the labor-force categories are defined in this crude fashion. A figure falling in this range equals about one-half of the number of persons who, at a 5 percent national unemployment rate, would be found unemployed for 15 weeks or longer in the country as a whole. Furthermore, a figure falling in this same range represents also the *difference between* unemployment of 15 weeks or longer duration when the national unemployment rate is 5 percent and the unemployment of such duration when the national rate is 3.8 percent. Any detailed study in terms of the relevant narrower categories would, of course, correct our figures in one direction in view of some considerations and in the other direction in view of others and I would not venture a guess as to just where one would come out. However, it is worth adding that at the present time the public sector is employing 12.7 million civilians of whom 2.7 million are employed by the federal government and the others by state and local governments. In addition, hospitals and educational institutions outside the public sector are jointly employing about 3 million persons. We are concerned here with an increase of these numbers in a very small proportion.

---

[4] See footnote 2.

But the problem has, of course, other important aspects beyond that of the "order of magnitude" in the foregoing sense, whatever the true figure might be. Some of these other aspects are admittedly troublesome, but it should be obvious that there exists no easy way out of the difficulties we are considering. As for the other aspects, the terms of employment would have to be satisfactory, not only with respect to wages but also in the sense that both the employing agencies and the workers would have to show interest in getting useful work done, and this requires careful planning in advance. At the same time the terms of employment would have to be such as not to tempt an exodus from conventional jobs. The program would have to be limited administratively to persons who can reasonably be expected to prove suitable and to persons belonging in categories with respect to which a strong presumption exists that at a national unemployment rate of, say, 5 percent they would otherwise be subject to an unemployment problem *beyond* what is involved in the desired degree of labor mobility in the economy at large. There would have to be mobility also into and out of the program itself as the demand-mix of the private sector changes. Quite aside from this, the employing agencies would have to have the power to fire workers who prove unsuitable. Some such workers would qualify for welfare-type payments while others would have to forgo support. Persons previously employed in the sectors in which the program offers employment would have to be made ineligible for an extended period in order to prevent the practice of first firing from the public sector workers who will thereby become eligible, then replacing them with workers belonging in the scarce categories, and finally rehiring the initially fired workers in the program. Nevertheless, on the crude numerical assumption we have made, such a program could reduce a 5 percent national unemployment rate to $4^{1}/_{2}$ percent without creating inflationary pressures, and it might well be possible to do better than that.

As was said above, one can only make the guess that the difficulties could be met at least successfully enough to make this kind of solution preferable to keeping idle a large number of individuals who are willing to work and many of whom would receive unemployment compensation or other welfare-type payments if they were given no work opportunity. Such a solution would be preferable also to generating full employment by conventional methods involving major inflationary pressures and thus producing alternations of inflationary phases with significant unemployment.

Acceptance of Major Chronic Inflationary Pressures Does Not Offer an Alternative. Any realistic explanation of the emergence of inflationary tendencies at full employment must place the emphasis on the joint effect of excess demand for scarce resource categories and of the market power of unions. Such a presentation suggests also the answer to the question whether keeping the national unemployment rate at a level at which specific labor shortages develop is apt to lead to a steady rate of inflation—i.e., to an inflation-unemployment trade-off along a stable "Phillips curve"—or to the *acceleration* of inflation. If we take it for granted that a significant rate of inflation—even a steady rate—should be avoided then we may proceed as I did in the foregoing analysis and conclude that we are *forced* to look for a second-best solution because conventional full-employment policies are significantly inflationary; yet not all participants in the debate consider an appreciable rate of inflation greatly injurious *provided* the inflation rate can be held steady. The behavior of the public and the institutional arrangements in the economy would according to some economists become geared to the correctly anticipated steady rate of price increases, and the important economic variables, including interest rates and presumably the foreign-exchange rates, would adjust accordingly. If one takes this position concerning a significant but steady rate of inflation, the foregoing discussion is unconvincing unless it is supplemented by an analysis of the question whether the inflation generated by conventional full-employment policies is likely at all to remain steady, i.e., not to accelerate. As was said a moment ago, by attributing the emergence of inflation to the bidding for scarce labor categories in an environment in which unions play a significant role, one comes close to implying acceleration but the problem requires closer analysis, particularly because recent econometric work performed on the subject has led some investigators to suggest nonacceleration.

Different countries differ greatly, of course, as to the level of activity at which the imperfect matching of the demand for with the supply of specific labor categories causes pronounced shortages, but once that level is reached in a country the efforts of enterprises to obtain more of the scarce categories must prove self-defeating. Hence even aside from union activity a permissive monetary-fiscal policy must be expected to bring about a sharpening of the bidding process, that is, acceleration of the inflation. Any attempt on the part of unions to raise the rate of increase of *real* wages beyond the rate of productivity increase will also prove self-defeating and hence the upward pressure unions exert on money wages will also increase from round to round. When shortages exist union pressure is

not a *necessary* condition of acceleration but it can make a significant contribution to acceleration, and it can start the process at a
level of activity at which competitive bidding for labor would not
yet generate the process. Furthermore, the tendency for wages paid
to nonscarce labor to rise at a similar rate is also enhanced by union
activity, as well as by other institutional characteristics of our
economy. After each round of self-defeating moves the individual
decision units are apt to try harder.

Our analysis implies a permissive monetary-fiscal policy, and it
is indeed essential to realize that a policy dedicated to maintaining
business activity at a level of major specific shortages is necessarily
permissive in the required sense. If it ceases to be permissive it
changes into a policy of preventing the inflation rate from rising
beyond some critical level by stop-and-go measures that become more
arduous the higher the inflation rate is allowed to rise before the
restraints are applied.[5]

This kind of reasoning establishes a strong presumption for
acceleration at any persistently maintained shortage level of the
national unemployment rate but it would admittedly be desirable
further to supplement the analysis with technical-statistical explora-
tions. Such attempts were made for our recent inflationary phase by
two investigators, Robert J. Gordon and George L. Perry,[6] but while
these authors suggest that there is no reason to fear acceleration
their findings leave a good many questions open.

In the first place—and this is perhaps the main point to remember—even if for the past years the validity of these models were
much more firmly established than is the case, and thus the accelerationist hypothesis could be rejected as concerns the past, this would
not answer the crucial questions for the future. It would have to be
kept in mind that the public would behave quite differently in circumstances where the policymakers would be committed to maintaining the system as a shortage level than in past circumstances in
which restraints sometimes came belatedly but were practically certain to bring about a recession in due time.

Secondly, it is very questionable whether even for the sixties the

---

[5] Along a line of reasoning that is not identical with that here presented, Arthur
M. Okun's analysis of these problems also led him to the conclusion that a
policy attempting to stabilize inflation at a significant rate would in fact result
in pronounced stop-and-go phases (see his "The Mirage of Steady Inflation,"
Brookings Papers on Economic Activity, 1971, 2).

[6] See Robert J. Gordon, "The Recent Acceleration of Inflation," *Brookings Papers
on Economic Activity*, 1970, 1; and "Inflation in Recession and Recovery," *ibid.*,
1971, 1. For Perry's contribution see *op. cit.* (cf. footnote 2).

data can be said to testify against the accelerationist hypothesis. Essentially the question reduces to whether in the second half of the sixties unemployment *decreased* at a sufficient rate to enable us to explain the historically observed acceleration of inflation during the period by the *reduction* of the unemployment rate. If we can explain the historical acceleration by changes in the unemployment rate, we may conclude that at a persistently maintained low rate of unemployment inflation would have continued at a *steady* rate. We have already seen that it is impossible to carry out satisfactory direct tests of the role of the level of unemployment, on the one hand, and of changes in that level on the other, because these two variables are very highly correlated in the data. But it is possible to test models in which the rate of inflation itself (not its rate of change) is assumed to depend on a number of explanatory variables including the rate of unemployment itself (but not the changes of the latter), and satisfactory results obtained with such a model may lead an investigator to suggest that inflation has tended to remain at a steady (nonaccelerating) rate in relation to the level of unemployment. The historically observed acceleration of inflation would then be attributed to changes of the explanatory variables, prominently including the reduction of the unemployment rate, not to an inherent tendency of inflation to accelerate at persistently maintained low unemployment levels. The results actually obtained by the method so described are of considerable interest but they have remained inconclusive for reasons I will summarize here merely in a few sentences because I discussed them in detail in another paper.[7]

During the inflationary years of the second half of the sixties, the official unemployment rate did *not* decline sufficiently to explain the historical acceleration of inflation, i.e., inflation *was* accelerating not merely in the historical sense but also in relation to the official unemployment rate. An argument can, however, be made for the proposition that the behavior of the official unemployment rate understates the decline of unemployment in the sense relevant to the present purpose, i.e., understates the reduction of *labor-market ease*. It is possible to carry out the corrections of the official unemployment rate in ways such that the resulting measure of labor-market ease should decline sufficiently to explain the historical acceleration of inflation in the second half of the decade. In other words, it is possible to adjust the unemployment measure by corrections that will keep inflation nonaccelerating *in relation to such a*

---

[7] See my "Phillips-type Approach or Acceleration?" *Brookings Papers on Economic Activity*, 1971, 2.

reconstructed measure of unemployment or of labor-market ease. The outcome depends on the size of the corrections made. Elsewhere I believe to have justified my view that the assumptions on which Gordon's corrections are based are farfetched. The basic logic behind Perry's argument is appealing but the data do not permit him, nor would they permit any other investigator, to proceed in close accordance with that logic and the expedients he relies upon at essential junctures are no more convincing than expedients that would fail to stabilize the inflation rate relative to the explanatory variables. At the present stage of inquiry, reliance on such expedients is inevitable.

We may then conclude that even as concerns the nineteensixties acceleration in relation to the explanatory variables of inflation disappears from the data *only if* particular techniques are used for correcting the official unemployment rate. Moreover, if future policy were committed to keeping constant a low rate of unemployment by methods involving the creation of specific shortages, the presumption of acceleration would increase greatly. The past behavior of the public was influenced by the knowledge that policymakers paid attention to the inflation rate, even if in the sixties the restraints were adopted too late and hence have led to a very burdensome adjustment process. A policy commitment to keep the economy at a shortage level would condition the public to different expectations which would almost certainly lead to acceleration. This strengthens the case for the kind of second best I am suggesting in this paper, since accelerating inflation is not a condition to which the economy could adjust. Allowing a high rate of inflation to develop that must subsequently be stopped by making the economy fall significantly behind its output trend is clearly not a reasonable program.

Throughout this analysis I have assumed that policymakers are not contemplating reliance on permanent controls for suppressing the chronic inflationary pressures that develop at high levels of activity when these levels are achieved by conventional methods. The controls recently introduced are not intended to serve this purpose. But we should add that whether or not some persons contemplate permanent direct controls for coping with chronic inflation at high levels of activity, such a course would not even be *feasible* under a political system similar to ours. There exist systems under which such a line of policy is technically manageable, with the result that acute shortages lead not to accelerating inflation but to significant limitations of the range of goods offered for sale at regulated prices. The approach calls for a very elaborate and rigorous enforcement apparatus, and its technical feasibility is enhanced under comprehensive government ownership where most sellers of goods depend for their jobs directly on the control agencies. Quite aside from technicalities, such a policy requires that the central government should have uncontested powers to decide in full detail what the priority ranking of various political objectives should be in relation to market efficiency, and in what specific ways the priority ranking so determined should express itself in the bill of available goods. This does not mean that even governments possessing these powers can for long remain heedless of the various group pressures emerging in their societies, but it does mean that such governments cannot operate in an environment in which open and sharp criticism of specific governmental decisions, and political activity directed against the decisionmakers, are the legitimate business of organized groups. Desirability or undesirability apart, maintaining the economy at a chronic level of shortages with a comprehensive and permanent system of direct controls is *not even technically feasible* in the contemporary United States.

Short-Run Problems of the Transition Toward a Sustainable Normal Growth Path

Economics and Politics Introduction. The controls that were introduced on August 15, 1971 are not intended to remain permanent. They were not adopted with the purpose of taking care of chronic inflationary pressures after the recovery from the recession which, according to dating by the National Bureau of Economic Research, lasted from November 1969 to November 1970. In relation to the long run, the official position is consistent with the negative conclusions presented in the preceding section concerning a system of direct controls for suppressing chronic inflation in our political setting. Nor does the official position suggest the *desirability* of such a line of approach, though we have heard much about the undesirability of direct controls even for an interim period and *on this* the top policymakers did change their minds.

They changed their minds when it was necessary to give up successive versions of unconvincing official optimism about the *speed* with which it was allegedly possible to achieve desirable employment-policy goals and at the same time to reduce to small size the sharp inflationary movement that the present administration had inherited from its predecessor. The last version of this official optimism concerning speed was put before the public in the February 1971 report of the Council of Economic Advisers.[8] That version was admitted to have been unrealistic in the summer of the same year.

The hypothesis underlying our temporary controls is that by keeping prices stable (or nearly so) for a while it will be possible to brake the inflationary *expectations* that the public had *carried over* from a period of overfull utilization into a period of underutilization. Inflationary price-expectations were raising the rate of increase of money wages significantly, and were therefore leading to a continuation of sharp price increases which in turn were leading to continued sharp wage increases, etc. While at shortage levels of activity union pressure is not a *necessary* condition of sharply inflationary price movements, this carry-over mechanism into periods of appreciable underemployment does presuppose union power in an essential way. The idea of using temporary controls during a period of underutilization for breaking the spiral generated by the carry-over mechanism must thus be distinguished clearly from the idea of suppressing the inflationary consequences of shortages by permanent controls. Yet the disadvantages of such temporary controls are weighty enough to suggest that if other methods of ending the period dominated by the carry-over effects are workable then they are *far* preferable. This is so unless the temporary controls shorten the transition significantly. On these grounds the case for the temporary controls was much weaker than was widely believed in the country.

Merely criteria of a very arbitrary kind could be invented for deciding what the wage *structure* and the price *structure* should be while the steepness of the rise of the general *level* of wages and prices is becoming reduced. This is the fundamental defect of the control policy to which we shifted in August 1971. There do indeed exist well-established criteria by which we rightly conclude that barriers to entry into specific areas of economic activity and limitations of competition lead in most cases to inefficiency as well as inequity. But, in the first place, eliminating or at least reducing such barriers is not a matter of short-run policy, hence not a task that could be performed effectively by those in charge of the transition from a steeply inflationary to an approximately noninflationary phase of development. Secondly, and equally importantly, elimination or reduction of barriers to entry is a very different act of policy than trying to set specific wage rates and prices "as if" these barriers did not exist.

---

[8] On this, see my "Case for Moderation in the Economic Recovery of 1971," Special Analysis Number 4, *American Enterprise Institute*, April 1971.

Even where there does exist a strong presumption that on grounds of efficiency specific wage rates or specific prices are too high in relation to others, knowledge of this is far from sufficient to serve as a basis for determining the "correct" level of the wage or of the price in question by efficiency criteria; and with respect to a limited period of transition even indications that a price is too high in relation to other prices become shaky. Not only is it impossible to ascertain during a brief period what a firm's profits *are in fact* in the relevant sense, but, given the need for long-run decisionmaking in a risky environment, the concept of the "normal" profit rate gives little guidance concerning the profits of which a controlling agency should approve in principle.

The decisions of the control agencies will necessarily relate to the wage and price *structure* and criticism of these decisions will be justifiably challenged on the grounds of efficiency as well as of equity. Objections will be justified on the latter grounds too, because the public can hardly feel that it has by some constitutional process given the control agencies powers to weigh in the name of the citizenry efficiency and equity considerations of a rather inarticulate kind across the wage and price structure. Indeed, the equity considerations will not be clearly distinguishable from considerations relating to the power of interest groups behind the scenes.

Despite these inherent deficiencies, our temporary direct controls were adopted at a time when in the light of the available data there existed a reasonable presumption that, given the additional fiscal stimuli [9] proposed by the administration in August 1971, the reduction of the unemployment rate to the neighborhood of 5 percent by the summer of 1972, with a further significant reduction of inflation by that time, was within reach in the absence of direct controls. While the large inflationary carry-over from the late sixties calls for keeping the recovery at a moderate pace, we should remember that in no postwar recovery did the unemployment rate decline by less than 1.5 percent in the first twelve months of its decline. It is exceedingly unlikely that the recovery process would be speeded up by the controls, even though the flattening of the price trend which had started many months earlier may conceivably become more abrupt (also more jerky, with ups and downs). Finally, not only is any speeding-up of the recovery very unlikely, but an appreciable risk exists that arbitrary interferences by the controlling agencies will

---

[9] The need for additional fiscal stimuli has existed for some time, as was also pointed out in my paper cited in the preceding footnote.

lead to slower recovery than would otherwise have developed. Yet, in spite of all this, a convincing case can be made for the proposition that introducing temporary direct controls had become "politically inevitable."

These statements require further elaboration.

Economics and Politics: Analysis of Facts. Let us now turn to an analysis of the information available at the time when the controls were introduced.

(1) In the United States price movements had all along shown a pronounced tendency to adjust to wage movements and to changes of productivity, when the latter changes are interpreted as *weighted averages* of past and of current productivity changes. Since all these data show an upward trend, this amounts to saying that prices have tended to rise to the extent that wage increases have exceeded weighted productivity increases. Alternatively expressed, wages have tended to rise in the same proportion as productivity plus prices, i.e., in proportion to the sum of the weighted productivity trend and the price trend. This relationship expresses itself clearly in Figure 2 which reflects year-to-year changes from 1952-53 to the present.

In this figure we measure the excess of wage increase over weighted productivity increase along the horizontal axis, and the price increase along the vertical axis. The straight line drawn in the figure shows the path along which all points of the graph would have been located if price increases had always precisely equalled the excess of wage over productivity increases. We do, of course, observe dispersion about this line, but the average deviation is not large and it is particularly small for the recent decade. However, as concerns the first half of 1971, we find for this short final period a large deviation because during these recent months price increases were *appreciably* smaller—wage increases appreciably larger—than would have corresponded to the relation expressed by the straight line.

The concepts employed in these statements need to be defined with precision and this is done in the footnote below.[10]

(2) Anything that could be said about the *direction* of adjust-

---

[10] Price increase, as the concept is here used, means increase in the private nonfarm GNP deflator; wage increase means the increase in compensation per manhour in the private nonfarm sector; weighted productivity increase means increase in output per man-hour in the private nonfarm sector, with the weight 0.8 assigned to the simple average of the past five years and the weight 0.2 attached to the current year.

Figure 2

RELATION OF PRICE INCREASE TO EXCESS OF WAGE INCREASE OVER WEIGHTED PRODUCTIVITY INCREASE

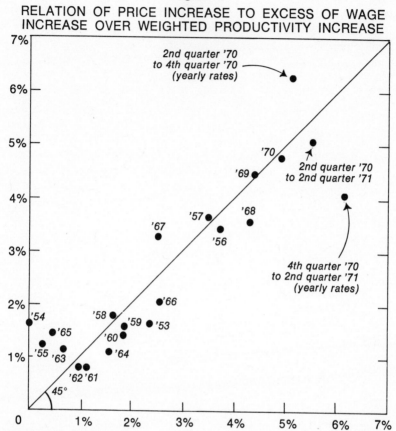

Horizontal Axis: Excess of current wage increase over weighted productivity increase (weight 0.8 assigned to average of past five years; 0.2 to current productivity increase).

Vertical Axis: Current increase in price deflator.

All data are for private nonfarm sector. Increases are from preceding year to year in question, except where differently marked.

ment—i.e., about which variables have adjusted to which others— would have to be much more speculative than the very safe statements we have just made. This is because mutual adjustments have taken place between our variables in ways that were strongly influenced by a considerable number of other economic variables not included in our statement. However, when yearly data are used we find that, in all instances in which the rate of price increase fell short of the excess of wage increase over weighted productivity increase, such a year of price-shortfall was promptly followed by a year in which rate of *wage increase declined*, and vice versa for price-overshooting. On the other hand, it is by no means a generally valid statement that, when price increases fell short of the excess of wage increase over weighted productivity increase, then such a year of price-shortfall was promptly followed by a *steepening of the price trend* (and vice versa). This second statement would not be generally valid, and examination of the data points clearly to the additional role of the height of business activity in determining whether the price trend did in fact steepen or flatten in the event of a preceding price-shortfall or overshooting. The wage trend *has* always flattened or steepened as stated above. Also the regularity concerning the *relationship* among price trend, wage trend, and productivity trend did come through promptly in practically all of the year-to-year data, i.e., a deviation from this relationship in one direction changed to (or moved toward) a deviation in the other direction promptly.[11]

(3) In these regards the inflationary period 1965-70 shows no abnormal traits whatever. The regularities continued to show throughout the period to which our data relate. What *was* "new" in the 1965-70 period was that during a five-year interval, which until 1969 was one of very high activity levels, any temporary overshooting of prices beyond the excess of wage over weighted productivity increases became reversed by a subsequent *large wage increase* combined with a further *small steepening* of the price trend (and in the late part of the period also by a weakening of the productivity trend); and temporary shortfalls of price increase in relation to the excess of wage increase over weighted productivity increase became reversed by a subsequent *significant* steepening of the price trend combined with an *insignificant* temporary flattening of the wage trend (a wage-trend flattening that in each case was preceded as well as followed by a significant steepening). Hence, the wage-price adjustment mechanism—the mechanism that has been operating all along with remarkable consistency—was placed on an escalator. The escalator had been put in motion by the highly inflationary methods of financing rapidly rising government expenditures.

(4) Given the basic tendencies reflecting themselves in Figure 2 and given the fact that in short-run data literal simultaneity practically never occurs, the anti-inflationary policies of the present

---

[11] Considering the rounding involved in the data we are using, this statement might have to be qualified for a *very* small number of quantitatively quite insignificant instances to all of which the principle of *de minimis non curat lex* is clearly applicable.

administration could have become effective in one of two ways. The wage trend could have flattened and the price trend could then have become adjusted, or a prior flattening of the price trend could have been followed by a flattening of the wage trend. Those who became impatient with the progress that was being made have repeatedly called attention to the fact that as of the summer of 1971 the wage trend failed to flatten. In this they were right since indeed some *steepening* of the wage trend was observable. But the assertion was frequently added that indications of a flattening of the price trend were inconclusive.

The general story of price developments over a period of two to three years can usually be summarized in many alternative ways depending on which indices are being stressed and on the length of successive subperiods regarded as meaningful units for comparison, but even on such general grounds the "impatient" version of the story seems unconvincing. This may be controversial. Yet what should not be controversial is that by the standards of the relation expressed by Figure 2 progress *was* being made.

The story of price developments "in general" can be reasonably summarized by the statement that in the first half of 1971 inflation was running at a yearly rate of about 4 percent. Both in terms of the consumer price index and of the private GNP deflator, this rate of increase was appreciably lower than had been the previous peak rates of close to 6 percent (to the "chain index" I shall return presently). The industrial component of the wholesale price index too was rising at about 4 percent which for this series marked no improvement but also no deterioration. The wholesale prices of farm products were rising more steeply in the first half of 1971 than earlier but the movements of these prices are strongly influenced by special factors and the present controls do not extend to them. The consumer-goods component of the GNP deflator with its 4 percent yearly rate of increase in the first half of 1971 was running well below its earlier peak rate. Unemployment had remained near its late-1970 peak level of about 6 percent but there was nothing in the experience of the period to suggest that a monetary and fiscal policy that would succeed in bringing about a gradual decline of the unemployment rate to the neighborhood of 5 percent by the summer of 1972 would interfere with a further reduction of inflation; and at present there is nothing to suggest that a faster noninflationary rise of the employment rate could be achieved with reliance on the controls which have been put into effect. The fiscal-policy stimulants proposed by the President in his August 15 announcement could have been adopted without the controls, and the long overdue severance of the tie between the dollar and gold was also a step they could have stood very well on its own merits. So even the general story can be told in a reasonable way by placing the emphasis on a reduction of the steepness of price inflation (though not yet of wage inflation) and by stressing the need to use a somewhat increased dose of the fiscal stimulants for stepping up the recovery process in order to bring about a gradual reduction of the rate of unemployment. So much for the "general story" told in what to me seems a reasonable way, though such "general accounts" of a two-year development can, of course, be given in a disturbingly large number of ways.

One reason for this ambiguity is that for some purposes it is preferable to use the Department of Commerce's "chain index" rather than its GNP deflator, and the rise of the chain index had not become moderated to the same extent as that of the deflator. But in the specific context of analysis based on Figure 2 the deflator should be used because the productivity indices imply an output measure defined in such a way that the deflator represents the price to be employed for translating the output into the money value from which wages are paid. Nor will we need the chain index for tracing real wages because at that point the consumer price index will have to be used.

By the specific standards suggested by Figure 2, we are indeed entitled to the conclusion that in the first half of 1971 a stage was reached in which the observed wage-price-productivity relations of two decades were very likely to lead to an appreciable flattening of the wage trend. During the first six months of 1971 the rate of price increase fell short of the excess of wage increase over weighted productivity increase by no less than 2.0 percent, and a large shortfall of the price increase has so far *always* led to a substantial reduction of wage increases. To be sure there existed past instances in which a shortfall of the price increase became reversed only *in part* by a flattening of the wage trend and in part by a steepening of the price trend itself but this *never happened* at unemployment rates and excess-capacity rates falling in the supernormal range in which they will be moving in the near future if unemployment declines gradually to the vicinity of 5 percent by the late summer of 1972.[12]

12 This statement disregards, as it should, the lag to which the cessation of the steepening of the price trend was subject in 1970, i.e., the height of the price increase shown in Figure 2 for the *half-yearly* interval from the second to the fourth quarter of 1970.

Aside from this, one might want to qualify the statement in the text with

By the summer of 1971 the stage *was* set for a significant flatten-ing of the wage trend with no steepening of the price trend; and if subsequently the increase of effective demand had been kept at a moderate rate, though at a somewhat higher rate than in the first half of 1971, then given a reduction of the rate of wage increase producers would have had a *very strong incentive to achieve higher capacity utilization rates by further moderating the rate of price increase.* After all, this price-moderating influence seems to have been quite effective *even* in the recent period of steepest wage increase!

During their spells of optimism most official experts seem to have expected a prior reduction of wage increases as a result of supernormal unemployment, and a reduction of the price increases as a result of wage moderation. We need not be astonished that it did not happen that way because during most of the period of steep money wage increases the rate of increase of *real* wages was very much below normal, in 1970 less than 1 percent. But this too changed in the first half of 1971 during which real wage rates rose at an annual rate of nearly 4 percent. This, of course, is a supernormal rate by a large margin, a rate at which real wages never rose for longer than a *very* brief period.

All along there has been good reason to expect that overcoming our difficulties would take an extended period of time. All along there has been good reason to expect also that a "game strategy" such as that of the administration could work only through induce-ments offered to producers to diminish the rate of price increase in order to raise capacity-utilization rates during a none-too-rapid recovery process *and* through the effect on wages of such price devel-opments as well as of the supernormal unemployment rate. The need for some additional fiscal-policy stimulants became clear several months prior to August 15.[13] When finally the stage was set for the second act—the first act of price-trend flattening was performed in

---

reference to a negligible exception in 1963, but it is questionable whether this should be considered an exception at all. That year was one of appreciable unemployment and yet as compared to the preceding year the rate of price increase changed from .9% to 1.2% in terms of the deflator and from 1.0% to 1.1% in terms of the consumer price index. However, not only can this be reasonably expressed by saying that the price level as measured by these indices remained practically stable in both years but it needs to be added that in 1963 as compared to 1962 the wholesale price index as a whole as well as its industrial component turned from a slight increase to a slight *decrease*.

[13] See footnote 8.

the first half of 1971—then the play was declared a failure and the economy was placed under a system of administrative controls.

What had happened?

(5) I think it was indeed impossible to eliminate the basic reason that made the shift "politically imperative." The situation became further complicated by what has seemed to me all along an unfortunate posture of various spokesmen for the government, a posture that had contributed to impatience by strongly suggesting the nonexistent possibility of moving fast and at very little cost. But whatever one may think of this posture the economically unjustified controls would probably have become politically inevitable in any event.

It was inevitable that dampening a sharp inflation to a tolerable level should be a long drawn-out process, except *perhaps* if in 1969 the new administration had subjected the economy to a "shock treatment," a course for which the new policymakers have not accepted responsibility and no one in their place would have. By 1971 the intense pressure toward direct controls was exerted from pretty nearly all sides. Intense pressure came from Congress, from the press, from many members of the business community, and from the proverbial man in the street alike. Almost all economists who would have held government positions if the 1968 elections had come out differently were strongly in favor of exerting direct influence on wage and price movements by means of administrative interference. While with the exception of the chairman of the Federal Reserve Board economists occupying official positions after January 1969 could not dissociate themselves from the President's initial program aimed at overcoming the difficulties *without* resort to direct controls, aversion against reliance on controls was certainly *not* shared by all economists working for the present administration.

It had been in the cards all along that at the time of the 1972 elections the country would not be in a state of nearly "full" employment combined with practical constancy of the price level, and it had gradually become obvious that whatever progress the country would have made by that time toward higher employment and lesser price increases would have been considered unduly small if the allegedly effective method of relying on direct controls had remained untried. The administration would have been highly vulnerable to the criticism that it did not use all available methods for achieving better results than are in fact capable of being reached. This must have gradually lowered the morale of the opponents of controls to the neighborhood of the zero point.

Advocates of a radical departure from past practices do, of

course, not always have this advantage over their opponents. There exist at least two reasons why in the present case they did have this advantage.

In the first place it is very tempting to believe that wage and price controls will be employed on balance to the benefit of the group to which one belongs. After all are one's own grudges and interests not clearly legitimate? And will the representatives of one's group not be able to use the right combination of reasoning and pressure to convince the authorities of the legitimacy of these group interests? The truth of the matter is that even in retrospect it is very difficult to judge in whose favor, relatively speaking, such controls have worked, and that there exists a strong presumption that specific interferences with the wage-price structure which are based on ill-defined criteria reduce the efficiency of the system at large.

Secondly, it has become tempting to believe that characteristics of different types of economic-political systems can be mixed almost indiscriminately. In this regard the truth of the matter is that some features of different economic-political blueprints do indeed mix— *pure* capitalism and *pure* socialism exist only in the propaganda literature—but on the other hand discrimination does have to be used in deciding which characteristics do mix and which do not. As was argued in this paper, comprehensive administrative regulation of wage rates and of prices does not mix well at all with the basic features of the contemporary American political system or with any system similar to it. The experience of other countries also strongly points in this direction.

Conclusions

(1) Full-employment policies are distinctly inflationary if they are pursued by the conventional method of raising effective demand to the point of pronounced shortages in specific resources. A policy committed to such a line would generate chronic inflationary pressures, and the resulting inflation would in all probability show a tendency to accelerate until the next stop-phase of stop-and-go alternations would put an end to the expansion. Returning to stop-and-go policies after a sharply inflationary interlude would, of course, mean giving up the commitment to full employment and it would mean doing so under particularly burdensome conditions.

(2) It is therefore imperative to explore alternatives to the *conventional type* of full-employment policy, even if the available alternatives are merely in the nature of second-best solutions. Such

265

an alternative was discussed and its further exploration was urged in the first part of this paper (pp. 247-50).

(3) The recent policy of temporary controls was adopted at a time when given the proposed additional fiscal stimuli [14] the stage was set for good progress toward an appreciably reduced rate of unemployment, a significant increase in the level of business activity, and a further appreciable reduction of the rate of price increases. This statement implies that a diminution of the rate of wage increases was also in the offing at that time as is indeed strongly suggested by the data we have examined. The controls now adopted are very unlikely to speed up the recovery process, even if they should make the flattening of the price trend more abrupt (yet also more jerky). Not only is such a speeding-up effect very unlikely but there exists the danger that the control agencies will not refrain from major arbitrary interferences with the wage and price structure and these would have major adverse effects on the speed of the recovery. Paradoxically, I am nevertheless inclined to the view that proclaiming the adoption of temporary controls had become "politically inevitable" in a reasonable sense of this term.

(4) The control agencies have a good chance of receiving part of the credit for what monetary and fiscal policy was already on the way to accomplishing, but they have this chance only if they follow mostly the principle of *keeping their eyes on the process and keeping their hands off it.* Assuming reasonable monetary and fiscal management and assuming a moderate pace in the return to the normal growth path of the economy, the agencies should be in a position to announce in the very near future that disinflation is progressing adequately; they should also be able to announce that if after each quarter the approach to end-of-1972 goals seems adequate, then administrative interferences will henceforth be very exceptional. Prenotification requirements could then be suspended even before the controls are ended.

(5) Differently expressed, if the public will interpret the objective of the control agencies as that of reducing the rate of inflation into a range no higher than 2 percent to 3 percent before the end of 1972, then *given the proper monetary and fiscal policies* the agencies can probably appear successful by remaining largely inactive and by refraining from the formulation of arbitrary criteria for specific wage rates and for the pricing of specific products. Implied in such a price target is a yearly rate of increase of private nonfarm compensation

---

[14] However, congressional action on these was forthcoming with a considerable delay.

per man-hour in the range between 5 percent and $5^1/_2$ percent with an increase in *real* compensation per man-hour somewhat in excess of 2.5 percent. In actual fact the long-run average of rates of productivity increase in the private nonfarm economy was 2.5 percent for the period 1952-70 and this figure rises to 2.8 percent only if we end the period in 1966, thereby wholly disregarding the exceptionally low average productivity increases of the last four years. With inclusion of the farm sector these two productivity increases were 2.9 percent and 3.2 percent respectively, and the average rates of increase of *real* private nonfarm compensation per man-hour were 2.8 percent and 2.9 percent respectively. It is often overlooked that some of the measured productivity increase leads automatically to higher average compensation per man-hour, *without* an increase of wage rates in any industry, because some of the measured productivity increase merely reflects the rising weight of the high-productivity and high-wage subsectors in the economy.

The control authorities—the need for which at the time of their inauguration was purely political, though understandably a "need" in *that* particular sense—will have done well if they will allow the tendencies generated by the appropriate monetary and fiscal policy to come through unimpeded. They could do much worse by yielding to the temptation to engage in a great deal of activity, thereby slowing the recovery. Fears that they will yield to this temptation, or rather will continue to yield to it, cannot be brushed aside at the time when this volume goes to press, but these fears are now shared by many and one may hope that this will have an effect on policy.

Cover and book design: Pat Taylor